The Triumph of Individual Style

9

20

10

14

18

31

1

The Triumph of Individual Style

A guide
to dressing
your body,
your beauty,
your self.

by
Carla Mason Mathis
and
Helen Villa Connor

Dancing Figure; Auguste Rodin,
National Gallery of Art,
Washington; Gift of Mrs. John
W. Simpson (detail).

Timeless Editions

Dedicated with love to our parents and grandparents.

Carla

Gwendolyn Effie McCuaig Mason Melgren
the late Carl Wilbur Mason (father)
the late Louis Melgren (stepfather)

Bertha Eichenberger Pfister Mason
Clara Asbach McCuaig
Jack McCuaig

Helen

Lydia Calica Villa
Romulo Silao Villa

Segunda Bambao Calica
Honorato Mendoza Calica
Tomasa Gabriel Silao Villa
Hilario Dizon Villa

ontents

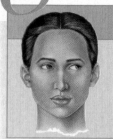

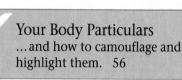
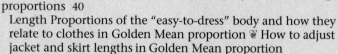

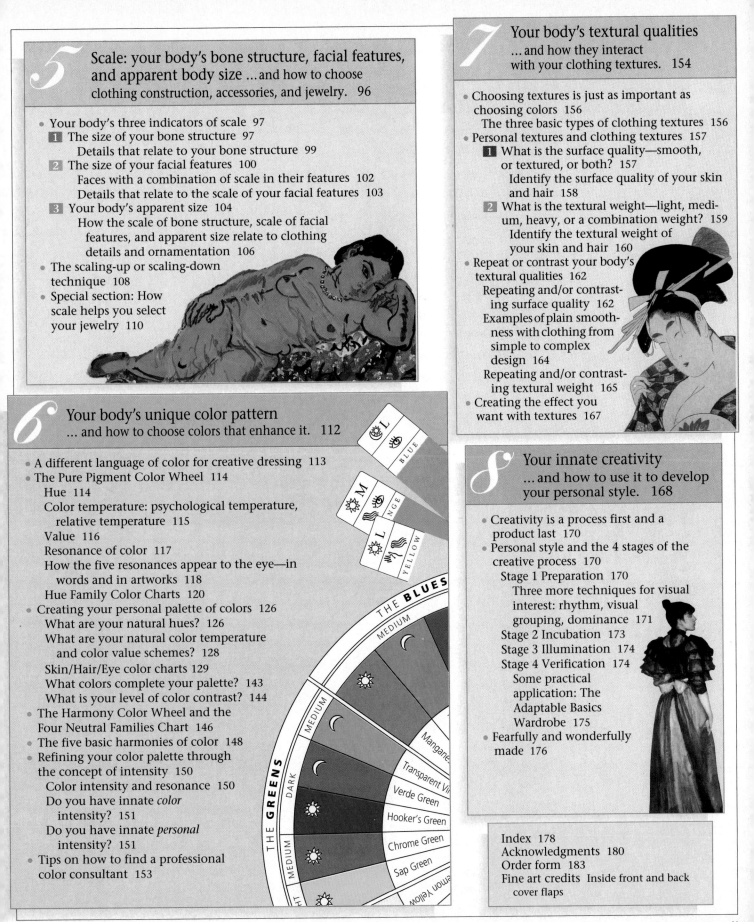

To be different just to be different is not the point. Here, one magnificent bloom, set apart, sits serenely in water—an image that serves to remind us that true Individual Style does not strain for effect. At its most triumphant, indeed, it is effortless. If the water lily could speak, might it not say, "You have but one life to live. Dare to be beautiful."

The Triumph of Individual Style

... a book for women on self-acceptance and personal style.

"Art is the imposing of a pattern on experience,
—our aesthetic enjoyment is recognition of the pattern."
—A.N. Whitehead, philosopher, 1861–1947, *Dialogues*

Beauty Today

In every age, women have wanted to feel beautiful and attractive for a variety of reasons.

Today, we are experiencing a dramatic shift in the meaning of beauty that has freed us from the shackles of all past ideals and standards of perfection. For most of us, it matters little how this change came about. We simply take for granted that women have earned the freedom to be unique and complex people. Feminine beauty today includes such qualities as confidence and self-acceptance, strength and intelligence, health and individual style.

More than anything else, individuality sums up the modern definition of beauty and style. Why is this such an exciting time for developing individual style? For one thing we have available today a wealth of clothing styles and colors that sets us free to put our own signature on fashion. For another, modern society supports the pursuit of individuality with more and more avenues for self-expression—in the arts, in education, and in our choice of work or lifestyle. Likewise, in the realm of beauty, we are also learning to value and enjoy our differences.

This book celebrates this era of real women who are breaking the molds. Each setting her own standard of beauty by playing up her uniqueness. Each experiencing the triumph of individual style.

The innovative approach of this book shows you how to see your face and body the way an artist would see it. Through illustrations, photographs, color charts, and well-known artworks we will open your eyes to a broader and richer definition of your physical beauty. In the process, we teach you the principles of design that will show you how easy it is to dress yourself like a work of art—whatever your size, shape, or color.

"Wait a minute," you may be saying skeptically. "We humans may be interesting because we are each different from one another, but we are not all beautiful." This book was created for you, too—those of you who think it is impossible to be beautiful on your own terms for whatever reason. Our belief is that everyone has the potential to be beautiful. Recognizing your beauty is simply a matter of perspective—a perspective that begins by taming, if not entirely conquering, the Beast.

Water lily,
Bill Terry Photography

Beauty and the beast of self-denial

The greatest obstacle to beauty is the beast that looms behind your mirrors and lurks in the shadows of your mind that goads self-consciousness to rear its ugly head. Time and time again, this beast may roar, "I hate your nose. Your eyes are too small." or "Why does your hair have to be so curly? And my God, your feet are HUGE!" Like a troll, it threatens to eat you alive each time you try to cross the bridge to the other side—where beauty lies.

> Lasting beauty begins with a self-awareness that goes beyond self-consciousness to self-acceptance.

By learning to love what others see on the outside, you open the avenues for expressing what you are inside and have others see your "whole self" as beautiful. We were all born beautiful by virtue of what every newborn represents—the miracle and promise of Life itself. Unless they are told otherwise, little children believe in themselves and are filled with the joy of living. A part of that joy is feeling they are pleasing to behold.

You may have forgotten that as you grew older. The key is to be able to recapture the childhood view; to "see" your beauty once again. And we have found the easiest way to do this is through the universal language of art.

Girl in Front of Mirror, Norman Rockwell, The Norman Rockwell Museum at Stockbridge (detail).

Beauty is an art

We can all learn to see the beauty of our faces and bodies, as ordinary as they may seem, through the language of art. Even if you have never seen beauty there before, you will! For this you need to understand these seven elements of art: line and space, shape, proportion, scale, color, and texture. All humans share these design elements; it is how they are arranged in our physical makeup that makes us each unique.

The artist sees that the way your body is put together creates an exciting design pattern of these elements; and that this design pattern is alive with your unique expressive qualities. The artist would say:

> "It will not be so much a question of painting that nose as it will be painting the expression of that nose."
> —Robert Henri, *The Art Spirit*

In other words, to the artist, there is a special expression found in every feature of your body, and in the colors or textures found in your skin, hair, or eyes. The artist tries to capture those expressions in his art; you will learn to capture them in the art of dressing.

Your Body's Design Pattern: your unique language of beauty

In this book, we will lead you chapter-by-chapter to discover Your Body's Design Pattern through the seven elements of art. With each element you will learn very specific things about your body, and in the process, develop self-acceptance. This in turn will lead you to our ultimate goal: to be highly selective in your clothing choices; to choose only those clothes and accessories that balance or are in harmony with Your Body's Design Pattern. By *balance* and *harmony* we mean capturing a visually pleasing relationship between you and your clothes so that your total presentation looks stable and in proportion, and that your clothes are "in tune with" the design elements found in your facial features and body. *Self acceptance* and *selectivity* are the basic prerequisites to the development of individual style. Carefully read the Overview on the next page. It describes this process of discovery.

The lily symbol

As you read through the book, you will come across many new ideas about how to "see" yourself relative to your clothing choices. These concepts have never been in print before. We have created a new language to describe art principles as they apply to the human body. These words merely describe what you most probably have instinctively or intuitively known. In order to help you quickly recognize these new ideas, this symbol appears next to them.

An overview: how to discover Your Body's Design Pattern

In every chapter just 3 simple steps.

1 From art...
In each chapter a different element of art is introduced to...

2 to body...
help you discover your Body's Design Pattern which leads you to a new level of **self-acceptance.**

3 to clothes
Then you learn about how to choose clothes that are in harmony with Your Body's Design Pattern which develops **selectivity.**

CHAPTER 1 Line	Your body type as defined by the contour lines of your body Line pattern in your face in terms of line movement and direction and of space	Best structural designs for your body type ❧ Best fabric choices and uses to achieve those structural design(s) Best use of line in your styling details ❧ Your best patterns and prints
CHAPTER 2 Shape	Your body's basic shape and width proportions	Your natural silhouette(s) in clothing, and how to change it for an alternate one(s)
CHAPTER 3 Proportion	Your body's length proportions and upper body balance points	How to combine tops and bottoms for your proportions ❧ How to wear any skirt length and jacket length you wish ❧ How to wear all neckline and collar styles
CHAPTER 4 Body Particulars	Your Body Particulars—your special features from head-to-toe that give your body character	How to use certain clothing techniques to highlight or camouflage your body particulars using line and space, shape, or proportion
CHAPTER 5 Scale	The scale pattern found in your body and face	How to select construction and styling details, jewelry and other ornamentation that are in harmony with your body's scale pattern ❧ How to upscale for drama
CHAPTER 6 Color	Your body's natural coloration as seen in your skin, hair, and eyes	How to select and use colors in harmony with your natural coloring ❧ How to use color to enhance your innate intensity ❧ How to use colors for different psychological effects
CHAPTER 7 Texture	Your body's textural qualities as seen in your skin and hair	How to select clothing textures that interact with your body's textural pattern (surface quality and textural weight)
CHAPTER 8 Your innate creativity	Your body's beauty as seen through self-acceptance, and a sense of wonder and creative freedom	How to express your individuality through dress ❧ How to be creative with your Design Pattern and set your own standard of beauty

Beauty across cultures

To demonstrate that each of you has a design pattern waiting to be discovered, look at these faces. Though they are of different racial backgrounds, these women have a similar appearance. Why? Because they have similar design elements: the shape and fullness of the lips, the largeness and spacing of the eyes, the thick and straight lines of the brows, and the curved hairline, among others. But they are different in other ways too—the most obvious being in their coloring and in the textures of their skin and hair.

Wild geranium

Your individuality is but a reflection of the uniqueness of others. In seeing the beauty in ourselves, we are more likely to see that everybody is, indeed, beautiful in his or her own way. In this basic truth lies the seed that can flower into a greater acceptance of other peoples; in effect, of all life—in all of its wonderful forms, shapes, sizes, and colors.

Stink bug

Red rose hips

Fern leaf

All photos:
Bill Terry
Photography

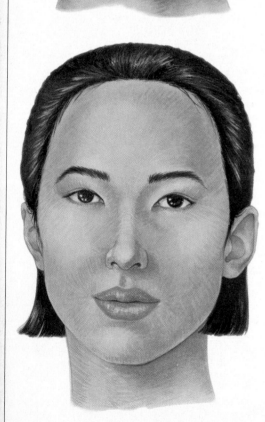

Timeless beauty

A predominant theme of this book is the belief that through the artist's perspective we can learn to see the commonplace as uncommonly beautiful. This theme stands at the heart of *The Triumph of Individual Style* and of a beauty that is timeless. Study the following images: The first is from the late nineteenth century by Edouard Manet. The second by Rembrandt was painted over three hundred years earlier. One subject is in her youth; the other is past her prime. The female image has always had a dominant place in art. Relatively speaking, both Manet and Rembrandt painted feminine beauty in rather realistic terms. Before Manet's time the nude figure in art was acceptable, for the most part, as long as it was depicted with biblical, classical or historical allusions. (Even Rembrandt's *Bathsheba*, though realistic, is a biblical figure). Then, in the late 1800's Edouard Manet exhibited his *L'Olympia*. This painting outraged the public, for Manet had dared to paint a woman nude without the customary classical body or back-drop to dignify her nakedness.

For years Manet stood alone, a maverick against the art world; but he opened the doors for many young artists who followed his lead. With unprecedented

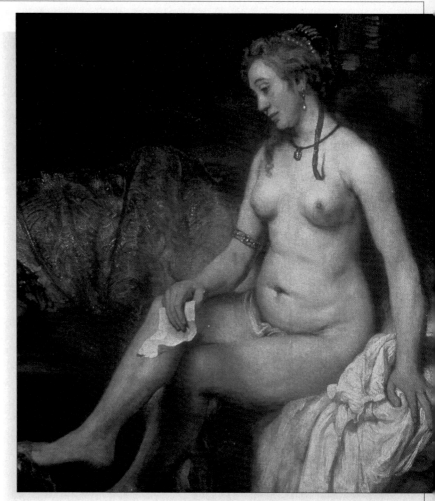

Bathsheba au bain, Rembrandt, Musée du Louvre, Paris (detail)

fervor and freedom, these artists tossed aside the historical or classical structures and painted the female figure solely for the beauty of the colors of her skin and the lines and shapes of her body. It was a celebration of feminine beauty that came in many different forms as shown in the examples displayed in our gallery on the following page:

L'Olympia, Edouard Manet,
Musée du Louvre, Paris. (detail).

Gallery of beauties

...the rosy, round and creamy-skinned women of Renoir...

Madame Hagen, Pierre-Auguste Renoir, The National Gallery of Art, Washington, Gift of Angelika Wertheim Frink, (detail).

...the serene, dark-skinned beauties of Gauguin...

Two Tahitian Women, Paul Gauguin, The Metropolitan Museum of Art, New York, (detail).

...the vibrant-colored elongated figures of Modigliani...

Girl in a Green Blouse, Amedeo Modigliani, The National Gallery of Art, Washington; Chester Dale Collection (detail).

...the glamorous females like Sargent's *Madame X*...

Madame X (Mme. Gautreau), John Singer Sargent, The Metropolitan Museum of Art, New York; Arthur H. Hearn Fund, 1916 (detail).

...and others we did not show... all foreshadowed our own era—a time ripe for the triumph of individual beauty and style.

We invite you now to imagine yourself as part of this gallery of women and to take pleasure in seeing the lines and shapes and colors that define your own physical qualities. By seeing yourself in artistic terms, you will cast aside all the stereotypes and ideals which have kept women from emerging as individuals and you can begin the journey of discovering your own timeless beauty.

"If you own only one original work of art in your life— let it be YOU!"

Individual beauty across time

Cultivating timeless beauty is a lifelong process. This is the lesson we can derive from Rembrandt's *Bathsheba* (see page 5). Rembrandt is considered one of the greatest masters of the unideal, and in his Bathsheba he set aside the perfect curves in order to depict the drama of the human body. In this image Rembrandt shows us the reality and the beauty of aging.

Though our bone structures remain relatively the same, we all know that our bodies change shape as we grow older and experience life. For example, sometimes after pregnancy many women's bosoms become larger or fall lower or their tummies aren't quite so tucked in, regardless of how much they exercise. Happily, we live in an era where there are ways to help us keep our youthful appearance. There is nothing wrong with taking advantage of "age-retarding" processes, but we all know they are only temporary adjustments.

On the other hand, the artistic viewpoint gives us a way to adjust beautifully to the flow of time. The artist sees that every phase in a woman's life has its special aesthetics. For example, color fades as one ages, especially in the eyes and hair. What does this mean to the creative mind? To us, it simply means that the colors you wear will also change. For some, the colors will be softened just as time softens the petals of a fading flower. They are still beautiful colors, just softer. For others, when the hair grows completely white, they seem to be able to wear stronger color, particularly those whose bodies still move with tensile strength in spite of a slower gait. Periodically throughout your life, you will also want to re-evaluate your body's silhouettes and reassess the kinds of clothing shapes that flatter your current form.

Whatever shape you're in, we will show you there is always a way to dress it artistically. Given that you have your health, you can always feel beautiful.

In short, by regarding yourself as a work of art at every stage or passage of your life, you will continue to revive your every feature with new character, so that it is never seen as an imperfection or flaw. Rather, each new line and shape, color or texture on your face and body is simply viewed as more new material for expressing yourself as a unique creation of time.

Best of all as we all grow older, though we may or may not lose interest in "dressing up", the look of confidence and self-esteem we've attained over a lifetime will allow us to project Time's true gift: the beauty of the soul and the spirit, which is the triumph of individual style at its greatest and most profound level.

May this book help guide you on your journey there.

Gwendolyn Mason Melgren
at ages 3, 14, 34, 44 and 79.

Water and reeds stage a
dance between line and
space. Any space, once
interrupted by a mere line
or dab of color, suddenly
brings to the eye a "figure"
in its background. Line is
the foundation, the beginning. Space supports it.

Line in your face and body

...and how to choose fabrics that work for you.

ine has movement. Traditionally line has been defined as a trace of a moving point.

The point can move in straight lines, curves, or a combination of both. In following lines with our eyes, we seem to move along more quickly with straight lines than the undulations of curved lines. We can easily feel this contrast in tempo between straight and curved lines when our eyes follow a line that is a combination of both. Notice in the next example how the eyes "zip" across the first straight line and slow down as they begin to trace the fluid, more graceful curves; then back to a quick streak across another straight line halting suddenly to maneuver the last rounded bend.

Since line is the foundation of design, we begin with the element of line (and its inevitable partner—space) in the discovery of your Body's Design Pattern. In this chapter the element of line will help you understand how to create a harmonious relationship between the language of line in your body and face with the fabrics you choose for your clothing. We begin with the body.

Line in the body

The contour or outline of your body can have predominantly straight lines and angles, or predominantly curved and rounded ones. By just looking at body contour lines in terms of straight and curved lines, we can distinguish five basic body types, which are represented by the five artworks on the following chart. Consider carefully the descriptions given for each type, and you will be able to identify your body as one of these five basic body types.

> Remember all you need to determine are your body's contour lines—whether they are straight or curved or both; forget for the moment your body's shape or size.

Chart of the five basic body types

❧

*W*hich one is yours?

SKELETAL	MOULDED
Overall bony appearance	Predominantly fleshy appearance
The bones show as though the skin is pulled over the bones, creating straight lines and angles. Look at these areas: • shoulders • upper chest • rib cage • knees • ankles	Flesh covers the bones, creating curved lines and general roundedness throughout the body. Look at these areas: • shoulders • upper arms • hips and thighs • tummy • derrière • knees and calves

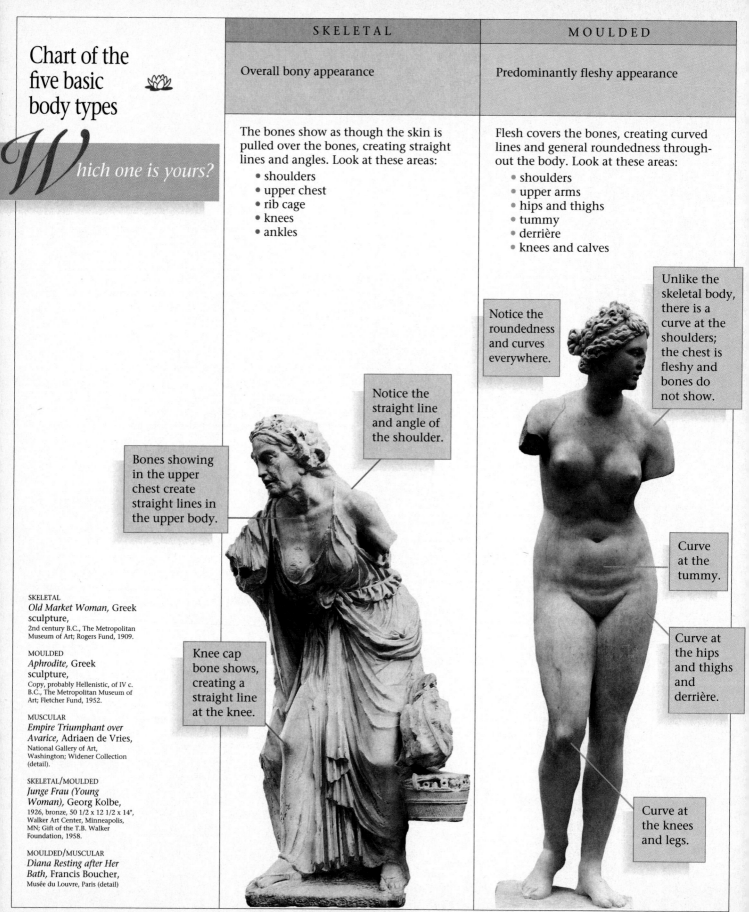

Notice the roundedness and curves everywhere.

Unlike the skeletal body, there is a curve at the shoulders; the chest is fleshy and bones do not show.

Notice the straight line and angle of the shoulder.

Bones showing in the upper chest create straight lines in the upper body.

Curve at the tummy.

SKELETAL
Old Market Woman, Greek sculpture,
2nd century B.C., The Metropolitan Museum of Art; Rogers Fund, 1909.

MOULDED
Aphrodite, Greek sculpture,
Copy, probably Hellenistic, of IV c. B.C., The Metropolitan Museum of Art; Fletcher Fund, 1952.

MUSCULAR
Empire Triumphant over Avarice, Adriaen de Vries,
National Gallery of Art, Washington; Widener Collection (detail).

SKELETAL/MOULDED
Junge Frau (Young Woman), Georg Kolbe,
1926, bronze, 50 1/2 x 12 1/2 x 14", Walker Art Center, Minneapolis, MN; Gift of the T.B. Walker Foundation, 1958.

MOULDED/MUSCULAR
Diana Resting after Her Bath, Francis Boucher,
Musée du Louvre, Paris (detail)

Knee cap bone shows, creating a straight line at the knee.

Curve at the hips and thighs and derrière.

Curve at the knees and legs.

MUSCULAR	SKELETAL/MOULDED	MOULDED/MUSCULAR
❦	❦	❦
Overall taut and muscular appearance	Both skeletal (bony and straight) and moulded (fleshy and curved) appearance	Both moulded (fleshy and curved) and muscular (taut and curved) appearance

Well-defined muscles create tautly-curved body with firm skin. Look at these areas:

- shoulders
- upper arm
- neck
- back
- thigh
- calves

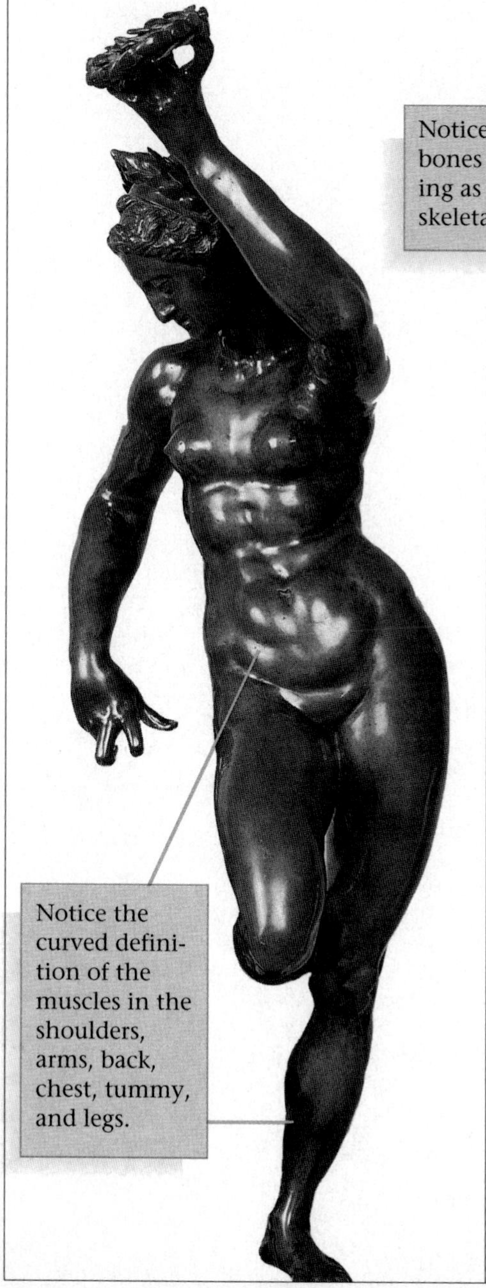

Skeletal (top of body). Bony in the
- shoulders • rib cage
- upper chest • (sometimes) hips

Moulded (bottom of body). Fleshy in the • hips (sometimes) • and/or
- thighs   derrière
- tummy

Like George Kolbe's *Junge Frau*, this combination body can be skeletal at the top, moulded in the lower body; or it can be the other way around—moulded top, skeletal bottom.

Muscular. Well-defined muscles in the
- neck
- arms
- back
- or elsewhere

Moulded. Fleshy in the
- hips
- thighs
- tummy

Like Boucher's *Diana*, this combination body can be muscular in the upper body and moulded in the lower body; or it can be the opposite—moulded top, muscular bottom.

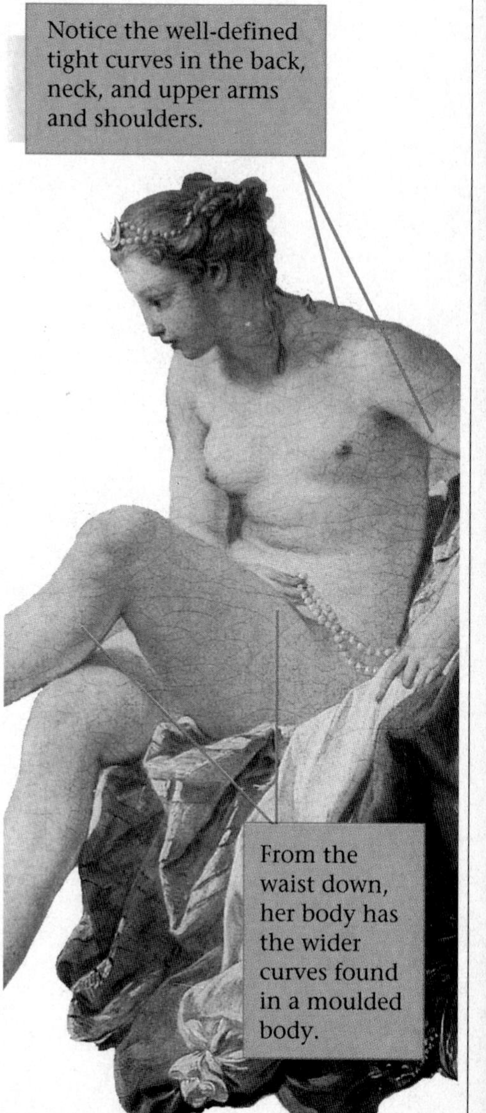

Notice the bones showing as in the skeletal body.

Notice the well-defined tight curves in the back, neck, and upper arms and shoulders.

Notice the curved definition of the muscles in the shoulders, arms, back, chest, tummy, and legs.

Notice the fleshy curves as in the moulded body.

From the waist down, her body has the wider curves found in a moulded body.

How to choose and use fabrics for your body type

Now that you know your body type based on its contour lines, in this next chart go to the column that shows your body type. The first section tells you what structural designs you need in your garments that will harmonize best with your body lines.

> Basically, the principle is: Where your body is straight, have straight lines in your clothing; where your body is curved, have curved lines in your garments.

Next, in the second section, you will find the categories of fabrics that work best to create this harmony. We call these your "inherent fabric" categories. Examples of clothing using these fabrics are shown in the section just below this.

Finally, to afford you greater freedom in your choice of fabric, in the bottom section of the column, we provide basic hints on how to adapt other fabrics that are not in your inherent fabric categories. Indeed, you may prefer to use these other fabrics, because you feel more comfortable with their effects.

Throughout, we speak of fabrics only in terms of how fabrics fall or work on the body. So we've divided fabrics into four categories:

1. fluid fabrics
2. medium-drape fabrics
3. medium-taut fabrics
4. taut fabrics

More information about these four fabric categories can be found on page 14.

Above: *Maud Dale*, Jean Lurcat, 1928, National Gallery of Art, Washington; Chester Dale Collection (detail).

	SKELETAL	MOULDED
Structural design of garment	You need straight lines and angles around your skeletal areas.	You need curves and drape over your moulded areas.
Your inherent fabric categories	You need *taut* to *medium-taut* fabrics (fabrics with body).	You need *medium-drape* to *fluid* fabrics (fabrics that move easily).
Examples of clothing using your fabrics	Use fabric with body to hold a straight line around arms and hips and to angle over the shoulders. Or, use medium-taut fabric to construct straight shoulders and straight side seams over your generally skeletal body.	Use fluid fabric to drape around the shoulders, hips, thighs, tummy and derrière. Or, use medium-drape fabric that easily follows the curves in your body.
Basic hints for adapting other fabrics to your body type	If you choose to wear medium-drape to fluid fabrics, use them in greater volume around the skeletal areas. For example, wear a garment that is gathered in volume around the shoulders, elbows and waist. Or, use gathers in skirts to drape with volume over hips and knees. Obviously, because the volume of fabric tends to create more fluid and curved lines, this is a way to achieve a softer, more graceful look for the skeletal body type. You may want to feel and dress this way most of the time, particularly if your walk is fluid. Also, this is especially effective if you have curved lines in your facial features — see Line in the face, page 15.	If you choose to wear medium-taut to taut fabrics, use them in a garment constructed with curves around your key moulded areas. For example, wear a garment using taut fabric with curved construction around the shoulders and hips (see examples for the Muscular body), and/or use slight gathering around the waist to create only a slight drape. If you have straight or angled facial features and/or have a strong, purposeful walk, you may wish to create straight shoulders rather than curved ones (see examples for the Skeletal body). With straight lines the look is less graceful and the overall effect becomes more straightforward and powerful.

MUSCULAR 	SKELETAL/MOULDED 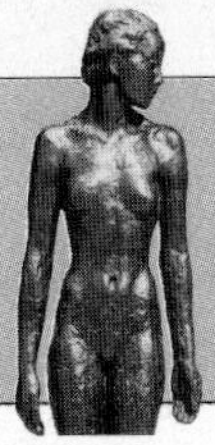	MOULDED/MUSCULAR 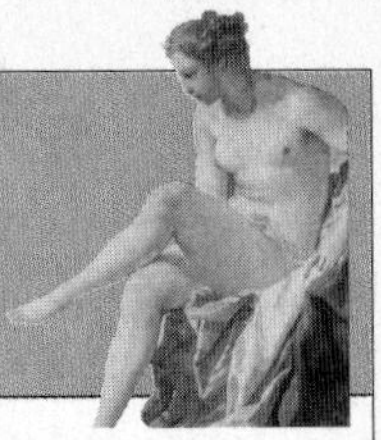
You need relatively taut curved lines to relate to the curves of your muscles.	You need straight lines where skeletal, and curved lines where moulded.	You need *taut* curved lines over your muscles, and soft curved lines and *drape* over your moulded areas.
You need *medium taut* to *medium drape* fabrics. (Fluid fabrics would be too droopy over a generally toned body.) The fabrics need to relate to the tautness of the toned body.	You need *medium-taut* fabrics where skeletal and *medium-drape* to *fluid* fabrics where moulded.	You need *medium-taut* to *medium-drape* where muscular and *medium-drape* to *fluid* fabric where moulded.

Use medium-taut fabric with curved construction over the shoulders and upper arms, and hips.

Use medium-taut to taut fabric at the top (constructed with straight lines over the shoulders if skeletal). This is combined with medium-drape fabric with some gathering for the skirt where you are curved.

Use medium-taut to taut fabric over your muscular areas, and medium-drape to fluid fabric over your moulded areas.

Or, use medium-drape fabric constructed with curves around your shoulders. The fabric generally drapes but never droops.

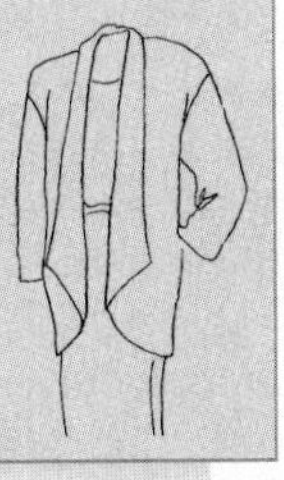

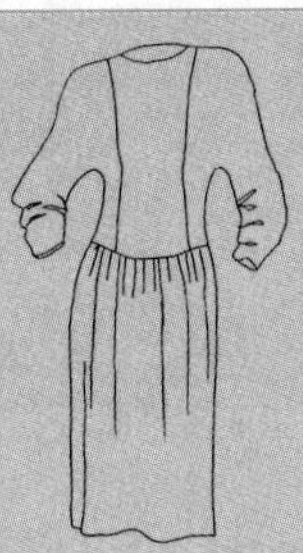

Or, use fluid fabric at the top to harmonize with your moulded upper body. This is combined with taut fabric for your skeletal lower body.

If you choose to use fluid fabrics, use them in volume and combine them with medium-taut fabrics elsewhere in the garment. For example, relatively taut fabric at the top, and fluid fabric in volume at the bottom.

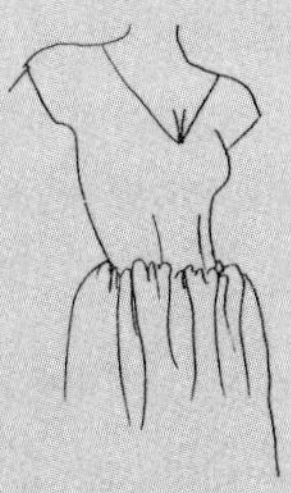

See hints under both skeletal and moulded body types.

See hints under both moulded and muscular body types.

Credits for art on top row, see page 10.

Understanding the four categories of fabrics

Fluid fabric

The fluid fabric falls loosely, is able to fall gently over body curves, and like the curved line, suggests something graceful in its movement. Fluid fabric is a perfect mate for the moulded body. Even in volume, when scrunched in the hand in gathers, fluid fabrics will still cascade effortlessly like a gentle waterfall. Some fluid fabrics are chiffon, silk jersey, lawn, rayon, sheer silks, sheer woolens, and sheer cottons.

Medium-drape fabric

The medium-drape fabric has a little more body than the fluid fabric. Not a waterfall, but more like waves that undulate, still moving with ease but with more force. Some medium-drape fabrics are wool challis, cotton jersey, wool jersey, velvet, soft wool crepe, fine knits, and silk crepe.

Ingres' *Mme. Rivière* is an excellent example of a moulded body type wearing fluid to medium-drape fabrics that are in complete harmony with her curved body.

lightweight linen

lightweight wool garbardine

wool flannel

medium-weight cotton

wool crepe

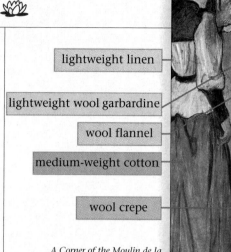

A Corner of the Moulin de la Galette, Henri Toulouse-Lautrec, National Gallery of Art, Washington; Chester Dale Collection.

Medium-taut fabric

The medium-taut fabric has more body than the fluid or drape fabrics. It is thicker, with slightly more dimension in its feel. We liken it more to a deep quiet lake—the water does not cascade or move in waves; it is still and smooth, but not frozen in place. It retains a subtle quality of movement. Some medium taut fabrics are lightweight wool gabardine, wool crepe, wool flannel, medium-weight cottons, and very lightweight linen, as seen in Toulouse-Lautrec's painting above.

Taut fabric

The taut fabric has more body and feels stiff to the touch. When scrunched in the hand and let go, it tries to spring back to its original flatness. No water analogy here. One is more likely to think of a touch of starch—perfect fabrics for creating straight lines that are in harmony with the skeletal body type. Some taut fabrics are heavy satin, silk taffeta, medium to heavy-weight linen, medium to heavy-weight gabardine, worsted wool and cotton duck.

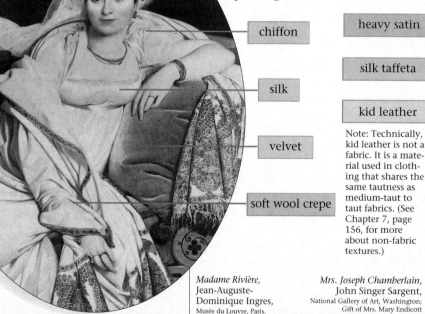

chiffon

silk

velvet

soft wool crepe

heavy satin

silk taffeta

kid leather

Note: Technically, kid leather is not a fabric. It is a material used in clothing that shares the same tautness as medium-taut to taut fabrics. (See Chapter 7, page 156, for more about non-fabric textures.)

Madame Rivière, Jean-Auguste-Dominique Ingres, Musée du Louvre, Paris.

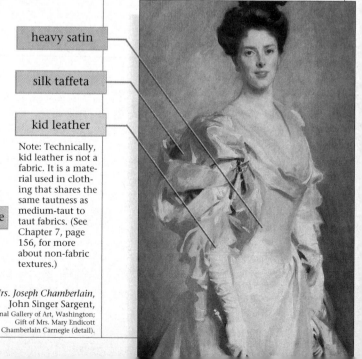

Mrs. Joseph Chamberlain, John Singer Sargent, National Gallery of Art, Washington; Gift of Mrs. Mary Endicott Chamberlain Carnegie (detail).

Line in the face

If line has movement, it must also have direction. The three basic directions of line are the horizontal, the vertical, and the diagonal; and each is associated with certain universal qualities.

Horizontal

The horizontal line, like a person lying down, suggests restfulness and quiet.

The Nymph of the Spring, Lucas Cranach, The Elder,
National Gallery of Art, Washington; Gift of Clarence Y. Palitz (detail).

Vertical

The vertical line, like a person upright, is associated with alertness and strength.

Head of a Woman,
Amedeo Modigliani,
National Gallery
of Art, Washington;
Chester Dale Collection.

Diagonal

The diagonal line is often related to dynamic action or restlessness.

Dancing Figure,
Auguste Rodin,
National Gallery of Art,
Washington; Gift of
Mrs. John W. Simpson.

As we have shown, the element of line in terms of movement gives us the clues to our body type and how to use fabrics for our body's design. Now we turn to the discovery of the element of line in the face. For the face we will look for both line movement and line direction.

All of your facial features can be described as either straight or curved, and can go in any of the three directions of line: horizontal, vertical, or diagonal. For instance, eyebrows or eyes can be slightly curved and slant downward in a diagonal direction as seen in Modigliani's *Madame Amedée*. The kinds of lines found in your facial features will show you what lines work best in the styling details within your garments such as in your necklines, collars, lapels, and/or pockets.

Madame Amedée (Woman with Cigarette),
Amedeo Modigliani,
National Gallery of Art, Washington; Chester Dale Collection (detail).

🪷 The basic concept is simple: To create harmony, repeat in your garment details the predominant line movement, and when appropriate, the line direction found in your facial features.

If you find that your features are predominantly straight, then repeat straight lines in your garment details, and if they also go in a diagonal direction, then angle those straight lines when appropriate. Likewise, if you have predominantly curved lines in your features, then use curves in your clothing, and when appropriate, in a similar direction.

Examples of how line in clothing can relate to the natural pattern of line in the face

Isabella Brant, Sir Anthony van Dyck, National Gallery of Art, Washington; Andrew W. Mellon Collection (detail).

Madame Henriot, Pierre-Auguste Renoir, National Gallery of Art, Washington; Gift of the Adele R. Levy Fund, Inc. (detail).

In this portrait of Isabella Brandt, notice the diagonal direction of her eyes, the straight diagonals in her eyebrows, nose tip, smiling mouth, the angles in her hairline with a widow's peak at the center, and even in the pointed shape of her jaw and chin. Her nose and the sides of her face have a straight vertical line. Her bottom lip has a strong straight horizontal line.

Her predominantly straight and angled line pattern is effectively repeated in her large outer collar and in the details in her bodice. The scalloped motif of the inner strapped bodice piece also repeats the less dominant tiny curved lines found in her hairline, upper lip and bottom of her eyes.

If we were to dress Isabella Brandt today, we might select these pieces of clothing. Can you see how straight diagonal lines in these outfits relate to the straight and angled line pattern found in her features? Only relatively taut fabrics can achieve these lines.

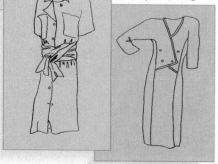

In this portrait of Mme. Henriot, notice the features are *mostly softly curved and in a horizontal direction: the eyebrows, the eyes, and the bottom lip. The contour of the sides of her face and chin are diagonal but also gently curved.* Her eyes are on a relatively horizontal plane from end to end; they are not angled like Isabella's eyes. The only straight angle Mme. Henriot has can be found in her nose tip. *Notice how the curve in her neckline relates to the line pattern found in her face.*

Here are other clothing choices that would be harmonious with this Renoir beauty. Only medium-drape to fluid fabrics can achieve these curved lines and soft effects.

In terms of the effect of line direction, which of the two faces above seems more animated and active, and which one seems quieter? Do you see that because we associate the straight diagonal line with dynamic action, the face with all the angles gives the impression of having a lot of activity? While the other face with curved horizontal lines in her face seems calmer, quieter, more graceful?

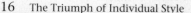

Discover the line pattern in your facial features

Perhaps you have never looked at your facial features in terms of line before, but it is really quite easy. The following two charts list the features you look at to determine the predominant line pattern in your face.

First look for line movement: All features listed in the Line Movement chart can be either relatively straight *or* curved, or can be both straight *and* curved.

Next look for line direction: In the Line Direction chart notice that only two features (the nose and sides of face) can have vertical direction.

> The predominance of one line movement and one line direction is what we want to look for in the line pattern of your face.

On the following charts:

1. Check each feature under the appropriate column or columns for your face. For example, if your eyebrows are straight, check Eyebrows under the Straight column in the Line Movement chart. If they go in both a horizontal and diagonal direction, check Eyebrows under the Horizontal and Diagonal columns in the Line Direction chart. Remember, it is possible for any feature to be a combination in both line movement and/or line direction, so look carefully at your features and check mark more than one column, if appropriate.

2. Count and total the number of checked features for each column. Which kinds of lines appear most in your features? You may find you have an equal distribution of all the lines, which simply means you have a greater latitude in your use of line movement and direction.

3. At the bottom of each chart, check off the box that describes the line pattern in your features.

> Before you analyze your face using the charts below, you may wish to practice looking for the line pattern on the two faces from the artworks of Ingres and Matisse, which are on the next two pages.

Line Movement	Straight	Curved
Eyebrows		
Eyes		
Sides of nose		
Tip of nose		
Mouth when:		
smiling		
not smiling		
Hairline		
Sides of face		
Jaw and/or chin		
Total		

The line movement of my features is
- ☐ Predominantly straight
- ☐ Predominantly curved
- ☐ Evenly distributed

Line Direction	Horizontal	Vertical	Diagonal
Eyebrows			
Eyes			
Nose *(can appear horizontal if very wide and short)*			
Tip of nose *(from nostril to tip to other nostril)*			
Mouth when:			
smiling			
not smiling			
Hairline			
Sides of face			
Jaw and/or chin			
Total			

- ☐ My features go predominantly in a horizontal direction.
- ☐ My features go predominantly in a vertical direction.
- ☐ My features go predominantly in a diagonal direction.
- ☐ My features go equally in _____ and _____ directions.

Practice looking for the natural pattern of line in the face

Madame Moitessier, Jean-Auguste-Dominique Ingres,
National Gallery of Art, Washington; Samuel H. Kress Collection (detail).

ere is something to remember: If you wish to highlight any of the features not included in your predominant lines, repeat their lines also by integrating them creatively with your predominant ones. For example, the Ingres beauty whose lines are predominantly horizontal (both curved and straight) could include the straight *vertical* lines seen in the sides of her nose and sides of her face in a neckline such as shown here:➜

Notice how both the horizontal and vertical lines of her features are highlighted. In fact, can you see how the vertical lines seem to give her sloping body and quiet appearance a sort of "lift" and "strength" which the horizontal line alone did not give? By repeating your line pattern in your clothing, it follows that you are also repeating the effects associated with those lines. You will appreciate these effects more clearly as you develop your skill in the creative use of line. *Throughout this book, we will show that the principal of repetition is basic to creating the harmony essential for beauty.* How you use the principal and its outcome depends upon your unique gift of creativity.

(For answers to charts, see page 182.)

Line Movement

	Straight	Curved
Eyebrows		
Eyes		
Sides of nose		
Tip of nose		
Mouth when:		
smiling (not shown)		
not smiling		
Hairline		
Sides of face		
Jaw and/or chin		
Total		

The line movement of Madame Moitessier's features is
☐ Predominantly straight
☐ Predominantly curved
☐ Evenly distributed

Line Direction

	Horizontal	Vertical	Diagonal
Eyebrows			
Eyes			
Nose *(can appear horizontal if very wide and short)*			
Tip of nose *(from nostril to tip to other nostril)*			
Mouth when:			
smiling (not shown)			
not smiling			
Hairline			
Sides of face			
Jaw and/or chin			
Total			

☐ Her features go predominantly in a horizontal direction.
☐ Her features go predominantly in a vertical direction.
☐ Her features go predominantly in a diagonal direction.
☐ Her features go equally in _____ and _____ directions.

Young Girl with Long Hair, Henri Matisse,
National Gallery of Art, Washington; Rosenwald Collection (detail).

What do you see?

The tops of her eyes are curved, and the bottoms are straight.

Her nose is straight on one side and curvy on the other.

Her nose tip has both straight and curved diagonal lines.

Her brows are straight horizontal lines.

From corner to corner, notice her eyes slant in a diagonal direction.

Her mouth, jaw and chin, and sides of her face are all curved diagonals.

Line Movement

	Straight	Curved
Eyebrows		✓
Eyes		✓
Sides of nose	✓	
Tip of nose		✓
Mouth when:		
smiling (not shown)		✓
not smiling	✓	
Hairline		✓
Sides of face		✓
Jaw and/or chin		✓
Total	2	7

The line movement of the young girl's features is
- [ ] Predominantly straight
- [x] Predominantly curved
- [ ] Evenly distributed

Line Direction

	Horizontal	Vertical	Diagonal
Eyebrows			✓
Eyes	✓		
Nose *(can appear horizontal if very wide and short)*			✓
Tip of nose *(from nostril to tip to other nostril)*			✓
Mouth when:			
smiling (not shown)			✓
not smiling			✓
Hairline			✓
Sides of face			✓
Jaw and/or chin			✓
Total	1	0	8

- [ ] Her features go predominantly in a horizontal direction.
- [ ] Her features go predominantly in a vertical direction.
- [x] Her features go predominantly in a diagonal direction.
- [ ] Her features go equally in _____ and _____ directions.

How to choose patterns and prints ✿

or most women, choosing a pattern or print that is beautiful on them is difficult, and so they go about it in a seemingly haphazard fashion.

Again, we suggest the solution is to find a harmony between you and the print. How do we go about this? There are so many kinds of prints, we feel that the first thing to do when confronted with a print is to ask yourself whether or not you like or love the basic motif of the print. If you do, then observe these four qualities common to all prints:

1. the *line* movement of the motif
2. the clarity or definition of the *line edge* in the motif
3. the *space* surrounding the pattern or print
4. the *scale* of the print.

Do the lines of the motif agree with the predominant line movement found in your facial features? If not, then consider another print. If they do, then analyze the print further.

Look at the following artworks numbered 1 through 4. Next to each is a print we feel is in harmony with her in terms of these four qualities. Through these well-known beauties, we will demonstrate how to see these qualities in your facial features. In the previous section we have already discussed line movement. For the other three qualities, we will be referring specifically to the *eyebrows, eyes, nose,* and *mouth*.

After line movement, the *clarity of the line edge* in the motif should be considered.

Four examples of relating print qualities to facial features

1

1. Predominant line movement: combination curved and straight
2. Clarity of line edge: well-defined
3. Space around print: moderate
4. Scale: small to medium

Ginevra de'Benci, Leonardo da Vinci, National Gallery of Art, Washington; Ailsa Mellon Bruce Fund (detail).

2

1. Predominant line movement: combination curved & straight
2. Clarity of line edge: moderately defined
3. Space around print: moderate
4. Scale: medium to large.

Two Tahitian Women, Paul Gauguin, The Metropolitan Museum of Art (detail).

3

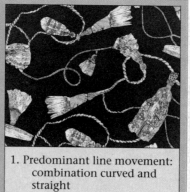

1. Predominant line movement: curved
2. Clarity of line edge: undefined
3. Space around print: little — and does not relate to her. So, she would wear this in small quantity, surrounded by an article of clothing that is solid and plain.
4. Scale: small to medium

Mona Lisa, Leonardo da Vinci, Louvre, Paris (detail).

4
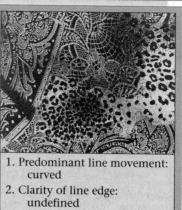

1. Predominant line movement: combination curved and straight
2. Clarity of line edge: combination well-defined, undefined
3. Space around print: little relative to the size of the shapes in the print
4. Scale: medium to large

La Mousme, Vincent van Gogh, National Gallery of Art, Washington; Chester Dale Collection (detail).

Clarity of line edge in the print

Da Vinci's portrait of *Ginevra de'Benci* (**1**) and his *Mona Lisa* (**3**) show us the extremes of line edge definition. On the one hand, **1** *has well-defined lines* in her features (look at the eyebrow, eyes, nose, and mouth), and so prints that have well-defined edges are excellent for her. On the other hand, **3** *has undefined features,* and print motifs that have soft edges or have a kind of blended effect will harmonize nicely with her.

Gauguin's *Tahitian Woman* (**2**) has facial features that come between these extremes; her features have *moderately defined* lines. Her prints will be neither hard-edged nor very soft-edged. Notice the moderately defined edge of the print we have chosen for her and contrast it with the other two.

Some faces can have a *combination of line edge* in their features, as in van Gogh's *La Mousme* (**4**). She is well-defined in the eyebrows and eyes and undefined in the nose and mouth. This contrast is repeated in the print we have chosen for her.

Space around the print

Next, the *space around the print* is very important, and it must relate to the space found around your facial features. Think of the arrangement of your features—eyebrows, eyes, nose, and mouth—as creating a design or "pattern", and think of your entire facial area as the background for that "pattern". Simply speaking, *prints can be widely spaced, moderately spaced, or densely spaced with little or no background.* The more facial space you have around your features, the more space or background you need in your print; and conversely, the less facial space around your features, the less background space you need in the prints you wear.

If a print does not relate to the spacing in your face—in other words, if the print is too dense—then consider not using the print. However, if the print is right for you in other ways in spite of its density, you might wish to use it in a small section of your outfit, such as in a scarf or blouse. In short, you must offset the print by surrounding it with non-printed pieces of clothing (See **3**, *Mona Lisa*).

How do you determine amount of space in your face? Look again at our artworks. In Ginevra's face (**1**), we see *a moderate amount of space* around the mouth and *much space* surrounding the nose and eyes. Notice the wide space in the eyelid and between the eye and eyebrow. In the Tahitian woman (**2**) we see a *moderate amount of space* around the features, generally all around the face. Then there are combination faces such as the *Mona Lisa* (**3**), which has *moderate to much space* (see her forehead) around her features. In the painting by van Gogh (**4**), the features are *not surrounded with a lot of space.* Notice the relatively short forehead, small chin, and lack of space around the eyes at the side of her face. The pattern of eyes, nose, and mouth covers most of the facial space. A print that takes up most of its surrounding background would be most harmonious with this face.

Scale of the print

Finally, consider the last quality: the *scale or relative size of the print.* We will have more to say about scale in Chapter 5.

For now, as you might have already guessed, remember the scale of the print should be relatively the same as the scale of your facial features, whether *small, and/or medium, and/or large scale.* Look again at our artworks:

1 has relatively small scale features except for her eyes which are medium in scale; therefore, her prints can be small to medium in scale, and with moderate to much space around the print motif.

2 has a combination of medium scale eyebrows and eyes, relatively large scale nose, and a medium to large scale mouth. Her prints or patterns can range from medium to large scale, surrounded by a moderate amount of space.

3 also has a combination—small scale mouth and medium scale in her other features. Her prints can range from small to medium.

4 has medium to large scale features, so her prints can range from medium to large scale, and as we've shown, the print motif can have little background.

With these four examples as a guide, fill in the following chart for your facial features.

🪷 Four qualities in your facial features to relate to prints

1. Predominant line movement:

curved

2. Clarity of line edge
(check features under the appropriate column):

	Well-defined	Moderately defined	Undefined
Eyebrows	✓		
Eyes	✓		
Nose	✓		
Mouth	✓		

3. Space:
- ☐ Much space, and/or
- ☒ Moderate space, and/ or
- ☐ Little space.

4. Scale:
- ☐ Small scale, and/or
- ☑ Medium scale, and/or
- ☐ Large scale.

Through the element of line, you have just learned how to choose the fabrics for your body type and prints that relate to your facial features. In the next chapter, you will learn to bring these fabrics to life through clothing silhouettes that relate to your *body's basic shape.*

Like a game of connect-the-dots, allow your eyes to follow the points along the outside edge of this thistle flower. Let your mind outline the invisible path that delineates this living form into its elementary shapes. If your eyes can see the two ovals in this bloom—one lying on its side atop the other oval which is nearly upright and tall—then you have the ability to see the basic shapes found everywhere in nature. In the same fashion, one can learn to see the basic shapes found in the human body.

Your body's basic shape

...and how to choose silhouettes for your wardrobe.

Shape is generally seen as a flat space enclosed by a line that has turned to meet itself.

It is also the outline of a form—form being a three-dimensional subject, such as your body or parts of your body.

In terms of the body and clothing, when we say the word "shape", we usually think of geometric shapes. These geometric shapes take on the effects of the lines that surround them, so that a triangle assumes the effect of diagonal lines—active, restless, and/or aggressive. Or an oval takes on the gracefulness that a curved line suggests.

The six basic silhouettes in clothing

The outline of a garment or outfit, be it a dress or a combination of tops and bottoms (skirts, trousers, or shorts), creates a geometric shape called a "silhouette".

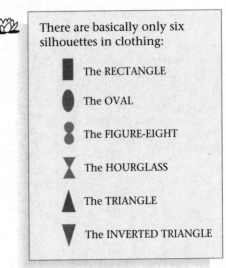

There are basically only six silhouettes in clothing:

■ The RECTANGLE

● The OVAL

⦿ The FIGURE-EIGHT

⧖ The HOURGLASS

▲ The TRIANGLE

▼ The INVERTED TRIANGLE

In the previous chapter, you discovered the first component of Your Body's Design Pattern—the attributes of line found in your body and face—and then learned how to relate them to your choice and use of fabrics in clothing. In this chapter you will discover the second component—*your body's basic shape*—and then relate it to one or more of the six silhouettes in clothing. Again, the goal is to create a harmony—this time, between the shape of your body and the silhouettes of your outfits.

Field Thistle, Bill Terry Photography

How to choose your natural silhouette 🪷

Your body's basic shape is the one created by the major part of the body that is defined by the shoulders, waist, and hips/thighs. In fact, by determining the width relationship between your shoulders, waist, and hips/thighs, you can quickly determine what we call your *natural silhouette* in clothing.

> 🪷 Your natural silhouette is the clothing shape that repeats your body's basic shape. As such, it is the one within which your body would generally feel most "at home".

In the following charts are art works that illustrate each basic body shape. As you can see, the great artists show us once again that there is beauty in all of them.

The descriptions given for each body shape will help you quickly determine your natural silhouette in clothing. **Remember, you are only determining your body's basic shape; disregard for the moment your body's size or body type.**

🪷 *Whatever your body's basic shape, that is also the shape of your natural silhouette.* The clothing examples shown with each of the figures in our artworks illustrate a few ways to achieve this harmonious match between body shape and clothing silhouette. Notice, too, that we differentiate the silhouettes as being either wide-waisted or narrow-waisted or both.

According to the width relationship between your shoulders, waist, and hips/thighs, what is your body's basic shape and which of the following is your natural silhouette?

My body's basic shape and natural silhouette is:

figure 8

Mars and Venus United by Love, Paolo Veronese, The Metropolitan Museum of Art; John Stewart Kennedy Fund, 1910 (detail).

RECTANGLE

Your natural silhouette is the rectangle if:

- Your shoulders are as wide as your hips/thighs
- And your waist is as wide as or just slightly narrower than your shoulders and hips/thighs.

OVAL 🪷

Your natural silhouette is the oval if:

- Your shoulders are narrower or as wide as your hips/thighs
- And from the front view, your waist appears the same width as, or slightly wider than, or noticeably wider than your shoulders and/or hips. And from the side view, your waist does not indent but seems to extend out in front and sometimes in back, giving a barrel-like impression from your shoulders to your hips.

Girl in Red, Edgar Degas, National Gallery of Art, Washington; Chester Dale Collection (detail).

This body shape dictates that garment pieces have straight vertical side seams, or give the impression of one continuous vertical seam line from shoulder to hem. This means:

- the waist is generally by-passed*
- the shoulders are never optically diminished
- the shoulders never extend beyond the hips
- and skirts do not taper or flare out at the bottom.

Any other straight vertical lines within the garment will add to the rectangular quality of this silhouette.

* If there is a slight waist, it is possible to give it a little emphasis with a narrow belt, loose belt, or with a blouson.

The Large Bathers, Paul Cézanne, National Gallery, London, (detail).

In both Cézanne's *The Large Bathers*, and Picasso's *Two Nudes*, you can see the oval shape of the body. *Though these bodies are on the large side, it is possible to have a slim oval shape for your body's silhouette.*

Two Nudes, Pablo Picasso. París (late 1906). Oil on canvas, 59-5/8" x 36-5/8", The Museum of Modern Art, New York. Gift of G. David Thompson in honor of Alfred H. Barr, Jr. (detail).

This body shape dictates that gar-ments have side seams that follow the curved line of the wide waist;

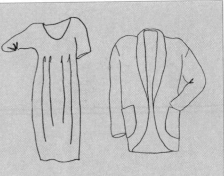

. . .as well as front and waist treatments that follow the curved line that begins at bosom level and extends out to bypass the waist line.

Parvati, standing, Islamic. Sculpture.
South Indian. Chola Dynasty, ca. 900, The Metropolitan Museum of Art; Cora Timken Burnett Collection of Persian Miniatures and other Persian Art Objects, Bequest of Cora Timken Burnett, 1956 (detail).

FIGURE-EIGHT

Your natural silhouette is the figure eight if:

* Your shoulders are curved and are relatively as wide as your hips/thighs
* And your waist is distinctly narrower than your shoulders and hips/thighs.

This body shape dictates that the outfit emphasizes the waist, has curved shoulders and hips, and has a bottom that tapers in at the hem.

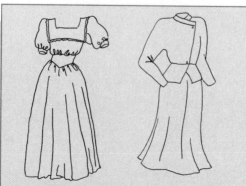

Madame X (Mme Gautreau), John Singer Sargent,
The Metropolitan Museum of Art; Arthur H. Hearn Fund, 1916 (detail).

HOURGLASS

Your natural silhouette is the hourglass if:

* Your shoulders are square and are relatively as wide as your hips/thighs
* And your waist is distinctly narrower than your shoulders and hips/thighs.

This body shape dictates that the outfit emphasizes the waist, has generally straight shoulders, and flares over the hips.

This silhouette can be full-length or short. A jacket with a flared peplum over a narrow skirt is an example of the shorter version of the hourglass silhouette.

flared peplum

▲ TRIANGLE

Your natural silhouette is the triangle if:

- Your shoulders and waist are narrower than your hips/thighs.

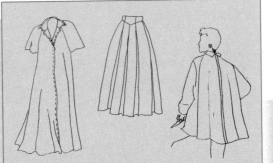

This body shape dictates that the bottom of the garment is wider or fuller than the bodice or top, whether the waist is emphasized or not. (Any top is okay as long as the shoulders are kept narrow.)

Bather Arranging Her Hair, Auguste Renoir,
National Gallery of Art, Washington; Chester Dale Collection (detail)..

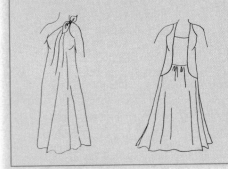

This silhouette is wide-waisted if your waist is as wide as or wider than the shoulders and gradually flares out and down to the wider hips.

This silhouette is narrow-waisted if your waist is distinctly narrower than the shoulders. The wide hips/thighs help to emphasize the narrowness of the waist. Generally, full skirts are used.

▼ INVERTED TRIANGLE

Your natural silhouette is the inverted triangle if:

- Your shoulders are wider than your waist and hips/thighs.

This body shape dictates that garment bottoms are always slimmer than the top, whether the waist is emphasized or not.

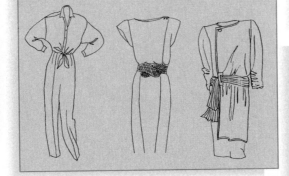

Nude, Roger de La Fresnaye,
National Gallery of Art, Washington;
Chester Dale Collection (detail).

This silhouette is wide-waisted if your waist is as wide as, or wider than, your hips. The hips are usually very narrow, so bypass the waist, or. . .

. . . you can widen the hips as with a peplum and create an illusion of a narrow-waisted inverted triangle.

This silhouette is narrow-waisted if your waist is distinctly narrower than your hips. (Even if your waist is narrow, you can bypass the waist with a wide jacket, and create a wide-waisted inverted triangle. You have a choice.)

One body, two silhouettes ✿

Can you be wide-waisted and narrow-waisted at the same time? The answer is yes! And consequently, you can have two different natural silhouettes, one in front and one in back. Here are four examples of such two-silhouetted bodies. Once you learn to observe the body in this way, you may discover that you have two natural silhouettes.

The first figure is wide-waisted in front with a rectangle silhouette. However, in the back she is narrow-waisted because of the way the back rib cage and hips bones allow her waist to come in. This indentation at the waist gives her back view the hourglass silhouette.

In the next example, indentation in the front waist (again because of the way the rib cage and hip bones are formed) gives us the impression of a figure eight silhouette, while the back is a rectangle.

The third example of a double-silhouetted figure is seen in Cézanne's painting of *The Large Bathers*. Here we see a woman with an oval silhouette in front and an inverted triangle silhouette in back.

The last figure demonstrates an overall inverted triangle silhouette, but gives an impression of an hourglass silhouette in back. In the front she has little or no indentation at her waist and in back she has an hourglass silhouette because of the back waist indentation.

The clothing examples for each figure show how the figure's two silhouettes can be integrated or expressed in one garment.

✿ The idea is: Where the waist narrows, create a waist in the garment.

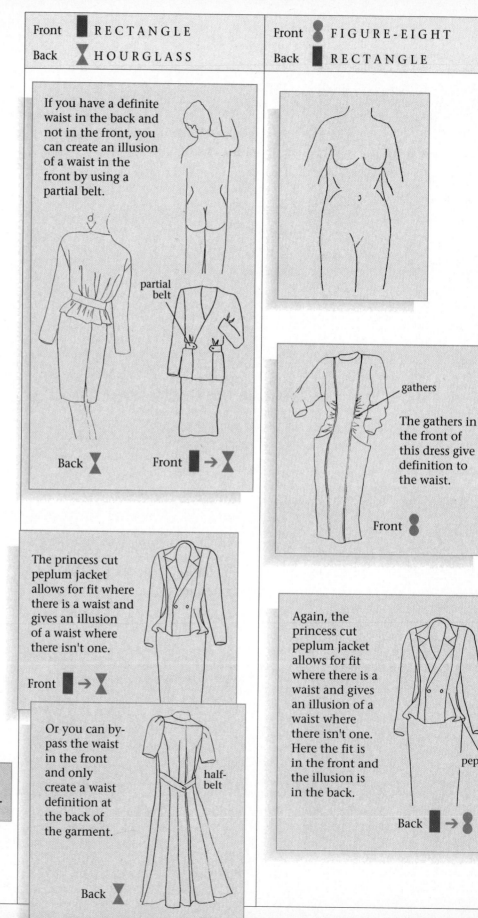

Front ▮ RECTANGLE
Back ⧗ HOURGLASS

If you have a definite waist in the back and not in the front, you can create an illusion of a waist in the front by using a partial belt.

partial belt

Back ⧗   Front ▮ → ⧗

The princess cut peplum jacket allows for fit where there is a waist and gives an illusion of a waist where there isn't one.

Front ▮ → ⧗

Or you can by-pass the waist in the front and only create a waist definition at the back of the garment.

half-belt

Back ⧗

Front ⧗ FIGURE-EIGHT
Back ▮ RECTANGLE

The gathers in the front of this dress give definition to the waist.

gathers

Front ⧗

Again, the princess cut peplum jacket allows for fit where there is a waist and gives an illusion of a waist where there isn't one. Here the fit is in the front and the illusion is in the back.

peplum

Back ▮ → ⧗

Front	**O V A L**
Back	▼ **I N V E R T E D T R I A N G L E**

Front	▼ **I N V E R T E D T R I A N G L E**
Back	⧖ or 8 **H O U R G L A S S** or **F I G U R E - E I G H T**

The Large Bathers, Paul Cézanne, National Gallery, London (detail).

Here is another figure, this time from the artwork of Cezanne. This figure is an oval in front. In the back her silhouette is the inverted triangle, which is created by her wide shoulders, a narrowing of the waist, and a small derrière that draws our eye inward away from the wide hips.

A nice garment for this combination would be this jacket, which has a simple drawstring at the back waist-line that helps to create the inverted triangle silhouette in the back.

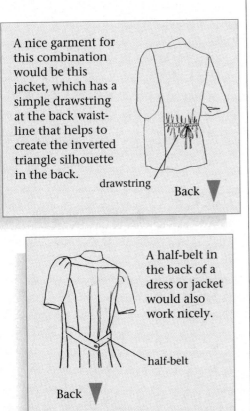

drawstring

Back ▼

A half-belt in the back of a dress or jacket would also work nicely.

half-belt

Back ▼

In this last example, we have a figure with an inverted triangle silhouette in front. (There is a slight or no indentation at the waist.) However, in the back while she is still an inverted triangle, there is more indentation at the waist, which gives the back the "impression" of having either an hour-glass or figure-eight silhouette. (The hourglass would have a square shoulder, while the fig-ure-eight would have a rounded shoulder.)

For example, in this jacket, while the overall look of it is an inverted triangle, the waisted back gives the impression of an hourglass. (If the shoulders were rounded and slightly sloped, this jacket would have a figure-eight silhouette.)

Back ▼ → ⧖

Knowing your natural sil-houette(s) is crucial in creating a personal style for two main reasons:

1. Because your body feels "comfortable" or "at home" in it, your natural silhouette can be the main framework for most of your clothing choices and for the outfits you may create from different pieces in your wardrobe. As long as an outfit stays within the natural silhouette, you will be certain to enhance your body's basic shape.

2. Your natural silhouette is also your frame-of-reference for the times when you wish to adapt alternate silhouettes into your wardrobe. In the next section, we discuss how to expand your wardrobe by adding these alternate silhou-ettes, which can add excite-ment, an element of surprise to your style, and a way to keep in step with any current fashion.

How to modify your natural silhouette to create alternate silhouettes ❧

"Variety is the spice of life."
"Everyone needs a change now and then."

We have all said these words or something to their effect at one time or another. As in life, we think every wardrobe needs variety now and then too, and there are many ways to do this. For example, you might buy a style in accessories you've never worn before or change the length of your hemline, or change the colors you wear. These changes are relatively easy to make.

To add variety to your wardrobe, you can also wear silhouettes other than your natural one. We call these your alternate silhouettes, because they are ones you can wear with relative comfort, but which require some adjustments to your natural one. Although changing your silhouette is not always easy to accomplish, it can add a dramatic change in your wardrobe. This is especially true if the silhouette goes from an angled silhouette (such as an inverted triangle) to a curved-line one (such as the figure-eight). Recall what we said at the opening of this chapter: Shapes take on the effects of the lines surrounding them, so that a triangle assumes the effect of diagonal lines—active, restless, and aggressive. Or an oval takes on the gracefulness that a curved line suggests.

In the following pages we show you ways to modify your natural silhouette to create one or more alternate ones. These are given simply to provide you with some ideas and inspiration.

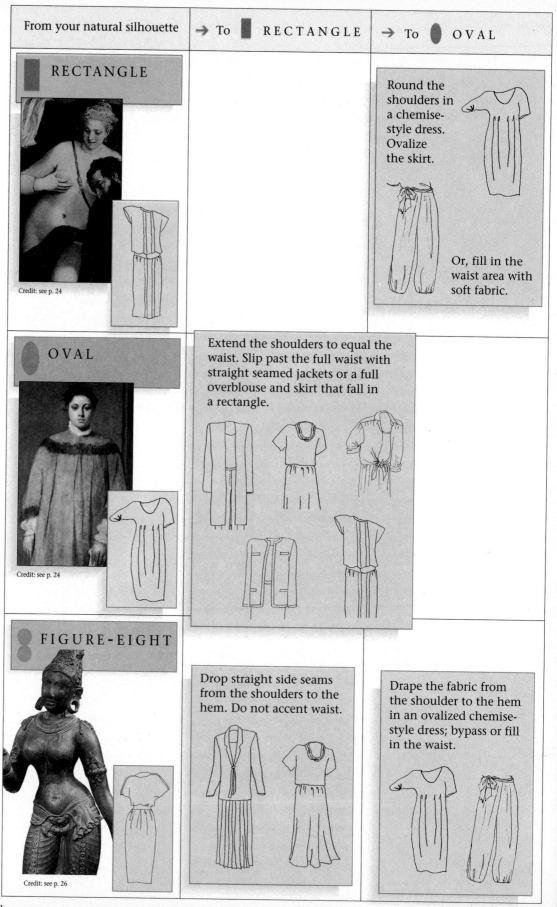

From your natural silhouette → To ■ RECTANGLE → To ⬭ OVAL

RECTANGLE

Credit: see p. 24

OVAL

Credit: see p. 24

FIGURE-EIGHT

Credit: see p. 26

Round the shoulders in a chemise-style dress. Ovalize the skirt.

Or, fill in the waist area with soft fabric.

Extend the shoulders to equal the waist. Slip past the full waist with straight seamed jackets or a full overblouse and skirt that fall in a rectangle.

Drop straight side seams from the shoulders to the hem. Do not accent waist.

Drape the fabric from the shoulder to the hem in an ovalized chemise-style dress; bypass or fill in the waist.

Curve the shoulder; give an impression of a waist with a half belt; ovalize the straight skirt. Or, have enough fabric above and below the waist to make the waist appear smaller.

Extend the shoulders. Create an impression of a narrower waist by using diagonals in the design or the construction. Flare out the skirt, either below the waist or at the bottom.

Optically narrow the shoulders with a dominant line from the neck to the underarm. Drop the body of the dress past the waist; then flare the skirt wider than the shoulders.

Extend the shoulders. Narrow the bottom of the skirt. You can bypass or accent the waist.

Difficult to do.

Difficult to do. However, you can create an impression of an hourglass, not with the waist but with narrowness at the bosom or by flaring the sleeves and flaring the skirt below the waist.

Keep shoulders narrow; flare the skirt over the tummy to a wider hem.

Extend the shoulders beyond the waist. Follow an ovalized line over the waist, then narrow the bottom of the skirt. If the tummy is large, then place dominant inverted triangle seam lines in a long jacket.

Create straight shoulders. Accent the waist. Create a short flare in a peplum, or a long flare in the skirt.

Give an impression of narrow shoulders and flare the skirt to create the triangle.

Extend the shoulders beyond the hips/thighs; keep the skirt narrow. The waist can, but need not, be accented.

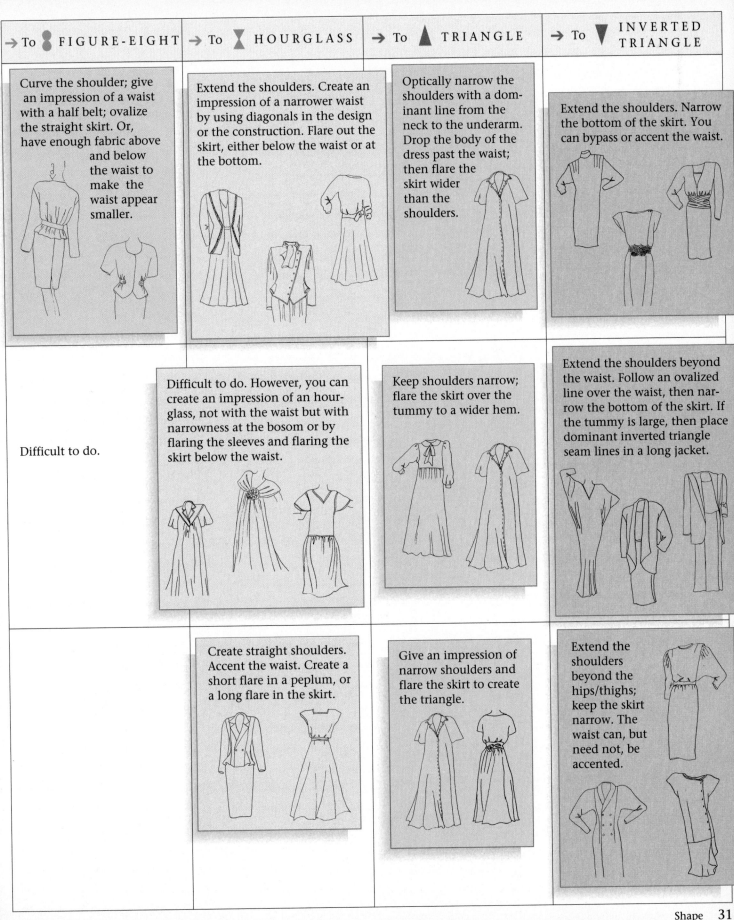

How to modify your natural
silhouette to create alternate
silhouettes *(Con't.)*

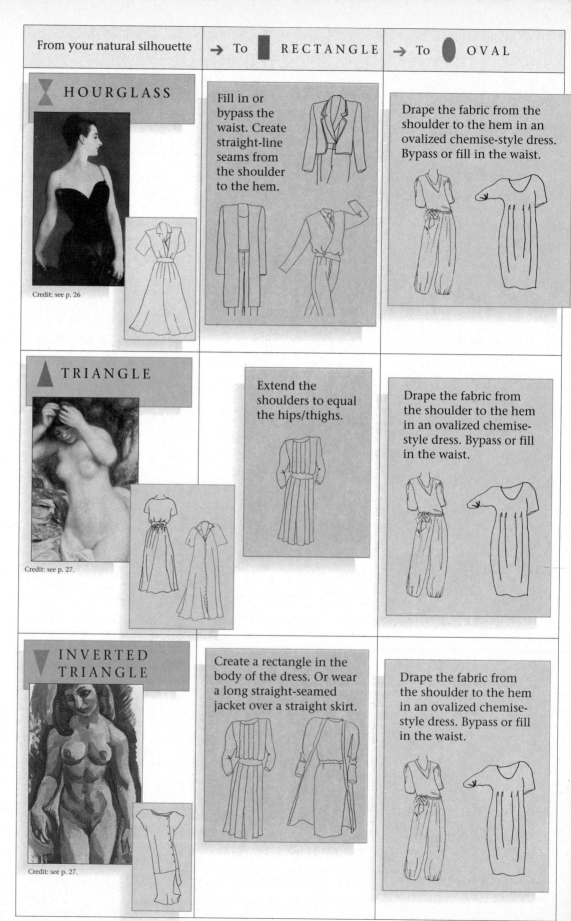

From your natural silhouette → To ▌ R E C T A N G L E → To ⬭ O V A L

H O U R G L A S S

Credit: see p. 26

Fill in or
bypass the
waist. Create
straight-line
seams from
the shoulder
to the hem.

Drape the fabric from the
shoulder to the hem in an
ovalized chemise-style dress.
Bypass or fill in the waist.

T R I A N G L E

Credit: see p. 27.

Extend the
shoulders to equal
the hips/thighs.

Drape the fabric from
the shoulder to the hem
in an ovalized chemise-
style dress. Bypass or fill
in the waist.

**I N V E R T E D
T R I A N G L E**

Credit: see p. 27.

Create a rectangle in the
body of the dress. Or wear
a long straight-seamed
jacket over a straight skirt.

Drape the fabric from
the shoulder to the hem
in an ovalized chemise-
style dress. Bypass or fill
in the waist.

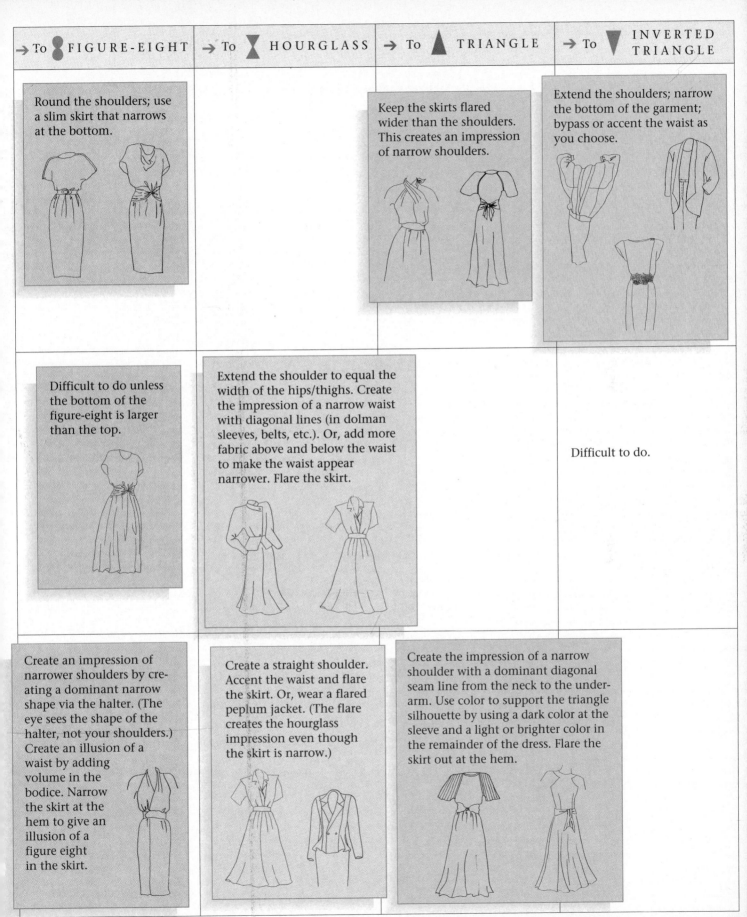

Round the shoulders; use a slim skirt that narrows at the bottom.

Keep the skirts flared wider than the shoulders. This creates an impression of narrow shoulders.

Extend the shoulders; narrow the bottom of the garment; bypass or accent the waist as you choose.

Difficult to do unless the bottom of the figure-eight is larger than the top.

Extend the shoulder to equal the width of the hips/thighs. Create the impression of a narrow waist with diagonal lines (in dolman sleeves, belts, etc.). Or, add more fabric above and below the waist to make the waist appear narrower. Flare the skirt.

Difficult to do.

Create an impression of narrower shoulders by creating a dominant narrow shape via the halter. (The eye sees the shape of the halter, not your shoulders.) Create an illusion of a waist by adding volume in the bodice. Narrow the skirt at the hem to give an illusion of a figure eight in the skirt.

Create a straight shoulder. Accent the waist and flare the skirt. Or, wear a flared peplum jacket. (The flare creates the hourglass impression even though the skirt is narrow.)

Create the impression of a narrow shoulder with a dominant diagonal seam line from the neck to the underarm. Use color to support the triangle silhouette by using a dark color at the sleeve and a light or brighter color in the remainder of the dress. Flare the skirt out at the hem.

Now you have it, now you don't—

The following is a summary of techniques for narrowing or widening your shoulders, waist, or hips when creating alternate silhouettes. The art of illusion is easier than you think. Basically, only two concepts are used:
1. the adding of more dimension with fabric and/or construction
2. the use of line—horizontal, vertical, and/or diagonal—to break up space.

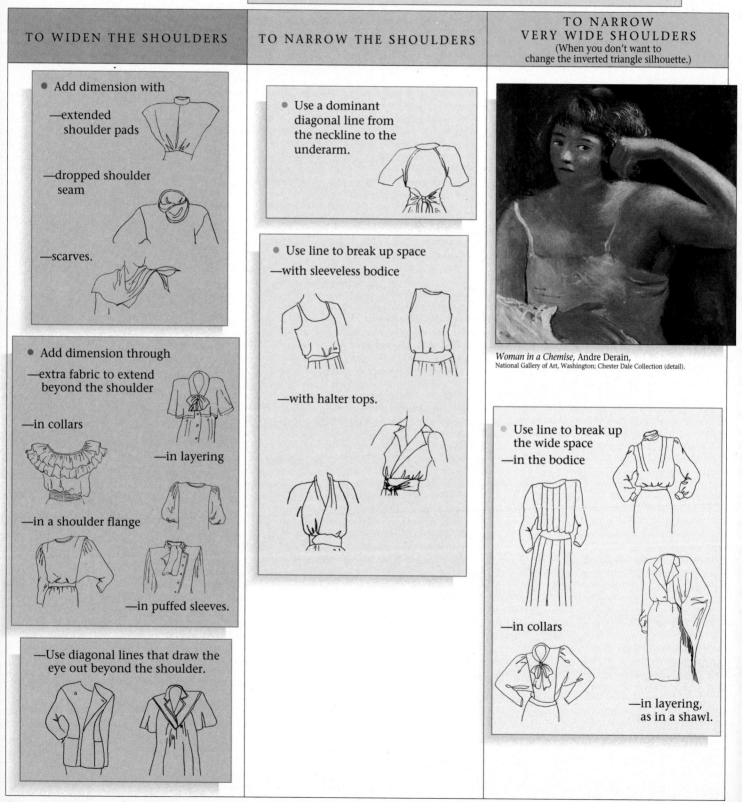

TO WIDEN THE SHOULDERS	TO NARROW THE SHOULDERS	TO NARROW VERY WIDE SHOULDERS (When you don't want to change the inverted triangle silhouette.)

TO WIDEN THE SHOULDERS

- Add dimension with
  —extended shoulder pads
  —dropped shoulder seam
  —scarves.

- Add dimension through
  —extra fabric to extend beyond the shoulder
  —in collars
  —in layering
  —in a shoulder flange
  —in puffed sleeves.

  —Use diagonal lines that draw the eye out beyond the shoulder.

TO NARROW THE SHOULDERS

- Use a dominant diagonal line from the neckline to the underarm.

- Use line to break up space
  —with sleeveless bodice
  —with halter tops.

TO NARROW VERY WIDE SHOULDERS

Woman in a Chemise, Andre Derain, National Gallery of Art, Washington; Chester Dale Collection (detail).

- Use line to break up the wide space
  —in the bodice
  —in collars
  —in layering, as in a shawl.

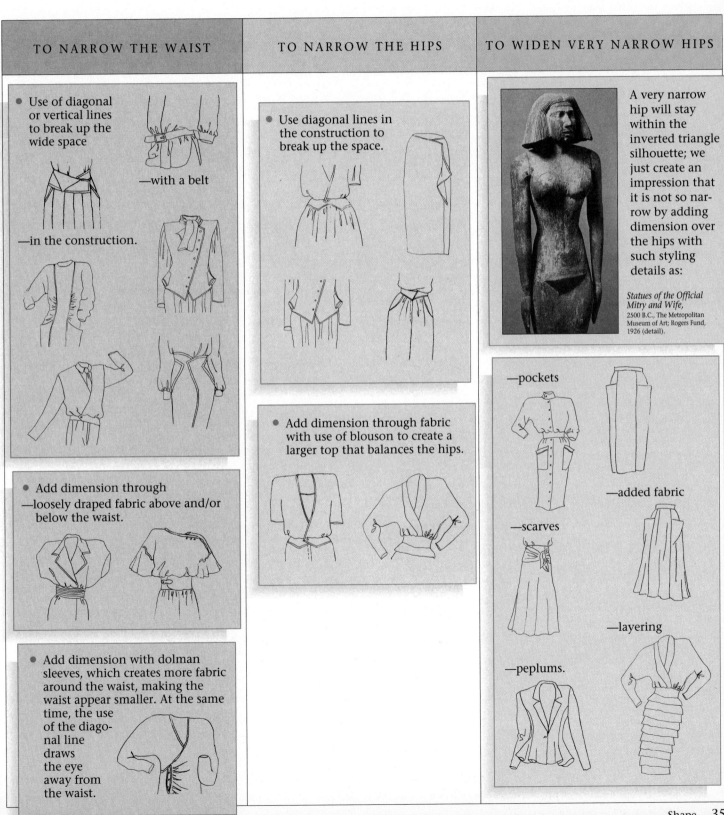

| TO NARROW THE WAIST | TO NARROW THE HIPS | TO WIDEN VERY NARROW HIPS |

TO NARROW THE WAIST

- Use of diagonal or vertical lines to break up the wide space

  —with a belt

  —in the construction.

- Add dimension through
  —loosely draped fabric above and/or below the waist.

- Add dimension with dolman sleeves, which creates more fabric around the waist, making the waist appear smaller. At the same time, the use of the diagonal line draws the eye away from the waist.

TO NARROW THE HIPS

- Use diagonal lines in the construction to break up the space.

- Add dimension through fabric with use of blouson to create a larger top that balances the hips.

TO WIDEN VERY NARROW HIPS

A very narrow hip will stay within the inverted triangle silhouette; we just create an impression that it is not so narrow by adding dimension over the hips with such styling details as:

Statues of the Official Mitry and Wife, 2500 B.C., The Metropolitan Museum of Art; Rogers Fund, 1926 (detail).

—pockets

—added fabric

—scarves

—layering

—peplums.

When can an alternate silhouette supercede the natural one?

Sometimes you may prefer your alternate silhouette to your natural one. This is especially true if you wish to balance the following two body considerations:
1. the wide head/narrow shoulder relationship
2. a body that is optically wide.

1 To balance the wide head/narrow shoulder relationship

The wide head/narrow shoulder can be found in art, as shown here in the drawing by Matisse and the Mosan Art sculpture. In these instances, the wide head/narrow shoulder relationship has been highlighted by simply exposing it.

Head of a Woman #2,
Henri Matisse,
The Santa Barbara Museum of Art,
Santa Barbara, CA; Gift of Wright S. Ludington (detail).

Aquamanile: Phyllis and Aristotle, Sculpture,
Bronze. French. XV, ca.1400, The Metropolitan Museum
of Art; Robert Lehman Collection, 1975 (detail).

If you choose not to highlight this feature, then modify your natural silhouette in a way that would extend the narrow shoulders. Depending on your waist and hips, this alternate silhouette might be a rectangle or the inverted triangle.

RECTANGLE

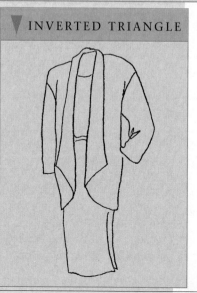

INVERTED TRIANGLE

2 To balance a body that is optically wide

The next artwork, *Girl Drying Herself,* by Degas shows that even a narrow-waisted silhouette, such as a figure-eight, can appear optically wide.

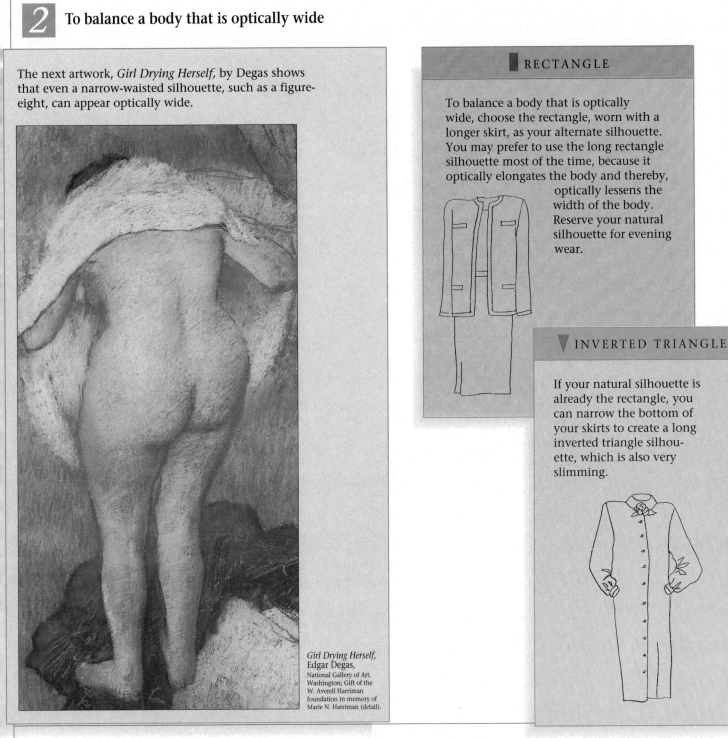

Girl Drying Herself,
Edgar Degas,
National Gallery of Art,
Washington; Gift of the
W. Averell Harriman
foundation in memory of
Marie N. Harriman (detail).

▮ RECTANGLE

To balance a body that is optically wide, choose the rectangle, worn with a longer skirt, as your alternate silhouette. You may prefer to use the long rectangle silhouette most of the time, because it optically elongates the body and thereby, optically lessens the width of the body. Reserve your natural silhouette for evening wear.

▼ INVERTED TRIANGLE

If your natural silhouette is already the rectangle, you can narrow the bottom of your skirts to create a long inverted triangle silhouette, which is also very slimming.

Whether you have one or two natural silhouettes, whether you prefer to use only your natural silhouette or choose alternate ones, once you establish the silhouette concept in your wardrobe, you will gain a tremendous sense of freedom in your creativity. Discover how quickly you can spot which clothes from a store rack or display will go with your body shape, and how easily you can eliminate those that do not. Know instantly how to make clothing adjustments to harmonize with your body shape. Do you realize that by choosing your most harmonious silhouettes, you have automatically taken care of the balance of the width proportions of your body? In the next chapter, we now turn to the other half of the balance—*your length proportions.*

On the underside of a tree branch, two mushrooms clinging side-by-side capture our attention. As we look more closely, they invite comparison. One is small. The other is about twice as wide. Even their stems measure so; and yet, the inner parts that delineate light and dark are comparable in height in spite of the size difference of the mushrooms. The bodies of each appear in fine proportion—to each other and within themselves.

Your body's length proportions

...and how to discover and balance them.

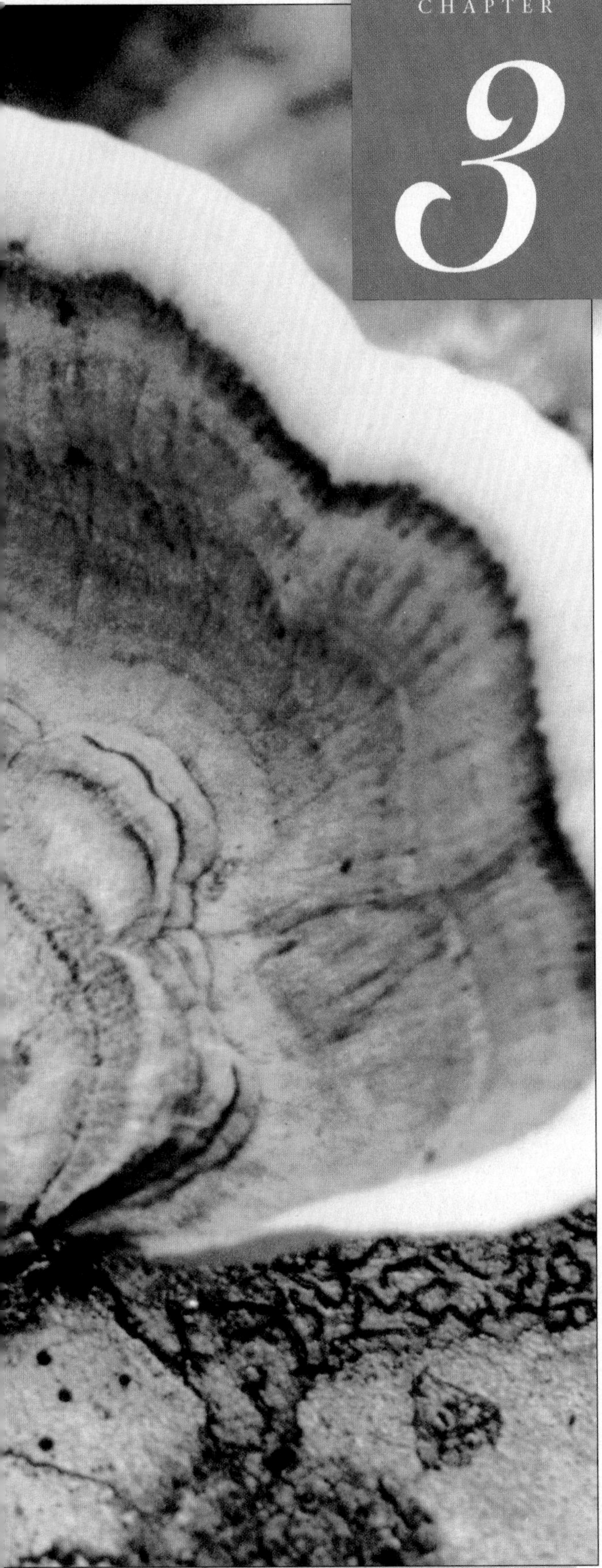

Proportion

Noun **1**: the relation of one part to another or to the whole with respect to magnitude, quantity, or degree; Ratio. **2**: harmonious relation of parts to each other or to the whole; balance. *Verb transitive* **1**: to adjust (a part or thing) in size relative to other parts or things *Verb transitive* **2**: to make the parts harmonious.

Webster's New Collegiate Dictionary

The essence of pleasing proportion

*L*ike all ideas of beauty, what makes for pleasing visual proportion is influenced by cultural preferences. However, certain concepts are accepted by many cultures and have stood the test of centuries. *Have enough difference for interest, but not so much that it creates imbalance.* This is the essence of pleasing proportion. To most people, a division of exact halves is the least interesting; it is quite often dull. When you look at a line or shape divided exactly in half, the brain quickly interprets them, and nothing is left to capture the eye's interest.

On the other hand, in an extreme relationship where one part overpowers the other, the imbalance makes us lose interest in the relationship altogether.

We create more interest and balance when the smaller part is large enough to be interesting and the larger part is small enough to entice the eye to compare them. In this regard, what the great masters of art have found and shown is that the closer we approach about ⅔ or ⅗ the measure of the other, the more interesting the relationship becomes. Here is a line divided about ⅗ along its length:

Here are two side-by-side rectangles. The one to the left is about ⅗ as large as the one to the right.

Traditionally, artists and architects have identified this proportion as the Golden Section or the Golden Mean.

When we think of proportion, we most often think of words such as these: *to relate* or compare size, relative importance or significance; *harmony*, arrangement, distribution; *to balance* and *to adjust*.

In this chapter we will use four of these words in the discovery of the third component of Your Body's Design Pattern: *your length proportions*.

To begin, on this page and the next, we will look at the Golden Mean as seen on the "easy-to-dress" body. With this as our departure point, first we will show you how *to relate* body parts to figure out length proportions for any figure.

Then the chart on page 42 will help you discover *your* length proportions so you can *adjust* your proportions through certain clothing techniques which are illustrated on pages 45 to 47.

Next, we will discuss how to make any hemline you choose be in *harmony* with your comfort zone, and how the Golden Mean ratios will help *balance* your tops and bottoms every time, whatever your length proportions.

Finally, we will show you how *to balance* your head and upper body proportions through your necklines, collars, and/or jewelry.

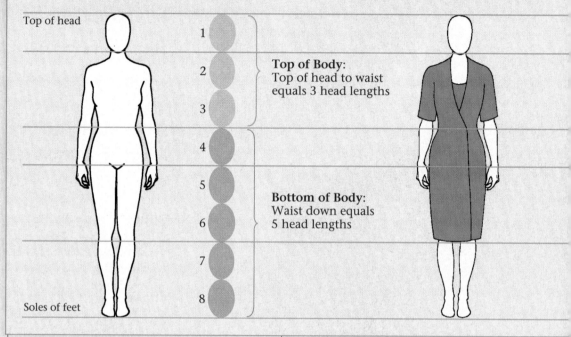

The easy-to-dress body unclothed, naturally has the 3:5 Golden Mean ratio between Top of Body and the Bottom of Body.

1 Here is an example of the 3:5 ratio between a dress (5 head lengths) and parts of the body that show—head, lower legs, and feet (3 head lengths).

Top of head

Top of Body:
Top of head to waist equals 3 head lengths

Bottom of Body:
Waist down equals 5 head lengths

Soles of feet

The "easy-to-dress" body: how to relate body parts to find length proportions. 🪷

To analyze length proportions for any figure, we need to relate the head length to the rest of the body. The Length Proportions chart above gives us the length proportions of the "easy-to-dress" body. Notice how this body divides conveniently into eight head lengths in the following way:

🪷 We've delineated the "top of body" from "bottom of body" at the waist because, when we think of clothes, we generally think of the top part of a dress or outfit as going to or near the waist, while a skirt or trousers goes from the waist down. In this respect, we see that the easy-to-dress body without clothing has the 3:5 Golden Mean ratio between top of body (3 head lengths) and bottom of body (5 head lengths).

The easy-to-dress body is rare. Yes, it is beautiful, but it does not negate the beauty found in all bodies. We present it here not as the ideal, but as an easy way to demonstrate the idea of the Golden Mean as applied to clothing. It will serve as a guide for creating pleasing proportions in clothing for your own unique body.

Generally clothes fall into three categories: dresses, tops (shirts, blouses, jackets, sweaters), or bottoms (skirts of many lengths, pants and trousers). As you can see in the chart, it is easy to execute the 2:3 or 3:5 relationship on the easy-to-dress body:

1 between dresses and the parts of the body that show (the head, lower legs, and feet),

2 between tops that come to the waist and knee-length skirts, or

3 when the outfit, head, legs and feet are integrated in a total look through the use of the same color, or a similar color value.

This may be the reason why clothing designers and manufacturers have chosen to mass produce most clothes to these proportions. It is simply easier to do.

To demonstrate how undemanding it is to design for the easy-to-dress body, consider how quickly it adapts to different jacket or skirt lengths. Under 3 in the chart above, we show an example of a relatively long jacket and long skirt. In the lower chart are other jacket lengths shown in Golden Mean proportion to skirts.

2 Here is an example of the 2:3 ratio between tops that come to the waist (2 head lengths) and knee-length skirts (3 head lengths).

3 Here are examples of the 3:5 ratio when the outfit, head, legs and feet are integrated in a total look through the use of color.

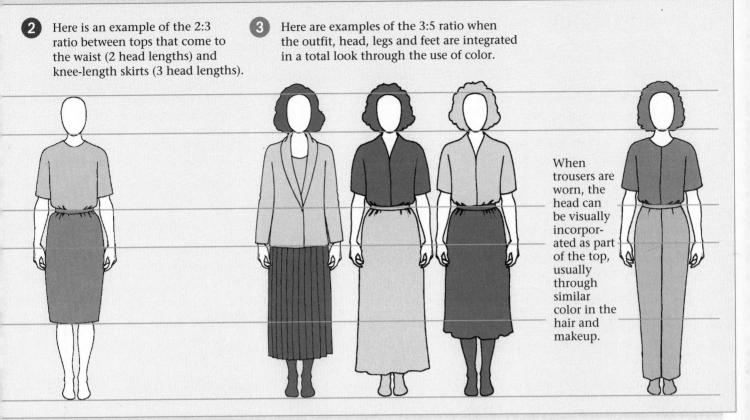

When trousers are worn, the head can be visually incorporated as part of the top, usually through similar color in the hair and makeup.

HOW TO ADJUST JACKET AND SKIRT LENGTHS IN GOLDEN MEAN PROPORTION

2:3 Notice in the first drawing that the jacket is smaller than the skirt. If the jacket comes down to the crotch and the skirt still goes to the knee, as shown in the second drawing, the 2:3 relationship remains. Here, the skirt is the smaller part, the jacket is the larger one.

3:5 Whatever the jacket length, the easy-to-dress body can easily adjust the skirt length to remain in good relationship with the jacket. For example, if the hemline is above the knee by one head length, a jacket whose length falls halfway between the waist and the crotch will create the 3:5 ratio between bottom and top.

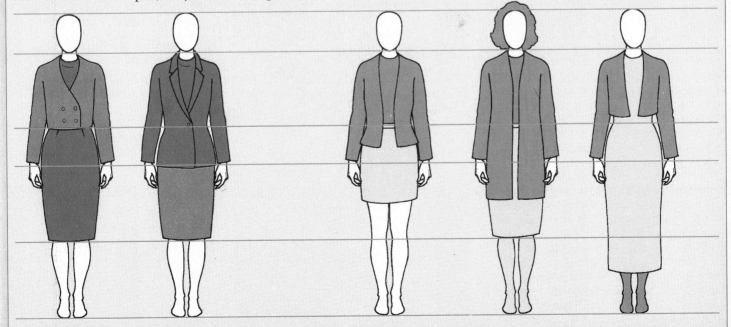

Discover your length proportions

*L*ike us, you are probably often dismayed to find nothing in the stores that fits, making you think there must be something wrong with your body. *Believe now and forever that there is nothing wrong with your body,* only that many clothes out there are cut for the easy-to-dress body proportions and not for your proportions. Not to be left out, you have probably adapted creatively to this situation by dressing in separates, by altering length proportions when you can, and by creating flexible wardrobes to go with your figure which does not fit the retail industry standard.

> Nevertheless, the concept to learn from our study of the easy-to-dress body is clear: a major aspect of visual beauty is a show of good proportion.

Specifically, we can summarize three key steps for consistently achieving good proportion in all the outfits you put together:
1. Balance your Top of Body with your Bottom of Body through certain clothing techniques that can be learned in minutes.
2. Choose skirt lengths that are in harmony with your Comfort Zone.
3. Stay within your silhouette and use the Golden Mean ratios to balance tops and bottoms.

We will show you how to implement these three steps shortly, but first you must learn how to determine your own length proportions, which is the topic of the next section. Once you know your length proportions, you can quickly relate them to the clothing techniques mentioned in step 1. And it will become clear how to make any skirt or jacket length you choose work for your proportions.

Now it's time to discover your length proportions based on head lengths. The following chart is provided to help guide you in your assessment. There are only four major measurements in length proportion that are important to know. Follow numbers 1 through 4 to discover these measurements for your unique body. With each measurement you will check off whether you are in proportion, short, or long.

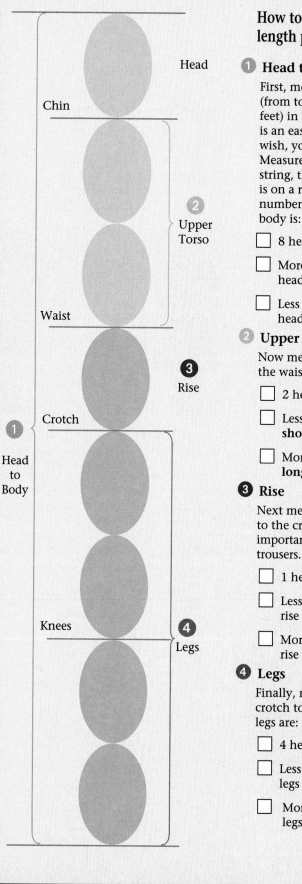

Head
Chin
Upper Torso
Waist
Rise
Crotch
Head to Body
Knees
Legs

How to measure your length proportions

1 Head to body proportion

First, measure your body's height (from top of head to soles of your feet) in head lengths. Using a string is an easy way to measure. If you wish, you may do it mathematically: Measure your head length with a string, then see how long your string is on a ruler. Finally divide that number into your total height. Your body is:

☐ 8 head lengths = **in proportion**

☐ More than 8 head lengths = head is **short**

☐ Less than 8 head lengths = head is **long**

2 Upper torso

Now measure just from the chin to the waist. It is:

☐ 2 head lengths = **in proportion**

☐ Less than 2 head lengths = **short-waisted**

☐ More than 2 head lengths = **long-waisted**

3 Rise

Next measure just from the waist to the crotch. This measurement is important only when you wear trousers. It is:

☐ 1 head length = **in proportion**

☐ Less than 1 head length = rise is **short**

☐ More than 1 head length = rise is **long**

4 Legs

Finally, measure just from the crotch to the soles of feet. Your legs are:

☐ 4 head lengths = **in proportion**

☐ Less than 4 head lengths = legs are **short**

☐ More than 4 head lengths = legs are **long**

How parts of the body relate in "not-so-perfect" bodies—like yours and mine.

Great works of art show us that relationships slightly off exact ratios are often more interesting than the "perfect" curves and proportions of the "easy-to-dress" body. Art by formula is rarely art.

In the words of Francis Bacon (1561–1626) from his *Essays; Of Beauty*,
"There is no excellent beauty that hath not some strangeness in the proportion."

In this spirit, we now shift our attention to two female figures from the works of Gauguin and Cranach.

Through these paintings, we are given a perspective of beauty that will help us develop a fine sensitivity to our own unique proportions. These two figures divide into eight head lengths like the easy-to-dress body. But unlike the easy-to-dress body, key places like the waist and rise do not fall in exact head lengths. In terms of head lengths, notice where these figures are in proportion, or short, or long.

While *Nave Nave Fenua* measures eight head lengths in her body, notice that she has a long waist, a slightly long rise, and short legs. But notice her lower legs with two head lengths are in proportion.

Venus also measures eight head lengths, but notice where her proportions differ: she has a short waist, a very long rise, and very long legs. Her lower legs, however, are in proportion like those of *Nave Nave*.

Nave Nave Fenua,
Paul Gauguin
National Gallery of Art;
Washington; Rosenwald
Collection (detail).

Venus in a Landscape,
Lucas Cranach,
The Elder,
Musée du Louvre, Paris (detail).

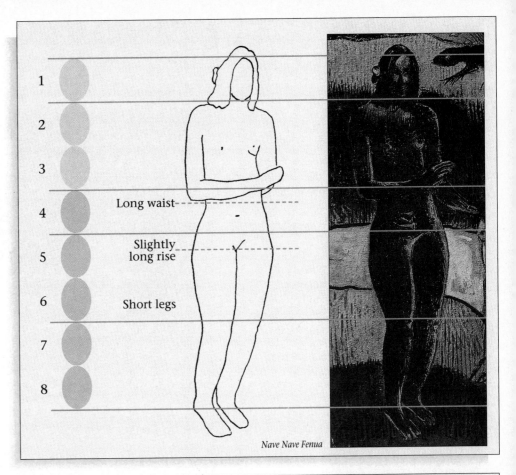

1
2
3
4   Long waist
5   Slightly long rise
6   Short legs
7
8

Nave Nave Fenua

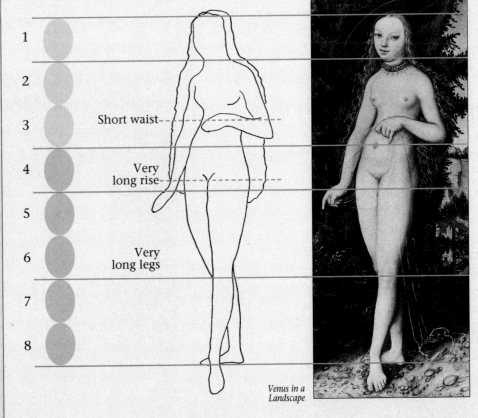

1
2
3   Short waist
4   Very long rise
5
6   Very long legs
7
8

Venus in a Landscape

Three key steps to creating good proportions ❧

With the knowledge of your length proportions as a starting point, we turn now to the three steps that will lead you to create good proportion in all clothing you wear.

Step 1. Balance the top of your body with the bottom of your body through clothing techniques you can learn in minutes.

These simple techniques generally entail using line direction to create certain illusions or effects.

If you remember this underlying principle—where you are short, optically lengthen; and where you are long, optically shorten—you will quickly master the art of balancing length proportion.

Let's look at the solutions for head and leg proportions first, because these are easy to do right away. They do not entail any special design idea. However, for the waist and the rise proportions, which will follow, style details are used to illustrate the underlying principle mentioned above. With this principle in mind, you will surely think of many other appropriate solutions.

SHORT HEAD

Optically lengthen your head by:

• Wearing fullness in your hair at the top of your head.

Mrs. Joseph Chamberlain,
John Singer Sargent,
National Gallery of Art, Washington;
Gift of Mrs. Mary Endicott Chamberlain Carnegie (detail).

Mrs. Richard Brinsley Sheridan,
Thomas Gainsborough,
National Gallery of Art, Washington;
Andrew W. Mellon Collection (detail).

LONG HEAD

Optically shorten your head length by:

• Wearing bangs of some sort.

Nude with Red Hair,
George Wesley Bellows,
National Gallery of Art,
Washington; Chester Dale Collection (detail).

Gypsy Woman with a Baby,
Amedeo Modigliani,
1919, National Gallery of Art,
Washington; Chester Dale Collection (detail).

|

Optically lengthen by:

1. pushing up sleeves (This works every single time.) ¾-length for short legs

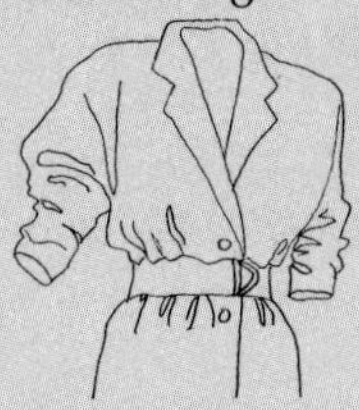

   ½-length for very short legs

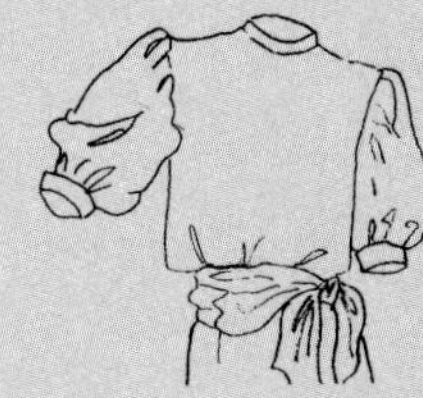

If you must wear sleeves long, use sleeves with deep cuffs or sleeves that taper at the wrist. Whenever possible, create interest in the upper body.

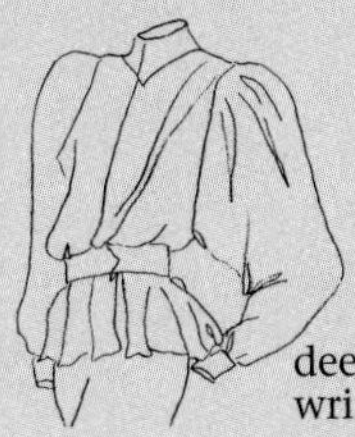

deep cuff or wrist band

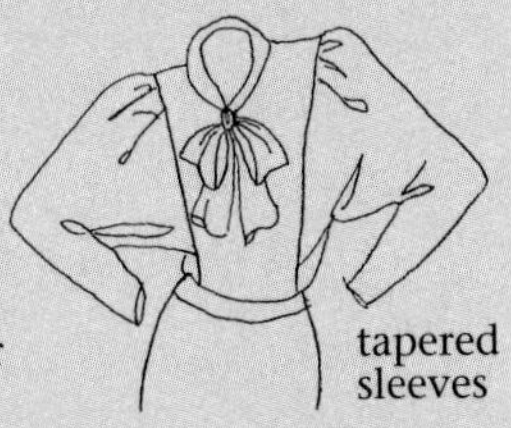

tapered sleeves

2. wearing pants that taper at the bottom

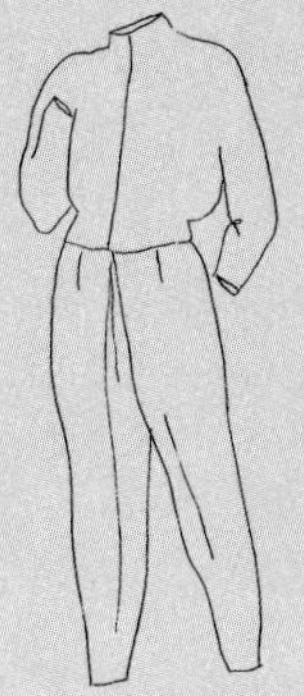

3. wearing a short jacket (at or above the waist) with a long skirt or trousers

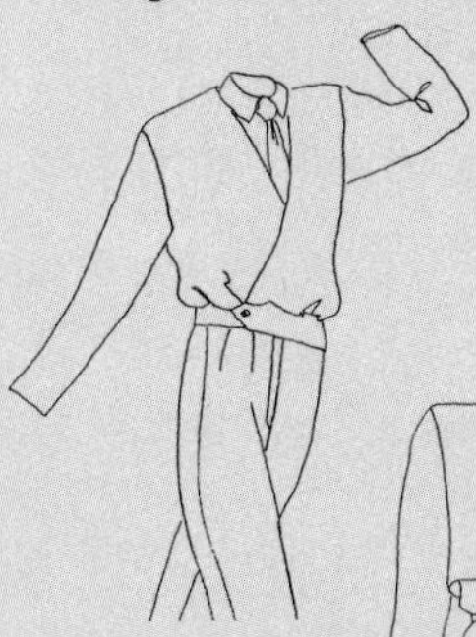

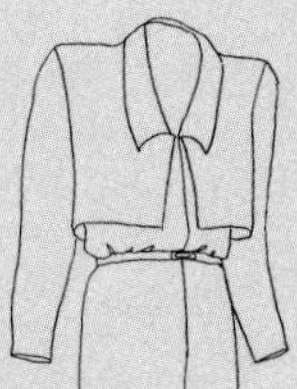

Note: You might not want to do this if you have a tummy.

4. wearing long jackets with short skirts, culottes, and/or walking shorts.

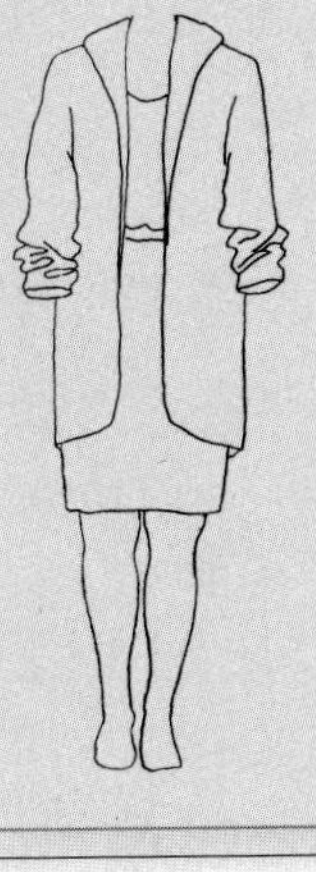

Optically shorten for better proportion by:

1. wearing medium length or long jackets

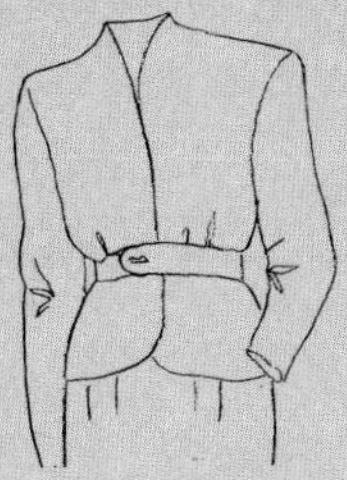

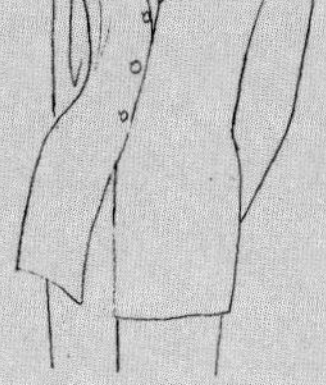

2. wearing long sleeves

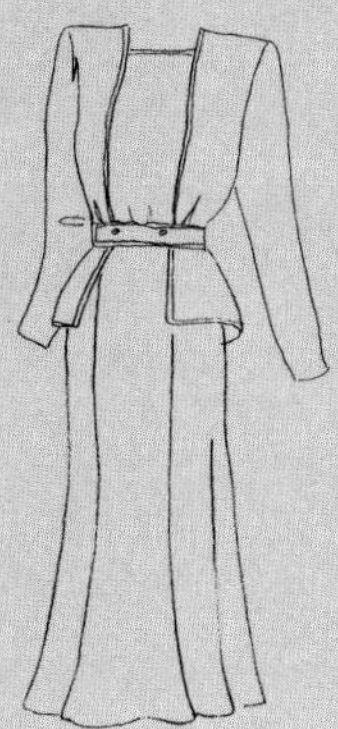

3. dropping the waist with jackets, belts or yokes

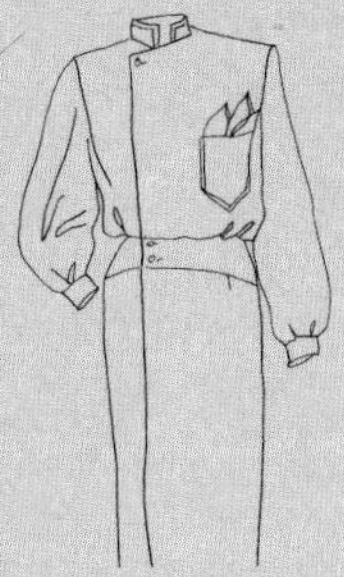

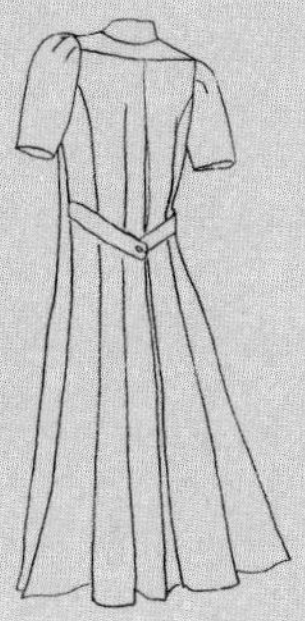

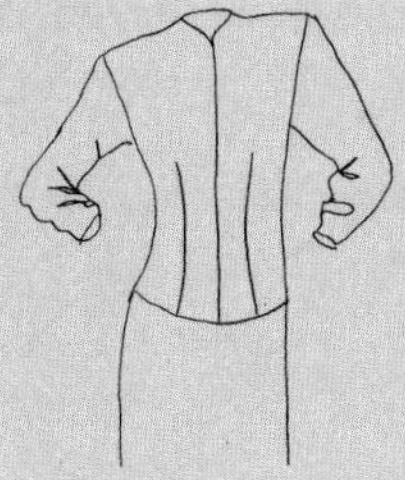

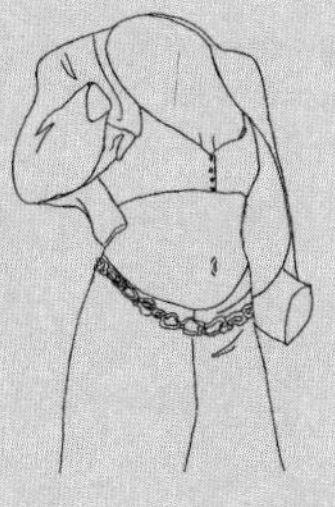

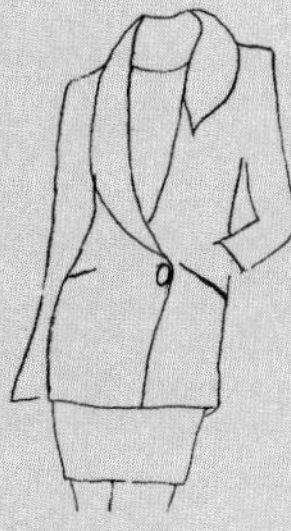

4. breaking up space of lower body.

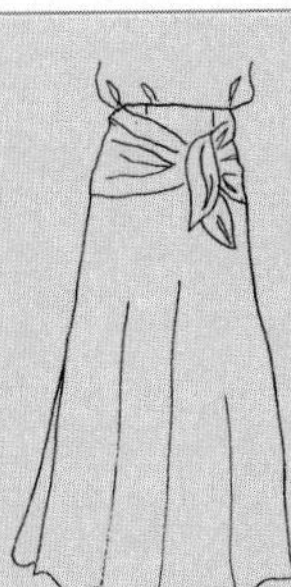

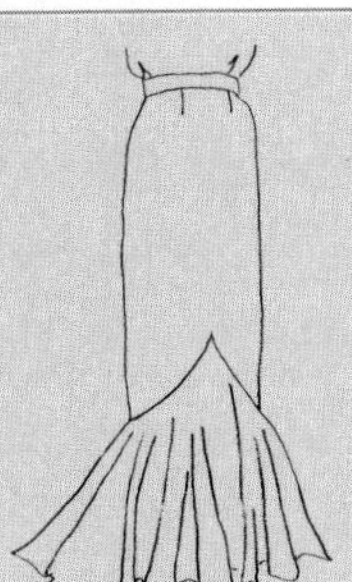

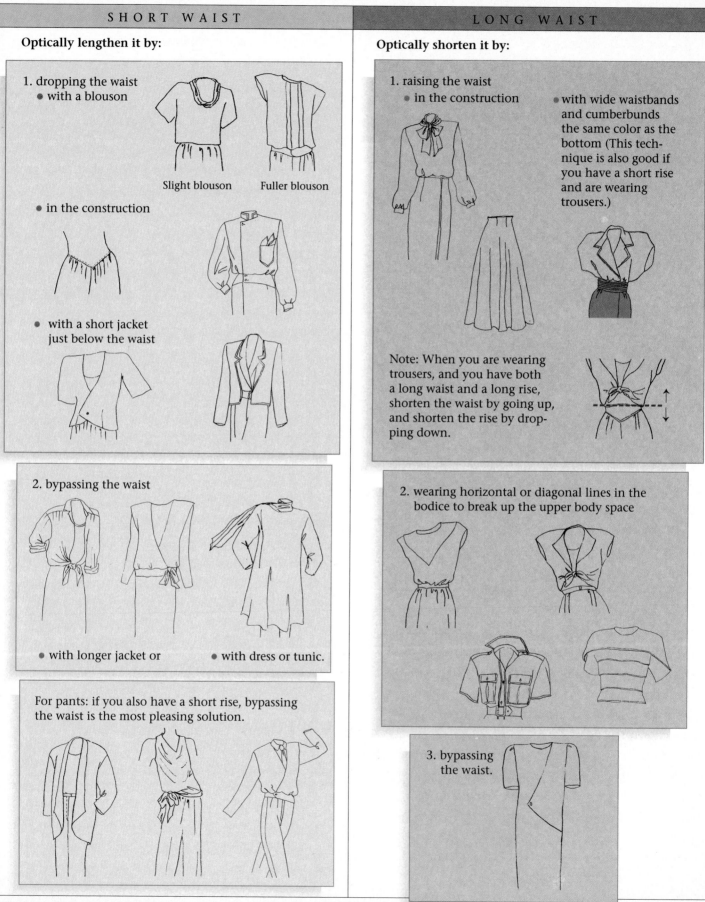

Optically lengthen it by:

1. dropping the waist
   - with a blouson

Slight blouson   Fuller blouson

   - in the construction

   - with a short jacket just below the waist

2. bypassing the waist

   - with longer jacket or   - with dress or tunic.

For pants: if you also have a short rise, bypassing the waist is the most pleasing solution.

Optically shorten it by:

1. raising the waist
   - in the construction

   - with wide waistbands and cumberbunds the same color as the bottom (This technique is also good if you have a short rise and are wearing trousers.)

Note: When you are wearing trousers, and you have both a long waist and a long rise, shorten the waist by going up, and shorten the rise by dropping down.

2. wearing horizontal or diagonal lines in the bodice to break up the upper body space

3. bypassing the waist.

Optically lengthen it by:

1. raising the waist in your trousers
   - with a belt that is the same color as the top
   - with a waistband placed above the waist

2. bypassing the waist. This is the most pleasing solution if you also have a short waist. If in addition to a short waist and short rise, you also have short legs, leave the waistline where it is, but then cover and bypass it with a tunic that goes below the rise. The key is to use one of the Golden Mean ratios in the relationship between tunic and pants, the tunic being the longer part. The following artwork of a reclining nude by Dufy shows us such proportions. She is only about 6 head lengths, because she has a short waist, a short rise, and short legs.

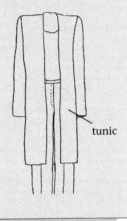

tunic

Relative to her head length, Dufy's nude has a very short waist, a short rise, and very short legs.

Reclining Nude, Raul Dufy,
National Gallery of Art, Washington; Chester Dale Collection (detail).

Optically shorten it by:

1. dropping the waist in your trousers
   - with a yoke

Note: If you also have a long waist, you raise and drop the waistline at the same time. Or, you can use diagonals in the bodice to break up the space of the top and then lower the waist to shorten the length of the rise.

- by wearing an overblouse

- with stitched-down pleats, (the eye focuses on the bottom of the stitch line)

- with a contoured waist or belt
- with a diagonally dropped waistband or belt.

In the following artwork, notice the figure's very long waist and very long rise combination. In addition, she also has very short legs. Like the very short figure of Dufy (left), the *Odalisque* would bypass the waist by wearing a tunic that falls below the rise. Again, use the Golden Mean ratio between the tunic and bottom of trousers, with the tunic being the longer part.

Odalisque in Grisaille, Jean-Auguste-Dominique Ingres,
The Metropolitan Museum of Art; Catherine Lorillard Wolfe Fund, 1938, (detail).

Step 2. Choose hemlines that are in harmony with your Comfort Zone.

This step is almost self-explanatory. Your hemline need not be dictated by fashion trends. Whatever is comfortable for you—and that may include two or more different lengths—is more in keeping with our goal of creating a harmony between you and your clothing. For example, you might have shapely legs and could wear shorter skirts to show them off, but you are modest and so you stay away from above-the-knee skirt lengths. Or, perhaps short skirts are not appropriate for your age or job position. Then short hemlines are not in your comfort zone. As you go through life's experiences and changes, you will widen or rethink your comfort zone accordingly.

Step 3. Stay within your silhouette and use the Golden Mean ratios when combining tops and bottoms.

Finally, always think of your body as a shape (your silhouette) that needs to be divided visually into pleasing proportions through clothing. *As a general rule, we could say that as long as you stay within your silhouette, you can wear any skirt length or jacket length you choose. The trick is to combine tops and bottoms within that silhouette so that together they reflect the Golden Mean relationship—the 2:3 and 3:5 ratios, or any other ratio that approximates these relationships.* Remember that whatever your length proportions, there will be times when you will want to integrate your hair color and/or stocking and shoe color to achieve these ratios.

Hint: The 2:3 ratio is easy to "eyeball." However, 3:5 is not as easy to see. If you have difficulty eyeballing these ratios, try using the 1:2 relationship. This is not a Golden Mean ratio; however, it is an easy and quick way to assess proportion, especially if your body is less than 8 head lengths. Here are three sketches showing the 1:2 ratio between tops and bottoms. Don't you agree they also look well-balanced?

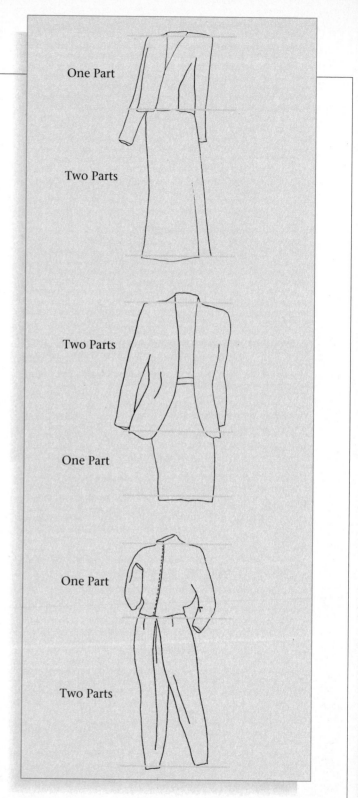

At this point you now know how to select styling details that adjust your body's length proportions and how to combine your wardrobe pieces so your overall look is visually balanced. There is just one more issue of balance that you must consider before the picture of proportion is complete—and this is discussed in the following section.

How to balance the head and upper body through necklines, collars, and jewelry

Have you ever said, "I can't wear that style neckline or collar because my neck is too short" or "my face is too wide" or something else or other? Well, we are about to show you that only your comfort zone should limit your choice of necklines or collars, not the style per se of a neck treatment. Contrary to what you may have been told, you can wear any neckline or collar style as long as it makes the head appear in balance with the upper body. To do this, at least two things must be included in the design of the neckline or collar:

1. A neckline opening or the collar construction needs to be at least as wide as the widest part of your face.
2. A neckline or collar opening or some detail of the collar treatment needs to fall at a balance point in the upper body.

Most people have two balance points.

What are balance points? Balance points are unique to you. It is a term we use to indicate how far down the bodice your neckline opening or collar should go. Your balance points also indicate the length of the necklaces you wear or how far down you should wear pins, corsages or the like, in order to balance your head with your neck and upper body. *In other words, the width of your necklines and collars are determined by the width of your face, and their lengths by your balance points.*

It is through the works of great artists, the masters of balance and proportion, that we can show you how to find your balance points. Some of you may already know this instinctively. If you do, we think you will still enjoy discovering how these great artists validate what you already know and do intuitively. For us it was great fun to see how the eye, indeed, naturally seeks balance and proportion.

FIRST BALANCE POINT

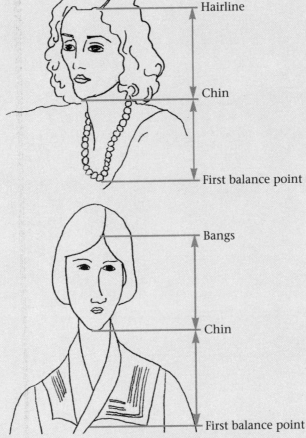

Hairline

Chin

First balance point

Bangs

Chin

First balance point

We have said most people have two balance points. Here is how to determine yours:

How to find your first balance point

1. Measure the length of your face from hairline to chin, or from bangs to chin if you wear bangs as shown in these well-known portraits. A string makes an easy measuring device.

2. Next take that distance and let it fall from the bottom of your chin down your chest. Where it ends is your first balance point. In our examples, notice that Tallulah's necklace is long enough so it falls at her first balance point, and the sailor collar of Modigliani's *Gypsy Woman with Baby* does the same. Ingres' *Portrait of Mme. Rivière* on page 50 gives us an example of a neckline that comes to her first balance point.

Tallulah Brockman Bankhead, Augustus John, The National Portrait Gallery, Smithsonian Institution; Gift of the Hon. and Mrs. John Hay Whitney (detail).

Gypsy Woman with Baby, Amedeo Modigliani, National Gallery of Art, Washington; Chester Dale Collection (detail).

Madame Rivière, Jean-Auguste-Dominique Ingres,
Musée du Louvre, Paris (detail).

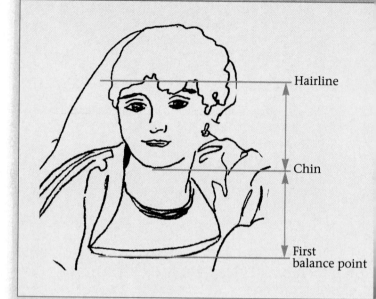

Hairline

Chin

First
balance point

Your second balance point gives you yet another choice that is also in harmony with you. Mme. Rivière is a wonderful example of someone using both her first and second balance points.

How to find your second balance point

1. Where is the widest part of your face? Imagine a horizontal line across your face where your face is widest, as we have illustrated here for Mme. Rivière.

2. Next imagine tracing a "shape" that begins from one side of the widest part of your face, around your jawline and chin, then back up to the other side of the widest part.

3. Finally, repeat the shape you have just traced (in your mind) at your shoulder line around your neck. Remember always to maintain the width of your face, or you will lose the shape. The bottom of that shape (x) indicates your second balance point.

If your neck is wider than your face, there are two ways to determine your second balance point. One way is to create greater optical width in your face with your hair first; then use that width in the shape that you repeat for your neckline. Another way is to narrow the neck with a collar or your hair (if it is long enough) to cover the sides of the neck; then repeat the shape of the jawline and chin as before.

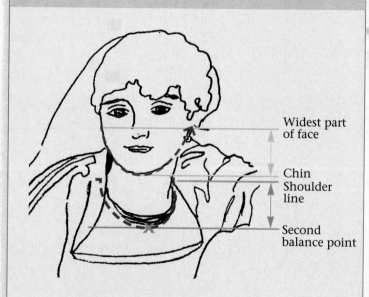

Widest part
of face

Chin
Shoulder
line

Second
balance point

Choosing the shape of your necklines and necklaces 🪷

*D*id you notice how Mme. Rivière's necklace not only falls exactly at her second balance point, but it also repeats the curved shape of her jawline and chin? Through the shape of her necklace, she creates a harmony that her straight neckline alone would not have achieved.

Imagine her without the necklace, and you will immediately see what we mean. However, we should note that the horizontal line of her neckline relates with the line movement of her eyebrows and creates its own harmony with her face.

Here is something to remember: For your most harmonious neckline or necklace shape, all you need to do is repeat the shape that begins and ends at the widest part of your face and includes your jawline and chin, as we have shown in the five sketches below. You can see this works for everyone, no matter how long or short, wide or narrow the neck.

Of course, you can choose shapes other than that of your jawline shape, as long as they relate to something else in your design and come down to one of your balance points. Besides the circular shapes, necklines can also be a square or a rectangular shape, or angled like the v-neck or shield shape.

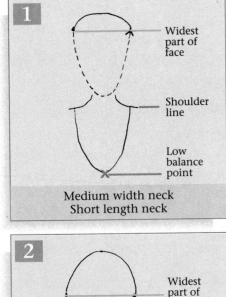

1
Widest part of face
Shoulder line
Low balance point

Medium width neck
Short length neck

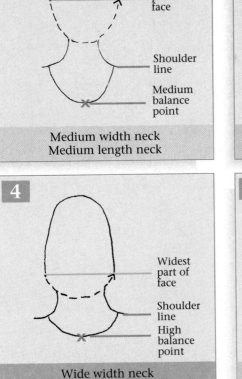

2
Widest part of face
Shoulder line
Medium balance point

Medium width neck
Medium length neck

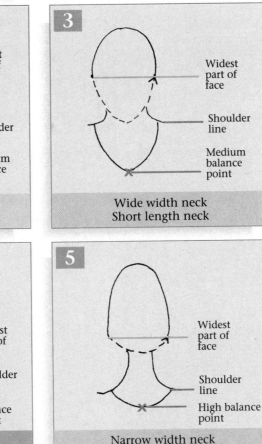

3
Widest part of face
Shoulder line
Medium balance point

Wide width neck
Short length neck

4
Widest part of face
Shoulder line
High balance point

Wide width neck
Medium length neck

5
Widest part of face
Shoulder line
High balance point

Narrow width neck
Long length neck

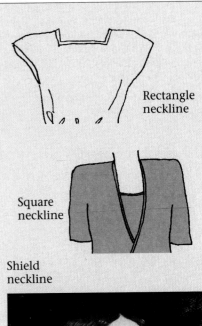

Rectangle neckline

Square neckline

Shield neckline

Ginevra de 'Benci, Leonardo da Vinci, 1474, National Gallery of Art, Washington; Ailsa Mellon Bruce Fund (detail).

Notice, too, that your balance points appear relatively high, medium, or low on the upper body. In the five neckline sketches (left), **1** has a low balance point. The higher the widest part of your face appears on your head, the lower your second balance point will be, and the closer it is to being at the same place as your first balance point, which is determined by your face length. Necklines **2** and **3** have medium balance points and **4** and **5** have high balance points.

What if a neckline opening is above your second balance point? If the neckline opening is as wide as your face but is above your second balance point, note how much farther above it is, then widen the neckline that same distance on each side of the opening. This creates what is called a bateau neckline.

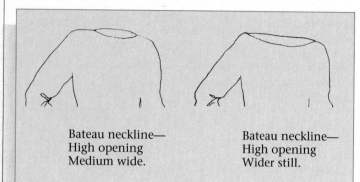

Bateau neckline—
High opening
Medium wide.

Bateau neckline—
High opening
Wider still.

If you wish to add an accent such as a brooch at your second balance point, this also helps to support the balance. Or, if the garment is in a print, something in the print might fall at the balance point which would again reinforce the balance. In this artwork by Rembrandt, not only is the neckline optically widened through the double pleats in the fabric at the neck, but also a brooch is placed at her second balance point.

Portrait of a Lady with an Ostrich Feather Fan, Rembrandt van Rijn, 1660, National Gallery of Art, Washington; Widener Collection (detail).

If a neckline is higher than your balance point but the opening is narrower than your face as in a jewel neckline, there are at least two ways to achieve balance:

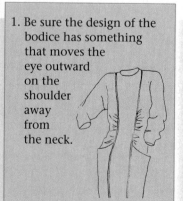

1. Be sure the design of the bodice has something that moves the eye outward on the shoulder away from the neck.

And/or:
2. Have something in the neckline treatment that moves the eye downward to a point of interest at the balance point or lower.

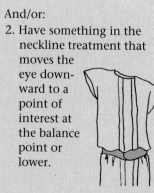

We have found a good way to maintain the balance is to move down the body with the same increment you used to find your balance point. Measure down with this increment as many times as you please until you have found where you want to place your point of interest. Often this point is at or near the waist. Sometimes it can be just below the bosom as in this artwork by Renoir. Here Mme. Henriot is wearing a choker that acts like a neckline. As a choker it is definitely above her second balance point. The sides of the actual neckline of her dress, however, move our eye downward to her cleavage and at the flower just beneath it—her chosen point of interest. Notice that this point of interest measures down at twice the increment that we use to locate her second balance point.

Madame Henriot,
Pierre-Auguste Renoir,
National Gallery of Art ,
Washington; Gift of the Adele
R. Levy Fund (detail).

Move the eye down to a point of interest using the same increment used to find your second balance point.

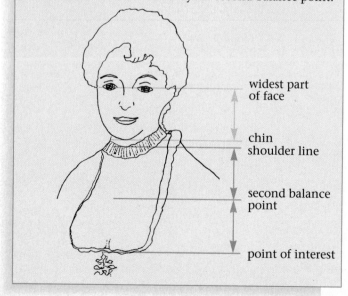

widest part of face

chin
shoulder line

second balance point

point of interest

Collars follow the same principles as necklines 🌸

We have said that all necklines (whether they are rounded, squared, or angled) can be created to have from a very high to a low opening. Where necklines fall for you depends on your balance points. When adapting necklines to your balance points, the opening should also be at least as wide as your face for good balance and harmony. These same principles apply to the *collars* you wear, with only a slight change: The opening of the collar can be narrower than your face, but something in the construction, for example the lapels, should extend out so the entire collar treatment is at least as wide as the face.

🌸 As for balance points, most collar styles can be constructed to accommodate a high, medium, or low balance point, whether it is through the collar opening itself or something else in the construction of the collar that hits the appropriate point.

The following chart shows six collar styles adapted for each of these balance points.

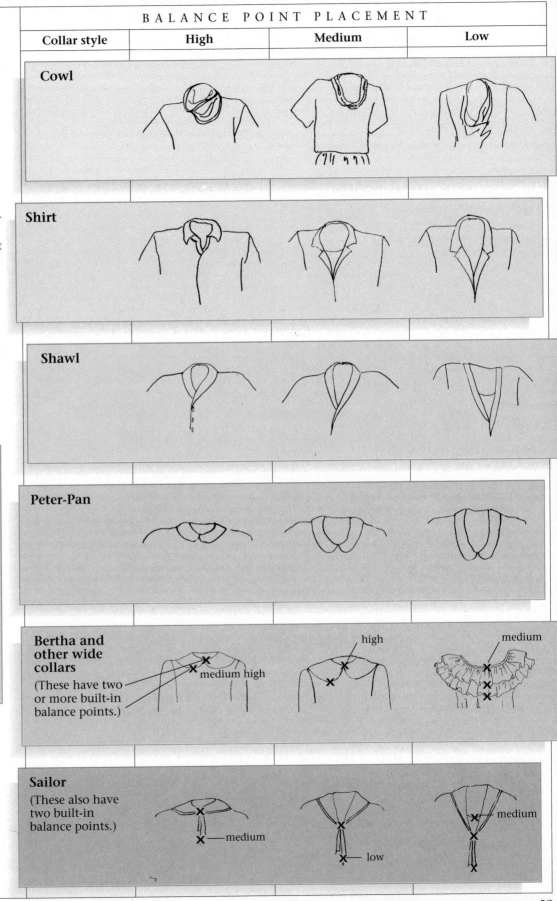

BALANCE POINT PLACEMENT

Collar style	High	Medium	Low
Cowl			
Shirt			
Shawl			
Peter-Pan			
Bertha and other wide collars (These have two or more built-in balance points.)	medium high	high	medium
Sailor (These also have two built-in balance points.)	medium	low	medium

High collars for all neck lengths

There are certain collar styles, such as the shirt collar, that can be adapted to look high and still easily provide the necessary balance points, as shown in the examples here.

A pushed-up collar around the neck provides a quick and simple high collar look, and the shirt opening can be adjusted to accommodate a high, medium, or low balance point.

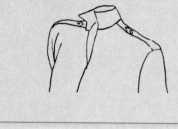

Here is a shirt collar buttoned all the way up to look like a high collar. The pullover ribbing widens the collar treatment as well as accommodates a medium-high balance point.

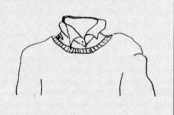

But what about the true high collar styles where the openings are all above anyone's balance points and are generally narrow? Long-necked people often instinctively gravitate to high collars to de-emphasize or camouflage the length of the neck. The fact that the opening is narrow is not a concern, because it is functioning as it should, that is, hiding the long neck. However, balance points are still important, so something of the collar, bodice construction or ornamentation must fall at the balance point.

In the following examples of high collars, the x's indicate where balance points are created within the style and/or construction of the collar or garment. Select those that appeal to you and that adapt easily to your balance points.

1. Collar band with a v-shaped cut into the bodice. The point of the v is good for a high balance point.

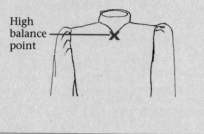

High balance point

2. High ruffle with bow. Balance points are created with the bow or where the lower ruffle ends.

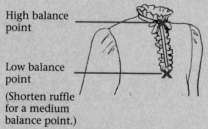

High balance point

Low balance point
(Shorten ruffle for a medium balance point.)

3. Funnel collar. This collar style can be created to have a high, medium, or low balance point at the v-opening.

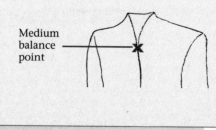

Medium balance point

4. Mandarin collar. In this example, there are two built-in balance points: the button near the collar, and the tips of the handkerchief in the pocket. The pocket treatment also helps to camouflage a long neck by creating a strong element of interest which draws our attention away from the neck area.

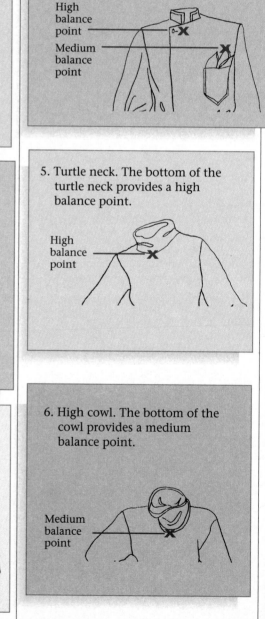

High balance point

Medium balance point

5. Turtle neck. The bottom of the turtle neck provides a high balance point.

High balance point

6. High cowl. The bottom of the cowl provides a medium balance point.

Medium balance point

The remarkable thing about the concept of balance points is that it breaks a long-standing fashion myth that short-necked people should never wear high collars. Contrary to popular belief, we believe anyone can use high collars regardless of neck length, as long as balance points are created. Remember, the idea behind the balance points is to keep the head and neck in balance with the upper body whether your neck is short, medium or long. We know many women with short necks who love wearing high collars and can easily wear the collars shown on page 54. Rather than camouflaging, these high collars highlight a short neck for the woman who is comfortable with emphasizing this particular feature.

Perhaps you have a short neck and like wearing high collars but you do not wish to highlight your short neck as such. There is a way to make it work. In addition to creating your balance point, also include these two camouflaging techniques:

1. Have something in the bodice that draws the eye outward away from the neck, and

2. Have something in the outfit that draws the eye downward lower than your balance point towards the waist or lower.

In the artworks by Renoir (at right), we have two women with short necks. Both are wearing ensembles with high collars along with elements that incorporate these two techniques.

Scarves, necklaces, collars and lapels are other means to accomplish these camouflage techniques for the woman who wants to wear high collars without emphasizing her short neck:

Here we have a collar band wrapped with a scarf that drapes downward toward the waist.

In this turtleneck, where the necklace falls can also be a balance point. The collar draws the eye outward and the lapels and sides of the jacket draw the eye in a long line downward, all creating interest away from the short neck.

The corsage on Caroline Remy's ensemble draws the eye outward away from the neck and is long enough to fall at her balance point. The corsage creates a dominant point that draws attention away from the short neck.

Caroline Remy ("Severine"), Pierre-Auguste Renoir, 1885, National Gallery of Art, Washington; Chester Dale Collection (detail).

Madame Hagen, Pierre-Auguste Renoir, National Gallery of Art, Washington; Gift of Angelika Wertheim Frink (detail).

In Mme. Hagen's outfit, the pleats in the bodice as well as the flowers in the print draw the eye outward away from the neck, and her full bow first falls at her balance point, then continues on toward the waist. The long line of the bow itself creates a dominant interest elsewhere away from the neck.

To camouflage or to highlight, to hide or to show off? That is the question we have touched on here with long and short necks. In the next chapter on Body Particulars, you will learn more about camouflaging or highlighting necks, not just long or short necks, but necks that have slopes and necks that slant forward as well. Most importantly, in the next chapter you will learn the eleven specific techniques of camouflaging and highlighting that can be applied to all your body particulars from head to toe. Once you learn these techniques and see how to implement them in various ways in clothing, you will see how quickly your own creativity will spawn other ideas to incorporate into your unique style.

Body Particulars overview chart

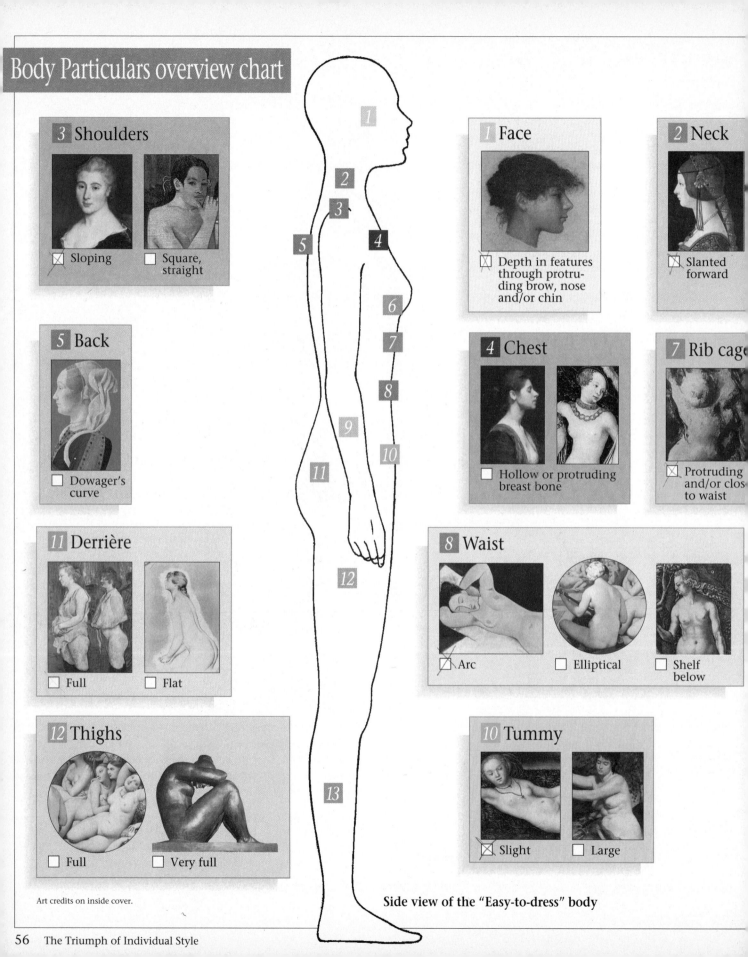

3 Shoulders

☒ Sloping
☐ Square, straight

5 Back

☐ Dowager's curve

11 Derrière

☒ Full
☐ Flat

12 Thighs

☐ Full
☐ Very full

Art credits on inside cover.

1 Face

☒ Depth in features through protruding brow, nose and/or chin

2 Neck

☒ Slanted forward

4 Chest

☐ Hollow or protruding breast bone

7 Rib cage

☒ Protruding and/or clos to waist

8 Waist

☒ Arc
☐ Elliptical
☐ Shelf below

10 Tummy

☒ Slight
☐ Large

Side view of the "Easy-to-dress" body

> Every part of your body has a creative meaning. To learn that meaning through the language of art—line, space, shape, proportion, color, and texture—is to elevate your personal style to an art form.

☐ Sloped

☐ Little indentation from chin to base of neck

☐ Long

☐ Short

6 Bosom

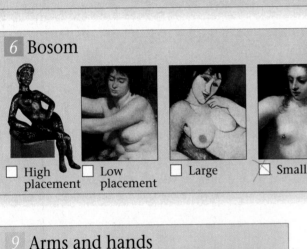

☐ High placement

☐ Low placement

☐ Large

☒ Small

9 Arms and hands

☐ Very full upper arms

☐ Very thin arms

☐ Large hands

13 Legs and feet

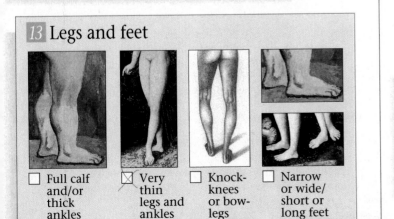

☐ Full calf and/or thick ankles

☒ Very thin legs and ankles

☐ Knock-knees or bow-legs

☐ Narrow or wide/short or long feet

4

Your Body Particulars

...and how to highlight or camouflage them.

Body Particulars are the features that give your body character. Look at the opening Body Particulars overview chart (left). It gives only a glimmer of how magnificent and varied the female body can be! You may have the same length proportions and silhouette as someone else you know; however, when you compare all your body particulars, it is unlikely you will be exactly the same (given that you are not identical twins, of course). In this chart, you see thirteen main areas from head-to-toe where you may look for body particulars. A box is provided in front of each body particular for you to check off, if appropriate. Each feature is depicted through a work of art to help you determine which of these features you possess. Artists are perhaps no more aware than we are of how unique is each human body, but they do seem more aware and accepting of the beauty found in all human features. We were astounded and elated to find that almost every human feature can be found in many fine works of art.

You already know that the easy-to-dress body is rare. Not only does this body have length proportions that divide easily into Golden Mean ratio, it also has none of the body particulars presented in this chapter. Take a moment, if you will, to imagine the easy-to-dress body assuming one or several of the body particulars shown. Imagine it taking on these features in different combinations. Can you see in your mind's eye how each body particular can give to its area of the body a different kind of expression? For example, a neck that slants forward makes a different statement than does a neck that is straight and erect. Or a bosom that is placed high on the chest has quite a different feeling than one that falls close to the waist. It is more difficult to see exactly how each body particular contributes to or changes the expression of the body as a whole, yet we know it does. What we are certain of and agree with is this statement by the artist, John Constable:

> "There is nothing ugly; I never saw an ugly thing in my life: for let the form of an object be what it may—light, shade, and perspective will always make it beautiful."
>
> —John Constable (1776-1837)
> Letter to John Fisher, 23 October, 1821

How to camouflage and highlight Your Body Particulars

Letting the beauty of your individuality shine through.

Body Particulars often present tough challenges to your dressing ingenuity. But our perspective is that every part of your body has a creative meaning. Your goal is to discover that meaning and learn to dress it artistically, always with your uniqueness in mind.

So far, you have discovered the types of fabrics that suit your body, how to determine your best silhouette shapes, how to successfully combine wardrobe pieces in good proportion, and how to select collars and necklines according to your balance points. Now it's time to add more detail in your well-proportioned silhouette, but with details that reflect

your individuality. This is where body particulars come in. In fact, if you think about it, the styling solutions you ultimately choose depend largely upon whether you want to conceal or to show off a particular feature. In other words, depending on your comfort zone, you may choose to camouflage or highlight

any body particular. The result: styling details created to do one or the other.

This chapter is divided into two parts to help you create styling details that are in harmony with your level of comfort relative to your body particulars:

Part I, called *How to camouflage and highlight Your Body Particulars* is devoted to showing you how to hide or show them off. Be prepared to be inspired by the many clothing examples given.

Part II is called *Whole body considerations*. Here we will discuss two issues that will add even greater refinement to the way you incorporate detail in your clothing presentation:

1. Symmetry in the face and body
2. Your body's side view contour lines

Be prepared for some exciting revelations in this section.

Art credits: see inside front cover.

Cultural or societal pressures often determine how you view certain parts of your body. If it is fashionable to have full bosoms for example, then you might feel you need to add layered fabric over your small breasts. You may want to camouflage in some way whatever part of your body you feel is out of the present norm. Since fashion trends are primarily about the "latest colors and fabrics" and about hemlines and silhouettes, most body particulars can't be viewed as either in or out of fashion. They just are. However, as you learn to accept and love each part of your body just as it is, you may well want to highlight that feature in an artistic way. By doing so you are making a personal statement, a show of self-acceptance and individuality, regardless of trends.

How to use Part I:

If you have not already check-marked your body particulars in the opening chart, do this now. The areas of the body appear in numbered boxes, 1 through 13. On each of the following pages in Part I, one of these area numbers is at the top left-hand corner of the page. Look for the numbers that pertain to you. Then look for the artwork representing your body particular in that area. To the left side of each artwork is the camouflage column showing ways to conceal that body particular. On the right side is the highlight column showing the opposite—ways to spotlight or show off the feature. The choice is yours.

🌸 There are six techniques for camouflaging and five for highlighting. These are shown in the key at the bottom of each page to help you learn the technique behind each clothing solution, so you will become adept at creating your own solutions. A brief study of these techniques is found on page 59. Throughout, keep in mind that the clothing suggestions that are presented focus on the particular feature. In order for *any* solution to "work", you must consider the balance of the entire visual presentation. It will be up to you to create this balance depending upon your unique body considerations.

> For some reason, when camouflaging a feature, it is relatively easy to create balance. On the other hand, it is more difficult to attain balance when highlighting. Therefore, if you choose to highlight a feature, you will have to be more aware of creating overall balance.

Sometimes, when highlighting a feature, a little camouflaging must be done first to carry off the desired highlighting. You will see a few examples of this. All examples are meant simply to give you ideas and interesting solutions.

❀ TECHNIQUES TO CAMOUFLAGE

1 Cover up creatively to hide the feature.
2 Use line to direct eye away from the feature and/or break up space.
3 Create more dimension in the clothing to change the contour line.
4 Surround a feature with more space to optically change its size.
5 Use dominance elsewhere to divert the eye away from the feature.
6 Surround a feature with a larger item to optically diminish its size.

Long neck

Mrs. William Crowninshield Endicott, John Singer Sargent, National Gallery of Art, Washington; Gift of Louise Thoron Endicott in memory of Mr. and Mrs. William Crowninshield Endicott (detail).

Notice how Mrs. Endicott in this portrait is camouflaging her long neck through creative cover-up (technique 1) with a high collar. She is also drawing attention away from the long neck with the long lacy shawl tied near her bosom, which is the use of dominance elsewhere (technique 5).

❀ TECHNIQUES TO HIGHLIGHT

1 Use creative exposure to show off the feature.
2 Repeat and/or extend the line of the feature to emphasize it.
3 Add more dimension in the clothing to make the feature appear larger.
4 Surround a feature with more space to optically change its size.
5 Place an eye-catching element at or around the feature to draw attention to it.

Full bosom

Madame Henriot, Pierre-Auguste Renoir, National Gallery of Art, Washington; Gift of the Adele R. Levy Fund, Inc. (detail).

Notice how Mme. Henriot in this portrait is highlighting her bosom through creative exposure (technique 1) and through the use of an eye catching element around the feature to draw attention to it (technique 5) with the flower brooch at her cleavage.

Face: protruding features ✿

TO CAMOUFLAGE

TO HIGHLIGHT

Notice how this woman's large hat and layered clothing come out beyond her protruding nose, thus optically diminishing the size of that feature ❻. Hair bangs can do the same, as seen in the *Head of Ana-Capri Girl* (right).

Head of Ana-Capri Girl,
John Singer Sargent;
Private collection, Richard
Ormond, London, England.

These ladies are *creatively* exposing their protruding features (nose, brow and/or chin) by pulling their hairdos back and allowing their features to show ❶. Also notice the *Lady in Yellow* has repeated the wavy line of her profile in the wave of her hair ❷. The Matisse woman has emphasized her large features even more by choosing large jewelry that are to scale with her large features ❷. (You'll learn more about scale in Chapter 5.)

Young Woman in White, Robert Henri,
National Gallery of Art, Washington; Gift of Violet Organ (detail).

Head of a Woman #2, Henri Matisse,
The Santa Barbara Museum of Art, Santa Barbara,
CA; Gift of Wright S. Ludington (detail).

Portrait of a Lady in Yellow, Alesso
Baldovinetti, National Gallery, London (detail).

This Gainsborough woman is wearing her hair very full around her face, thus optically diminishing the size of her features ❻.

Mrs. Richard Brinsley Sheridan, Thomas Gainsborough,
National Gallery of Art, Washington; Andrew W. Mellon Collection (detail).

In this portrait, this woman is both high-lighting *and camou-flaging* her protruding nose. By pulling her hair back she exposes the feature ❶, but by wearing fancy hair ornaments she *camouflages* her nose somewhat by creating dominance elsewhere ❺*.

Portrait of a Young Woman, Piero del Pollaiulol,
The Metropolitan Museum of Art; Bequest of Edward S. Harkness, 1940 (detail).

❶ Cover up creatively to hide the feature.
❷ Use line to direct eye away from the feature and/or break up space.
❸ Create more dimension in the clothing to change the contour line.
❹ Surround a feature with more space to optically change its size.
*❺ Use dominance elsewhere to divert the eye away from the feature.
❻ Surround a feature with a larger item to optically diminish its size.

❶ Use creative exposure to show off the feature.
❷ Repeat and/or extend the line of the feature to emphasize it.
❸ Add more dimension in the clothing to make the feature appear larger.
❹ Surround a feature with more space to optically change its size.
❺ Place an eye-catching element at or around the feature to draw attention to it.

Neck: slanted forward

Cover up the neck with a hood ❶. The drape of the hood adds dimension and fills in the slant of the neck ❸.

A medium length hair style can do the same thing if the hair covers the slant of the neck ❶.

Tallulah Brockman Bankhead,
Augustus John,
The National Portrait Gallery of Art,
Smithsonian Institution; Gift of the Hon.
and Mrs. John Hay Whitney (detail).

Bianca Maria Sforza,
Ambrogio de Predis,
National Gallery of Art,
Washington; Widener
Collection (detail).

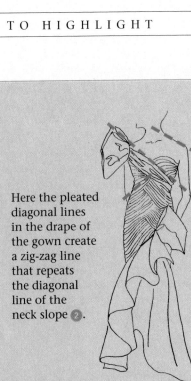

Here the pleated diagonal lines in the drape of the gown create a zig-zag line that repeats the diagonal line of the neck slope ❷.

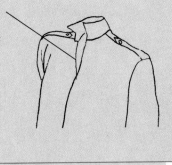

Cover up the neck with a pushed-up collar, keeping the neckline open around the slant of the neck ❶.

Cover up the neck with a high collar ❶, then add a long scarf to add dimension around the slant ❸, and to create a long line downward away from the neck ❷.

Again, the diagonals in the design of this dress repeat the diagonal of the neck slope ❷.

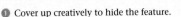

❶ Cover up creatively to hide the feature.
❷ Use line to direct eye away from the feature and/or break up space.
❸ Create more dimension in the clothing to change the contour line.
❹ Surround a feature with more space to optically change its size.
❺ Use dominance elsewhere to divert the eye away from the feature.
❻ Surround a feature with a larger item to optically diminish its size.

❶ Use creative exposure to show off the feature.
❷ Repeat and/or extend the line of the feature to emphasize it.
❸ Add more dimension in the clothing to make the feature appear larger.
❹ Surround a feature with more space to optically change its size.
❺ Place an eye-catching element at or around the feature to draw attention to it.

Neck: sloped

Cover up the neck and chin area with a collar ❶. (Remember your balance points when choosing your collar styles.) A shoulder length hair style can also cover up the slope.

Madame Jacques Louis Leblanc, Jean-Auguste-Dominique Ingres, The Metropolitan Museum of Art; Wolfe Fund, Catharine Lorillard Wolfe Collection, 1918 (detail).

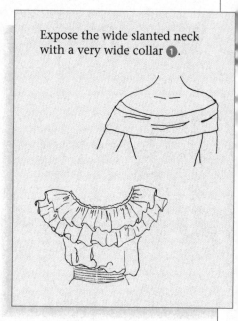

Expose the wide slanted neck with a very wide collar ❶.

Diagonals in an opened shirt collar break up the width of the sloped neck ❷.

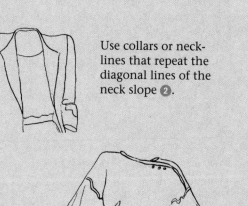

Use collars or necklines that repeat the diagonal lines of the neck slope ❷.

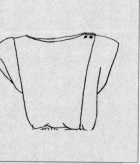

Use a neckline that is wider than the sloped sides of the base of the neck ❹.

❶ Cover up creatively to hide the feature.
❷ Use line to direct eye away from the feature and/or break up space.
❸ Create more dimension in the clothing to change the contour line.
❹ Surround a feature with more space to optically change its size.
❺ Use dominance elsewhere to divert the eye away from the feature.
❻ Surround a feature with a larger item to optically diminish its size.

❶ Use creative exposure to show off the feature.
❷ Repeat and/or extend the line of the feature to emphasize it.
❸ Add more dimension in the clothing to make the feature appear larger.
❹ Surround a feature with more space to optically change its size.
❺ Place an eye-catching element at or around the feature to draw attention to it.

Neck: little indentation from chin to base of neck ⚜

(In general, use collars rather than necklines.) This high cowl covers the chin and neck area ❶. The collars need to be bigger than the neck size in order for the chin to appear smaller ❹.

Madame Amédée (Woman with Cigarette), Amedeo Modigliani, National Gallery of Art, Washington; Chester Dale Collection (detail).

Madame Amédée has exposed her neck and chin by wearing a low neckline ❶ that repeats the diagonal line of her chin and neck (as seen in side view), which comes from not having a well-defined chin apart from the neck. Her neckline also repeats in a reversed or inverted fashion the diagonal line in her slanted eyes, slanted brows, and shoulders ❷. This repetition creates an overall diamond-shaped effect between her slanted features and her neck-line. Notice how her earrings further enhance this diamond-shaped effect and the diagonal line of her chin and neck.

This collar creates diagonal lines across the neck and chin area ❷. The opened collar creates space around the area ❹. The tie draws the eye away from the neck and chin ❺.

First, camouflage by covering the chin and neck area with a large necklace that adds dimension ❶*, ❸*. Then to highlight, be sure the strands conform with the shape and line of the chin ❷. Use eye-catching colors and textures in the necklace to create dominance around the features ❺.
Note: If you have features that protrude, when you highlight your neck in this way, the depth and dimension of the necklace also balances the protrusion of the features.

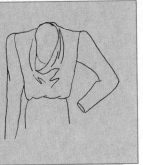

The low cowl creates space around the neck and chin area ❷ and creates dimension below it ❸. And, the drape of cowl draws attention away from it ❺.

---

* ❶ Cover up creatively to hide the feature.
   ❷ Use line to direct eye away from the feature and/or break up space.
* ❸ Create more dimension in the clothing to change the contour line.
   ❹ Surround a feature with more space to optically change its size.
   ❺ Use dominance elsewhere to divert the eye away from the feature.
   ❻ Surround a feature with a larger item to optically diminish its size.

❶ Use creative exposure to show off the feature.
❷ Repeat and or extend the line of the feature to emphasize it.
❸ Add more dimension in the clothing to make the feature appear larger.
❹ Surround a feature with more space to optically change its size.
❺ Place an eye-catching element at or around the feature to draw attention to it.

Cover up with a scarf as shown in Modigliani's *Gypsy Woman,* or a hood, or high collars ❶. And always remember to create your balance points in the neck treatment, as discussed in chapter 3.

Gypsy Woman with Baby, Amedeo Modigliani, National Gallery of Art, Washington; Chester Dale Collection (detail).

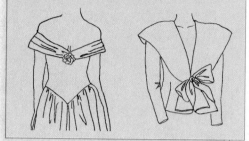

The easiest way to highlight a long neck is simply to expose it creatively ❶ as shown in these examples.

In this portrait by Sargent, Mrs. Endicott has covered her long neck with a dark-colored high collar ❶, and has also created dominance elsewhere with the lace collar treatment below it ❺.

Mrs. William Crowninshield Endicott, John Singer Sargent, National Gallery of Art, Washington; Gift of Louise Thoron Endicott in memory of Mr. and Mrs. William Crowninshield Endicott (detail).

In addition to simply being exposed, the line of this long neck is repeated in the long earrings ❷ and the necklace draws even more attention to the neck ❺.

In this outfit, dominance at the asymmetrically belted waist draws attention away from the neck area ❺.

In addition to the high collars in these drawings ❶, the downward lines in the scarves and in the jacket construction camouflage by drawing the eye away from the neck area ❷.

In Dewing's *Lady with a Lute,* her exposed long neck ❶ is further emphasized by the very low neckline that extends the line of the neck ❷.

Lady with a Lute, Thomas Wilmer Dewing, National Gallery of Art, Washington; Gift of Dr. and Mrs. Walter Timme (detail).

❶ Cover up creatively to hide the feature.
❷ Use line to direct eye away from the feature and/or break up space.
❸ Create more dimension in the clothing to change the contour line.
❹ Surround a feature with more space to optically change its size.
❺ Use dominance elsewhere to divert the eye away from the feature.
❻ Surround a feature with a larger item to optically diminish its size.

❶ Use creative exposure to show off the feature.
❷ Repeat and/or extend the line of the feature to emphasize it.
❸ Add more dimension in the clothing to make the feature appear larger.
❹ Surround a feature with more space to optically change its size.
❺ Place an eye-catching element at or around the feature to draw attention to it.

Neck: short

The easiest way to camouflage a short neck is simply to create space around and below it with open collars or necklines. Showing more skin optically gives the short neck more length ❹.

Madame Hagen,
Pierre-Auguste Renoir,
National Gallery of Art,
Washington; Gift of Angelika
Wertheim Frink (detail).

Opposite from the long neck, covering up a short neck with a high collar will highlight it. In a sense, a high collar "exposes" the shortness of the neck ❶, as shown in these drawings and in Renoir's *Madame Hagen* (left).

In addition to the open neckline and collar ❹, the shirt tied at the waist creates dominance elsewhere to divert the eye away from the neck area ❺.

As discussed in Chapter 3, always remember to create your balance points in the design of a high neck treatment—a bow, ruffles, flounce, scarf tie, corsage or other ornamentation. Any of these can also become eye-catching elements that highlight the short neck ❺ while creating balance points.

Caroline Remy ("Severine"), Pierre-Auguste Renoir,
National Gallery of Art, Washington; Chester Dale Collection (detail).

In this open v-neckline ❹, the line to the waist also directs the eye away from the neck area ❷.

Renoir's *Madame Henriot* illustrates how to *first camouflage then highlight* a relatively short neck: Camouflage with a low neckline that adds more space below it ❹*, then highlight the neck with an eye-catching element close to the neck, such as a choker necklace ❺.

Madame Henriot, Pierre-Auguste Renoir,
National Gallery of Art, Washington; Gift of the Adele R. Levy Fund, Inc. (detail).

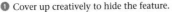

❶ Cover up creatively to hide the feature.
❷ Use line to direct eye away from the feature and/or break up space.
❸ Create more dimension in the clothing to change the contour line.
*❹ Surround a feature with more space to optically change its size.
❺ Use dominance elsewhere to divert the eye away from the feature.
❻ Surround a feature with a larger item to optically diminish its size.

❶ Use creative exposure to show off the feature.
❷ Repeat and/or extend the line of the feature to emphasize it.
❸ Add more dimension in the clothing to make the feature appear larger.
❹ Surround a feature with more space to optically change its size.
❺ Place an eye-catching element at or around the feature to draw attention to it.

Shoulders: sloping

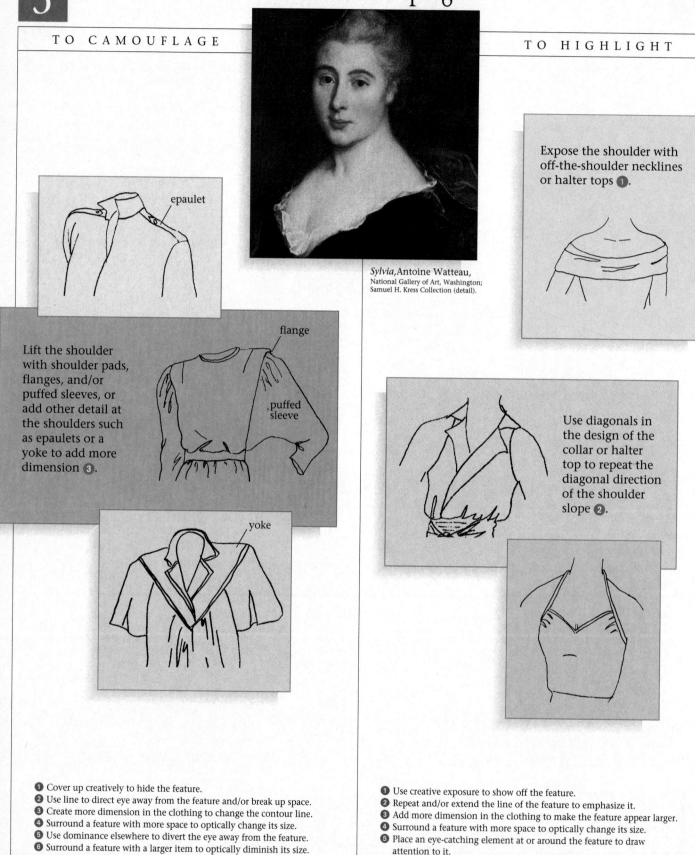

epaulet

Sylvia, Antoine Watteau,
National Gallery of Art, Washington;
Samuel H. Kress Collection (detail).

Expose the shoulder with off-the-shoulder necklines or halter tops ❶.

Lift the shoulder with shoulder pads, flanges, and/or puffed sleeves, or add other detail at the shoulders such as epaulets or a yoke to add more dimension ❸.

flange

puffed sleeve

Use diagonals in the design of the collar or halter top to repeat the diagonal direction of the shoulder slope ❷.

yoke

❶ Cover up creatively to hide the feature.
❷ Use line to direct eye away from the feature and/or break up space.
❸ Create more dimension in the clothing to change the contour line.
❹ Surround a feature with more space to optically change its size.
❺ Use dominance elsewhere to divert the eye away from the feature.
❻ Surround a feature with a larger item to optically diminish its size.

❶ Use creative exposure to show off the feature.
❷ Repeat and/or extend the line of the feature to emphasize it.
❸ Add more dimension in the clothing to make the feature appear larger.
❹ Surround a feature with more space to optically change its size.
❺ Place an eye-catching element at or around the feature to draw attention to it.

Shoulders: square, straight

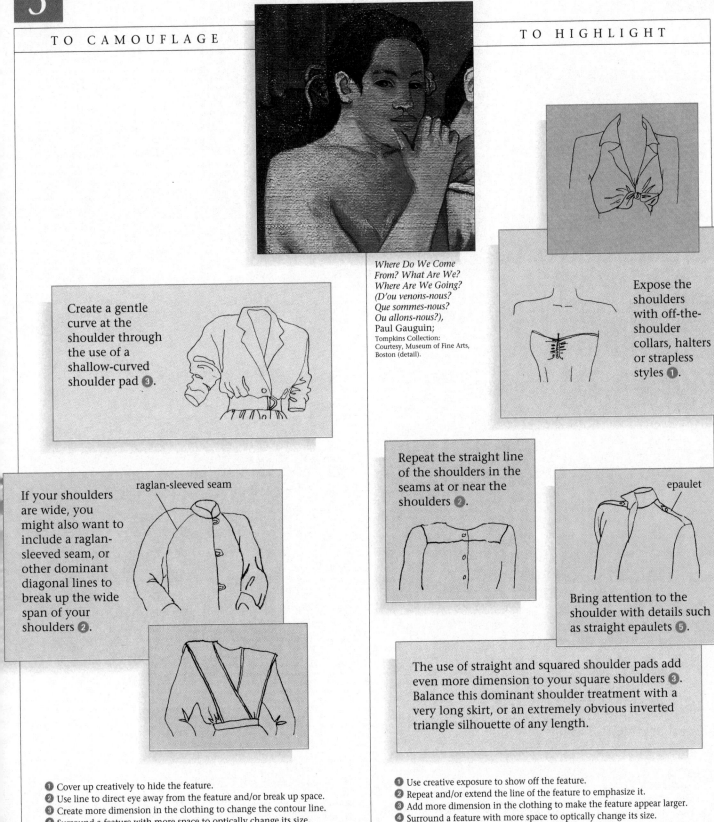

Where Do We Come From? What Are We? Where Are We Going? (D'ou venons-nous? Que sommes-nous? Ou allons-nous?), Paul Gauguin; Tompkins Collection: Courtesy, Museum of Fine Arts, Boston (detail).

Create a gentle curve at the shoulder through the use of a shallow-curved shoulder pad ❸.

Expose the shoulders with off-the-shoulder collars, halters or strapless styles ❶.

raglan-sleeved seam

If your shoulders are wide, you might also want to include a raglan-sleeved seam, or other dominant diagonal lines to break up the wide span of your shoulders ❷.

Repeat the straight line of the shoulders in the seams at or near the shoulders ❷.

epaulet

Bring attention to the shoulder with details such as straight epaulets ❺.

The use of straight and squared shoulder pads add even more dimension to your square shoulders ❸. Balance this dominant shoulder treatment with a very long skirt, or an extremely obvious inverted triangle silhouette of any length.

❶ Cover up creatively to hide the feature.
❷ Use line to direct eye away from the feature and/or break up space.
❸ Create more dimension in the clothing to change the contour line.
❹ Surround a feature with more space to optically change its size.
❺ Use dominance elsewhere to divert the eye away from the feature.
❻ Surround a feature with a larger item to optically diminish its size.

❶ Use creative exposure to show off the feature.
❷ Repeat and/or extend the line of the feature to emphasize it.
❸ Add more dimension in the clothing to make the feature appear larger.
❹ Surround a feature with more space to optically change its size.
❺ Place an eye-catching element at or around the feature to draw attention to it.

Chest: hollow or protruding breast bone

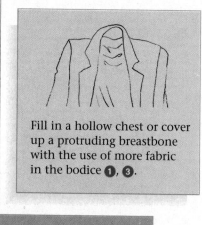

Fill in a hollow chest or cover up a protruding breastbone with the use of more fabric in the bodice ❶, ❸.

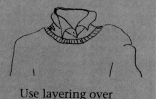

Use layering over the area ❶, ❸.

Lady with a Lute,
Thomas Wilmer Dewing,
National Gallery of Art,
Washington; Gift of Dr. and
Mrs. Walter Timme (detail).

The Judgment of Paris,
Lucas Cranach, The Elder,
1928, The Metropolitan Museum
of Art; Rogers Fund (detail).

For both the protruding breast bone and the hollow chest, you can create dominance with eye-catching jewelry such as a necklace or brooch. Rest the jewelry in the hollow, or place it on the garment near the breast bone ❺. For both, choose jewelry that repeats the shape of the hollow or protruding breast bone ❷.

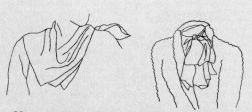

Use scarves, ruffles or bows over the area ❶, ❸.

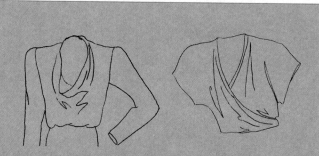

The draping fabric in these necklines will *highlight* a hollow by having the dimension around it ❸. For a protruding breastbone, these same neck treatments highlight through creative exposure ❶. However, the depth of the fabric around it *camouflages* it slightly ❸*.

Cover up in the front of the dress ❶, and open up the back of a dress to create visual interest ❺.

❶ Cover up creatively to hide the feature.
❷ Use line to direct eye away from the feature and/or break up space.
* ❸ Create more dimension in the clothing to change the contour line.
❹ Surround a feature with more space to optically change its size.
❺ Use dominance elsewhere to divert the eye away from the feature.
❻ Surround a feature with a larger item to opptically diminish its size.

❶ Use creative exposure to show off the feature.
❷ Repeat and/or extend the line of the feature to emphasize it.
❸ Add more dimension in the clothing to make the feature appear larger.
❹ Surround a feature with more space to optically change its size.
❺ Place an eye-catching element at or around the feature to draw attention to it.

Back: dowager's curve

Ginevra Bentivoglio,
Ercole de' Roberti,
National Gallery of Art,
Washington; Samuel H.
Kress Collection (detail).

Repeat the curved line of the back in the design of the hair and/or the garment curve ❶, ❷. In this particular gown the added dimension of the stand-up ruffle camouflages the curved back slightly ❻*.

Cover the curve ❶ and add fullness above or below it ❸.

Cover the curve with fabric ❶ and add interest below it that adds dimension to change the contour ❸. The added fabric should have relatively as much depth as the curve.

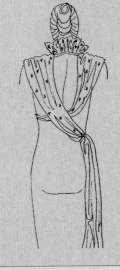

First *camouflage* by having fabric with dimension around the curve ❸*, then *highlight* by exposing the back ❶ and/or adding an eye-catching color and/or decorative sequins or such ❺.

❶ Cover up creatively to hide the feature.
❷ Use line to direct eye away from the feature and/or break up space.
* ❸ Create more dimension in the clothing to change the contour line.
❹ Surround a feature with more space to optically change its size.
❺ Use dominance elsewhere to divert the eye away from the feature.
* ❻ Surround a feature with a larger item to optically diminish its size.

❶ Use creative exposure to show off the feature.
❷ Repeat and/or extend the line of the feature to emphasize it.
❸ Add more dimension in the clothing to make the feature appear larger.
❹ Surround a feature with more space to optically change its size.
❺ Place an eye-catching element at or around the feature to draw attention to it.

TO CAMOUFLAGE	TO HIGHLIGHT

First cover up ❶. Then place jewelry or another point of interest higher than the bosom ❺.

First *camouflage* by using a dickey or insert that is placed high ❶*. Remember to use shallow arm holes which relate to the high bosom ❶*. The diagonal line in the neckline opening directs the eye away from the high bosom ❷*. Next, *highlight* by emphasizing the dickey with color or trim ❺.

Place the pocket higher than usual, to fool the eye ❶.

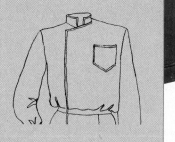

Decorative Figure, Henri-Emile-Benoit Matisse, 1908, Hirshhorn Museum and Sculpture Garden, Smithsonian Institution; Gift of Joseph H. Hirshhorn, 1966 (detail).

Place a dominant decorative element at the high bosom ❺.

Cover up the high small bosom with a large bow or layers of fabric ❸.

Cover up the high bosom with more volume in the fabric ❶, ❸, and add a high bow for dominance elsewhere ❺.

Wear a high-necked, tight-fitting halter that shows the high bosom placement ❶. The high collar balances the high placement.

* ❶ Cover up creatively to hide the feature.
* ❷ Use line to direct eye away from the feature and/or break up space.
 ❸ Create more dimension in the clothing to change the contour line.
 ❹ Surround a feature with more space to optically change its size.
 ❺ Use dominance elsewhere to divert the eye away from the feature.
 ❻ Surround a feature with a larger item to optically diminish its size.

❶ Use creative exposure to show off the feature.
❷ Repeat and/or extend the line of the feature to emphasize it.
❸ Add more dimension in the clothing to make the feature appear larger.
❹ Surround a feature with more space to optically change its size.
❺ Place an eye-catching element at or around the feature to draw attention to it.

Bosom: low placement ❧

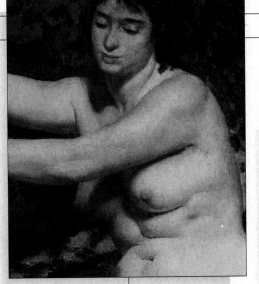

Diana, Pierre-Auguste Renoir,
National Gallery of Art, Washington; Chester Dale Collection (detail).

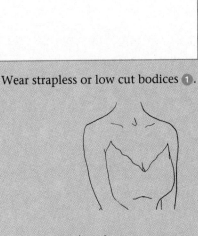

TO CAMOUFLAGE

Wear a skirt or dress with a dropped waist to direct the eye away from the bosom ❷. The dropped effect can be with accessories or in the construction.

Wear a full bodice with armholes that are dropped to the level of the bosom ❶. Then add interest below the bosom with a diagonal belt that drops below the waist ❷, ❺.

TO HIGHLIGHT

Wear strapless or low cut bodices ❶.

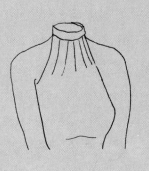

Wear tight-fitting bodices with high armholes to emphasize the contrast of the low bosom ❶. Then balance this effect with a very long skirt or with trousers.

❶ Cover up creatively to hide the feature.
❷ Use line to direct eye away from the feature and/or break up space.
❸ Create more dimension in the clothing to change the contour line.
❹ Surround a feature with more space to optically change its size.
❺ Use dominance elsewhere to divert the eye away from the feature.
❻ Surround a feature with a larger item to optically diminish its size.

❶ Use creative exposure to show off the feature.
❷ Repeat and/or extend the line of the feature to emphasize it.
❸ Add more dimension in the clothing to make the feature appear larger.
❹ Surround a feature with more space to optically change its size.
❺ Place an eye-catching element at or around the feature to draw attention to it.

Bosom: large

Nude on a Blue Cushion,
Amedeo Modigliani,
National Gallery of Art,
Washington; Chester Dale
Collection (detail).

Cover-up with a jacket ❶, use shoulder pads that extend the shoulder slightly to balance bosom ❸, and then use vertical and diagonal lines to draw the eye away from the width of the bosom ❷.

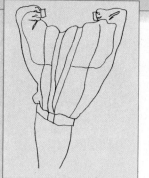

Use a diagonal line in the collar or accessory such as a large shawl or scarf ❷.

Use sleeves and bodice that are fuller than the bosom ❻. Use diagonal lines in the collar to break up the space ❷.

Show the large bosom with revealing tops ❶. Balance with long sleeves and/or a long skirt.

Show the fullness of the bosom with a halter top ❶. In this particular dress, the drape around the bosom adds an element of grace and camouflages slightly.

If you like dressing in layers, *highlight* by wearing a form-fitting top that shows the full bosom ❶. *Camouflage* slightly by wearing an unstructured coat over it to create a diagonal line that diminishes the size of the bosom ❷ *. You can also create interest below the bosom with detailing in the skirt ❺ *.

❶ Cover up creatively to hide the feature.
* ❷ Use line to direct eye away from the feature and/or break up space.
❸ Create more dimension in the clothing to change the contour line.
❹ Surround a feature with more space to optically change its size.
* ❺ Use dominance elsewhere to divert the eye away from the feature.
❻ Surround a feature with a larger item to optically diminish its size.

❶ Use creative exposure to show off the feature.
❷ Repeat and/or extend the line of the feature to emphasize it.
❸ Add more dimension in the clothing to make the feature appear larger.
❹ Surround a feature with more space to optically change its size.
❺ Place an eye-catching element at or around the feature to draw attention to it.

Bosom: small

Susanna, Jacopo Tintoretto,
National Gallery of Art, Washington;
Samuel H. Kress Collection (detail).

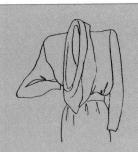

Add dimension over the
bosom with layers, bows,
ruffles, or draping ③.

Wear tight-fitted bodices ①.

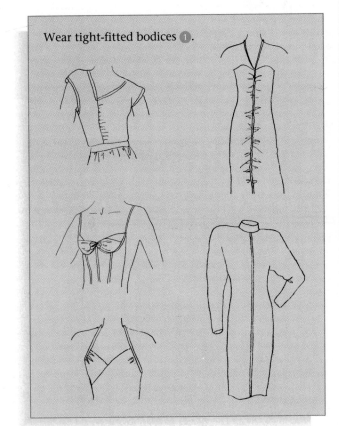

① Cover up creatively to hide the feature.
② Use line to direct eye away from the feature and/or break up space.
③ Create more dimension in the clothing to change the contour line.
④ Surround a feature with more space to optically change its size.
⑤ Use dominance elsewhere to divert the eye away from the feature.
⑥ Surround a feature with a larger item to optically diminish its size.

① Use creative exposure to show off the feature.
② Repeat and/or extend the line of the feature to emphasize it.
③ Add more dimension in the clothing to make the feature appear larger.
④ Surround a feature with more space to optically change its size.
⑤ Place an eye-catching element at or around the feature to draw
   attention to it.

TO CAMOUFLAGE　　　　　　　　　　TO HIGHLIGHT

Simply cover the ribs by either blousing over the ribcage or by bypassing the waist area altogether ❶.

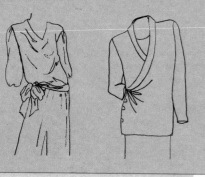

Nude with Upraised Arms, Georges Rouault, National Gallery of Art, Washington; Chester Dale Collection (detail).

Show the rib cage with a close-fitting bodice ❶ that has an elasticized gathering that creates a ripple. This ripple effect repeats the line of the protruding ribcage ❷. The added dimension of the gathering balances the protrusion.

elasticized gathering

Wear a skirt that does not have a waist band but has a contoured waist and/or yoke that falls below the low rib cage ❷.

contoured waist

yoke

Repeat the rippling line of the ribcage in tight-fitting dresses that drape back and forth across the body ❷.

Use a dropped diagonal belt that is lower in front than the low rib cage ❷. And/or blouson the top above a belt ❶.

blouson

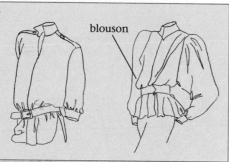

Surround rib cage with a short full cropped-top that stands out farther than the rib cage ❹.

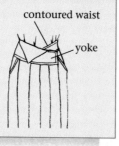

Highlight by showing the rib cage ❶. In this case a halter top is used that also *camouflages* slightly because of the front tie. The bunching of the fabric and the tie stand out further than the ribs ❻*.

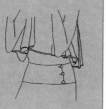

❶ Cover up creatively to hide the feature.
❷ Use line to direct eye away from the feature and/or break up space.
❸ Create more dimension in the clothing to change the contour line.
❹ Surround a feature with more space to optically change its size.
❺ Use dominance elsewhere to divert the eye away from the feature.
* ❻ Surround a feature with a larger item to optically diminish its size.

❶ Use creative exposure to show off the feature.
❷ Repeat and/or extend the line of the feature to emphasize it.
❸ Add more dimension in the clothing to make the feature appear larger.
❹ Surround a feature with more space to optically change its size.
❺ Place an eye-catching element at or around the feature to draw attention to it.

Waist: arc

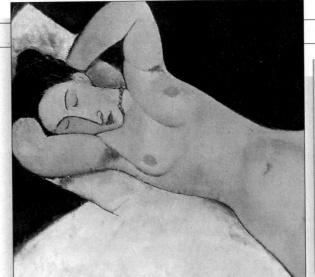

Nude, Amedeo Modigliani, 1917; oil on canvas, 28-3/4" x 45-7/8"; Photo: Robert E. Mates, Photograph c. 1991; Solomon R. Guggenheim Foundation, New York (detail).

TO CAMOUFLAGE

What is the arc waist?
The arc waist is the long concave shallow curved line that begins at or near the under-arm and arcs in bow-fashion to the widest part of the hip. If you have an arc waist, you will recognize that there is no waist 'niche' on which a belt can easily rest. This is why you cannot easily wear a belt horizontally where the arc defines the smallest part of your waist.

Use diagonal and/or vertical lines in the construction of the garment to create an illusion of a waist. It is best to avoid horizontal lines at the waist ❷.

Simply bypass the waist altogether ❶.

Create the illusion of a smaller waist by wearing a midriff-style dress that has gathers at the top and bottom of the mid-section ❸. Use horizontal lines above and below the waist in order to break the long line of the arc waist, thus creating a defined mid-section ❷.

midriff

blouson

Use diagonal lines in the construction in the mid-section to break-up the long line of arc ❷. Add a slight blouson above the diagonally draped mid-section ❸.

TO HIGHLIGHT

Wear a dress that is cut on the bias. A bias cut follows the contour of the body: in this case, the long arc waist ❷. In addition, add a curve in the construction that repeats the line of the arc waist ❷.

bias cut

A princess cut is also an excellent design to empha-size the arc waist, because it does not have a strong horizontal line, yet it does come in at the waist ❷.

Expose the waist in a form-fitting bodice ❶. Balance with either diagonals at the waist or a flared top above it.

Expose the waist as in hip-hugger pants and a short cropped top ❶. Remember to stay away from a horizontal line at the waist.

❶ Cover up creatively to hide the feature.
❷ Use line to direct eye away from the feature and/or break up space.
❸ Create more dimension in the clothing to change the contour line.
❹ Surround a feature with more space to optically change its size.
❺ Use dominance elsewhere to divert the eye away from the feature.
❻ Surround a feature with a larger item to optically diminish its size.

❶ Use creative exposure to show off the feature.
❷ Repeat and/or extend the line of the feature to emphasize it.
❸ Add more dimension in the clothing to make the feature appear larger.
❹ Surround a feature with more space to optically change its size.
❺ Place an eye-catching element at or around the feature to draw attention to it.

Waist: elliptical

What is the elliptical waist?

The woman who has an elliptical waist appears to be flat and quite wide at the waist from the front and back views; however, the waist looks very narrow from the side view.

It is essential for this body particular to optically break up the wide space of the front and back, which will make the narrow side view appear in better proportion. This is true whether you want to camouflage or highlight.

Avoid gathers at the front and back of the waist.

*Le bain turc
(The Turkish Bath)*,
Jean-Auguste-
Dominique Ingres,
Musée du Louvre, Paris (detail).

Use vertical and/or diagonal lines to break-up width of the waist ❷.

Let the waist show with a bias cut dress that conforms to the elliptical body. The slightly diagonal line optically extends the width of the waist from the front view ❷.

Along with the diagonal and vertical lines at the waist ❷, you can make the waist appear even smaller by adding something wider below it, as in the flare of this jacket ❻.

Repeat the flat horizontal line at the waist to emphasize its narrow width ❷.

❶ Cover up creatively to hide the feature.
❷ Use line to direct eye away from the feature and/or break up space.
❸ Create more dimension in the clothing to change the contour line.
❹ Surround a feature with more space to optically change its size.
❺ Use dominance elsewhere to divert the eye away from the feature.
❻ Surround a feature with a larger item to optically diminish its size.

❶ Use creative exposure to show off the feature.
❷ Repeat and/or extend the line of the feature to emphasize it.
❸ Add more dimension in the clothing to make the feature appear larger.
❹ Surround a feature with more space to optically change its size.
❺ Place an eye-catching element at or around the feature to draw attention to it.

Waist: shelf below ⚜

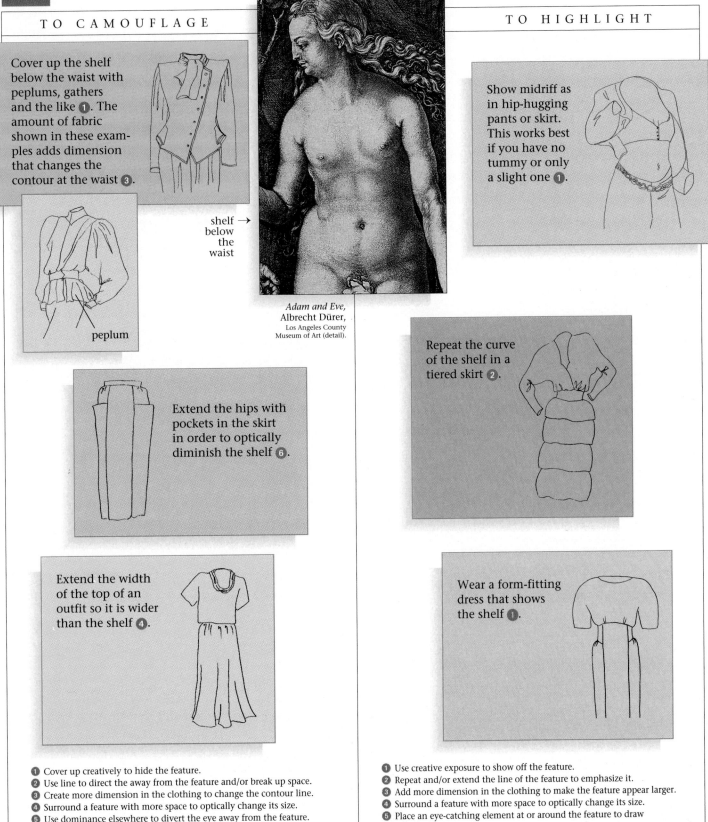

TO CAMOUFLAGE

Cover up the shelf below the waist with peplums, gathers and the like ❶. The amount of fabric shown in these examples adds dimension that changes the contour at the waist ❸.

peplum

Adam and Eve,
Albrecht Dürer,
Los Angeles County
Museum of Art (detail).

shelf →
below
the
waist

Extend the hips with pockets in the skirt in order to optically diminish the shelf ❻.

Extend the width of the top of an outfit so it is wider than the shelf ❹.

TO HIGHLIGHT

Show midriff as in hip-hugging pants or skirt. This works best if you have no tummy or only a slight one ❶.

Repeat the curve of the shelf in a tiered skirt ❷.

Wear a form-fitting dress that shows the shelf ❶.

❶ Cover up creatively to hide the feature.
❷ Use line to direct the away from the feature and/or break up space.
❸ Create more dimension in the clothing to change the contour line.
❹ Surround a feature with more space to optically change its size.
❺ Use dominance elsewhere to divert the eye away from the feature.
❻ Surround a feature with a larger item to optically diminish its size.

❶ Use creative exposure to show off the feature.
❷ Repeat and/or extend the line of the feature to emphasize it.
❸ Add more dimension in the clothing to make the feature appear larger.
❹ Surround a feature with more space to optically change its size.
❺ Place an eye-catching element at or around the feature to draw attention to it.

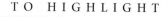

Use diagonal lines in a flared sleeve to optically break up the arm width ②. The fullness of the flare makes the arm appear smaller ④.

Notice in Renoir's painting (left) that the arms are exposed ①, and the curves of the arms are repeated in the curves of the ornamentation throughout the costume ②.

Dancer with Castanets,
Pierre-Auguste Renoir,
National Gallery, London (detail).

Tilla Durieux, Pierre-Auguste Renoir,
1960, The Metropolitan Museum of Art; Bequest of
Stephen C. Clark (detail).

In this painting, also by Renoir, interest is created at the arm by covering it with a sheer shawl ①, ⑤.

Extend the shoulder at least as far out as, or further than, the widest part of the upper arm. This optically adds dimension to change the contour ③, and optically diminishes the size of the upper arm ⑥.

First *highlight* by exposing the full arm ①. Then, *camouflage* by making certain the width and volume of the ruffles are larger than the fullest part of the upper arm ⑥*.

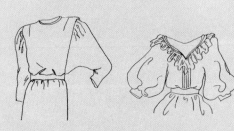

Either use lots of fabric or just loosely draped fabric in the sleeves to cover up the arm width ①.

First *camouflage* by surrounding the arm with relatively more space to diminish the width of the arm ④*. Then, *highlight* by using cut-work in the fabric so that the skin shows through ①, ⑤.

① Cover up creatively to hide the feature.
② Use line to direct eye away from the feature and/or break up space.
③ Create more dimension in the clothing to change the contour line.
* ④ Surround a feature with more space to optically change its size.
⑤ Use dominance elsewhere to divert the eye away from the feature.
* ⑥ Surround a feature with a larger item to optically diminish its size.

① Use creative exposure to show off the feature.
② Repeat and/or extend the line of the feature to emphasize it.
③ Add more dimension in the clothing to make the feature appear larger.
④ Surround a feature with more space to optically change its size.
⑤ Place an eye-catching element at or around the feature to draw attention to it.

Arms and hands: very thin arms

TO CAMOUFLAGE

TO HIGHLIGHT

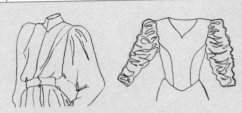

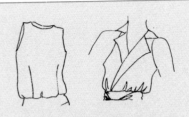

Add fabric in the sleeve to cover up the arm ①, or to create more dimension around the arm ③.

Depending upon your comfort zone, show the arm in a cut-in sleeveless top or a halter ①.

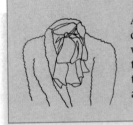

Add dimension with fabrics that have thickness and loft ③.

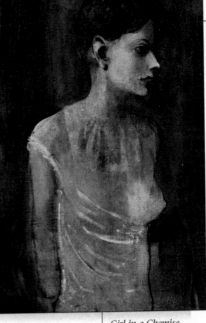

Girl in a Chemise,
Pablo Picasso,
Tate Gallery, London/
Art Resources, N.Y. (detail).

Repeat the line in the garment for a "wavy" thin arm ②.

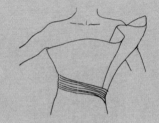

Arms and hands: large hands

Partially cover the hands with long sleeves that have a ruffle or a flounce that hangs over part of the top of the hands. Create the same effect with small to medium scale bracelets that hang down over the hand ①.

Wear large-scaled rings and bracelets that draw attention to the hands. If you choose to wear nail polish, choose a bright color, and wear longer nails ⑤.

If you don't want these ornamentations, just wear full sleeves that have a wrist band that falls slightly longer onto the hand ③.

Keep the emphasis in other parts of the body. If you wear nail polish keep it natural or very subtle ⑤.

Lady with a Fan,
Pablo Picasso,
National Gallery of Art,
Washington; Gift of the
W. Averell Harriman
Foundation in memory
of Marie N. Harriman
(detail).

Wear large or many smaller interesting pieces of jewelry or tight large wrist band bracelets. ⑤.

Madame Moitessier,
Jean-Auguste-
Dominique Ingres,
National Gallery of Art,
Washington; Samuel H. Kress
Collection (detail).

① Cover up creatively to hide the feature.
② Use line to direct the eye away from the feature.and/or break up space
③ Create more dimension in the clothing to change the contour line.
④ Surround a feature with more space to optically change its size.
⑤ Use dominance elsewhere to divert the eye away from the feature.
⑥ Surround a feature with a larger item to optically diminish its size.

① Use creative exposure to show off the feature.
② Repeat and/or extend the line of the feature to emphasize it.
③ Add more dimension in the clothing to make the feature appear larger.
④ Surround a feature with more space to optically change its size.
⑤ Place an eye-catching element at or around the feature to draw attention to it.

Tummy: slight

TO CAMOUFLAGE

Cover up with a jacket or overblouse ❶. Create diagonals over the tummy at the bottom of the jacket ❷. The tied overblouse also adds dimension above the tummy to change the contour line ❸.

Wear draped fabric over the bulge ❸, with diagonal lines in the styling detail ❷.

Wear a peplum jacket or top that is bloused slightly farther out than the tummy ❻.

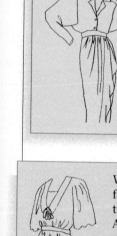

Wear gathers that fall easily over the tummy ❶. Add a detail elsewhere to draw eye away from the tummy area, as in the bow ❺.

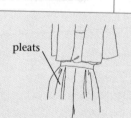

pleats

Wear pleats on each side of the tummy to create an illusion of a flatter tummy ❸.

The Nymph of the Spring, Lucas Cranach, The Elder, National Gallery of Art, Washington; Gift of Clarence Y. Palitz (detail).

TO HIGHLIGHT

flared skirt

Show the tummy by wearing a diagonally wrapped form-fitting dress or gown over the tummy ❶, ❷. Balance the effect with a flared skirt.

Wrap the tummy to highlight it ❶. Balance the fullness of the tummy with a full drape at the back.

❶ Cover up creatively to hide the feature.
❷ Use line to direct the eye away from the feature.and/or break up space
❸ Create more dimension in the clothing to change the contour line.
❹ Surround a feature with more space to optically change its size.
❺ Use dominance elsewhere to divert the eye away from the feature.
❻ Surround a feature with a larger item to optically diminish its size.

❶ Use creative exposure to show off the feature.
❷ Repeat and/or extend the line of the feature to emphasize it.
❸ Add more dimension in the clothing to make the feature appear larger.
❹ Surround a feature with more space to optically change its size.
❺ Place an eye-catching element at or around the feature to draw attention to it.

Tummy: large

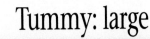

Diana, Pierre-Auguste Renoir,
National Gallery of Art,
Washington; Chester Dale Collection (detail).

Bypass the tummy with a full-shouldered top or dress that narrows below the tummy ❶, ❻.

When highlighting a large tummy, you must always consider *balance*. Have some part of your visual presentation be optically fuller (as in a hair style) or larger than the tummy (as in fullness at the back of the skirt). The bigger the tummy the *grander* the total design must be.

If the top is slightly darker in color than the skirt, then the eye is drawn to the narrow skirt ❺.

Place a dramatic ornament at the top of the tummy ❺. Then loosely drape fabric over the tummy in a large sweep of fabric ❸. This effect dramatizes the tummy if the back of the gown is relatively flat.

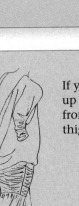

If your thighs are narrow, cover up the tummy by draping fabric from the shoulder to a dramatic thigh band ❶, ❺.

Show off the tummy by highlighting it with a striking draped effect that goes around the tummy as seen in Renoir's *Dancer with Castanets* ❶. Notice that the tummy is balanced by the long skirt that is flared at the back. Also notice that the curve of the tummy is repeated in the garlands of flowers that cascade down the skirt. These garlands tend to camouflage the tummy slightly by drawing the attention to other parts of the body as well ❷*.

Dancer with Castanets, Pierre-Auguste Renoir,
National Gallery, London.

❶ Cover up creatively to hide the feature.
*❷ Use line to direct the eye away from the feature and/or break up space.
❸ Create more dimension in the clothing to change the contour line.
❹ Surround a feature with more space to optically change its size.
❺ Use dominance elsewhere to divert the eye away from the feature.
❻ Surround a feature with a larger item to optically diminish its size.

❶ Use creative exposure to show off the feature.
❷ Repeat and/or extend the line of the feature to emphasize it.
❸ Add more dimension in the clothing to make the feature appear larger.
❹ Surround a feature with more space to optically change its size.
❺ Place an eye-catching element at or around the feature to draw attention to it.

TO CAMOUFLAGE

Create some fullness at the back to cover-up the derrière ❶, ❻. Add detailing that draws the eye away from the derrière ❺. The vertical lines of the pleating break up the large span of the derrière ❷. The full-ness at the bottom of the skirt diminishes the derrière ❻.

In this full skirt the soft pleating adds vertical and slightly diago-nal lines that break up the width ❷.

If you have a waist, wear a full skirt that simply covers the derrière ❶.

Wear a long, lightweight, and unstruc-tured coat or jacket that skims over the derrière ❶.

Wear a short jacket with full-ness that flares out farther than the derrière ❻.

Wear a jacket that has a full peplum ❶. The diagonal line at the bottom of this jacket optically diminishes the size of the derrière ❷.

Fill in the area above the full derrière with fabric such as a gathered bow or tie ❸.

Rue des Moulins, Henri de Toulouse-Lautrec, National Gallery of Art, Washington; Chester Dale Collection, 1894 (detail).

TO HIGHLIGHT

Highlight by creating interest at the back of a form-fitting suit jacket or dress ❺. Balance by extending the shoulders as wide as the hip or derrière.

Show off the derrière with a dress that fits tightly over it ❶. Create eye-catching interest at or around the derrière to draw attention there ❺.

Show off the derrière with a dress that fits snugly over the derrière ❶. Flare the skirt out below it for balance ❻*. The larger the derrière, the more important it is to balance it with a full hairdo, a hat, or a full wide collar.

Repeat the line of the derrière curve in the construction of the dress ❷.

❶ Cover up creatively to hide the feature.
❷ Use line to direct the eye away from the feature and/or break up space.
❸ Create more dimension in the clothing to change the contour line.
❹ Surround a feature with more space to optically change its size.
❺ Use dominance elsewhere to divert the eye away from the feature.
* ❻ Surround a feature with a larger item to optically diminish its size.

❶ Use creative exposure to show off the feature.
❷ Repeat and/or extend the line of the feature to emphasize it.
❸ Add more dimension in the clothing to make the feature appear larger.
❹ Surround a feature with more space to optically change its size.
❺ Place an eye-catching element at or around the feature to draw attention to it.

TO CAMOUFLAGE

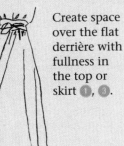

Create space over the flat derrière with fullness in the top or skirt ❶, ❸.

Study for "The Bathers", **Pierre-Auguste Renoir,** French, 1814-1919, red, black, and white chalk over graphite, touched with brush, c.1884/85, 98.5 x 64 cm.; Bequest of Kate l. Brewster, 1949.514. c.1990, The Art Institute of Chicago.

TO HIGHLIGHT

Wear a slim skirt over the flat derrière ❶; you can also flare out the skirt at the bottom to make the derrière appear even smaller ❹.

Draw attention to the flat derrière with a dramatic flat bow or ornament ❺.

gathers in back

eye-catching detail

Create small gathers at the back of the skirt or trouser ❶ and place eye-catching details elsewhere ❺.

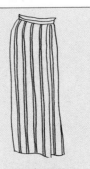

Wear straight stripes in a tight-fitting skirt. When the stripes remain straight, it emphasizes the flatness of the derrière ❷.

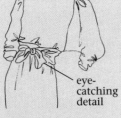

eye-catching detail

gathers

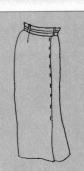

Contrast the flatness of the derrière with a flared short jacket ❹, which balances the derrière while drawing attention to it ❺.

Copy the flatness of the derrière with flat design in the skirt or dress ❷.

❶ Cover up creatively to hide the feature.
❷ Use line to direct the eye away from the feature and/or break up space.
❸ Create more dimension in the clothing to change the contour line.
❹ Surround a feature with more space to optically change its size.
❺ Use dominance elsewhere to divert the eye away from the feature.
❻ Surround a feature with a larger item to optically diminish its size.

❶ Use creative exposure to show off the feature.
❷ Repeat and/or extend the line of the feature to emphasize it.
❸ Add more dimension in the clothing to make the feature appear larger.
❹ Surround a feature with more space to optically change its size.
❺ Place an eye-catching element at or around the feature to draw attention to it.

Thighs: full

Wear a flared
skirt that
falls over
the thigh
area ❶, ❻.

*Le bain turc
(The Turkish
Bath),*
Jean-Auguste-
Dominique Ingres,
Musée du Louvre, Paris (detail).

Walking Woman,
Gaston Lachaise,
1922, Hirshhorn Museum and Sculpture
Garden, Smithsonian Institution; Gift of
Joseph H. Hirshhorn, 1966.

Wear a long tunic jacket
that falls over the thigh
area ❶. The waist
may or may not
be bypassed.

Wear a slightly or
moderately full dirndl
skirt that allows room
for the thigh ❶.

Wear an ovalized skirt
or pant that gently
follows the curved
line of the thighs ❷.
To ovalize a pant or
skirt, the side seam is
tapered from below
the thigh to the
hem in a
seam that
curves in
at the
hem.

Wear a tight-fitting
dress that follows the
curve of the thigh ❶.
In this example
the flare at the
bottom of the skirt
creates balance.

Choose skirts
or trousers that
are designed
with ample
fabric ❹, ❻.

In these two
examples the
curve of the
thigh is
repeated in the
seams of the
bodice or waist
treatments ❷.

❶ Cover up creatively to hide the feature.
❷ Use line to direct the eye away from the feature and/or break up space.
❸ Create more dimension in the clothing to change the contour line.
❹ Surround a feature with more space to optically change its size.
❺ Use dominance elsewhere to divert the eye away from the feature.
❻ Surround a feature with a larger item to optically diminish its size.

❶ Use creative exposure to show off the feature.
❷ Repeat and/or extend the line of the feature to emphasize it.
❸ Add more dimension in the clothing to make the feature appear larger.
❹ Surround a feature with more space to optically change its size.
❺ Place an eye-catching element at or around the feature to draw
attention to it.

12

Thighs: very full

From a gathered waistline, flare the moderately draped fabric over the thigh ①, ⑥.

Night, Aristide Joseph Bonaventure Maillol, The Metropolitan Museum of Art; Gift of Maurice Wertheim, 1950.

Wear full loosely draped pantaloons in a dark color ①, ③. The trousers should taper at the ankle.

The Dancer with Castanets is highlighting her full thighs by drawing attention to that area of her body with the garlands of flowers, and by the sheer fabric that reveals her legs ⑤. The line of the garlands also repeats the curve of the thigh ②. The sheer full skirt flares out in back to provide the balance for her full-figured body.

Dancer with Castanets, Auguste Renoir, National Gallery, London.

Wear a long jacket that covers the thigh ①. Slightly taper the skirt below the thigh.

It is often most comfortable for a person with very large thighs to wear a long jacket when wearing trousers.

The full long oval shapes that balloon over the thigh area not only *camouflage* ①, ⑥* by creatively covering up, but they also *highlight* if they are the same or a brighter color because they repeat the line of the full thigh ②. Keep the pant slim for balance.

---

* ① Cover up creatively to hide the feature.
  ② Use line to direct the eye away from the feature and/or break up space.
  ③ Create more dimension in the clothing to change the contour line.
  ④ Surround a feature with more space to optically change its size.
  ⑤ Use dominance elsewhere to divert the eye away from the feature.
* ⑥ Surround a feature with a larger item to optically diminish its size.

① Use creative exposure to show off the feature.
② Repeat and/or extend the line of the feature to emphasize it.
③ Add more dimension in the clothing to make the feature appear larger.
④ Surround a feature with more space to optically change its size.
⑤ Place an eye-catching element at or around the feature to draw attention to it.

Legs and feet: full calf and/or thick ankles

TO CAMOUFLAGE   **TO HIGHLIGHT**

Two Nudes,
Pablo Picasso.
París (late 1906).
Oil on canvas,
59-5/8" x 36-5/8",
The Museum of
Modern Art, New York
Gift of G. David
Thompson in honor
of Alfred H. Barr, Jr.
(detail).

Add relative space at the bottom of skirts and in the legs of trousers to add something fuller around the full ankle or calf ➍.

The fuller the calf and ankle, the fuller the skirt ➍.

Wear tight fitting pants with wide top short boots ➌.

Wear brightly colored socks that are scrunched at the ankle. Wear with substantial shoes such as tennis shoes, or wear softly-crushed boots ➌, ➎.

➊ Cover up creatively to hide the feature.
➋ Use line to direct the eye away from the feature and/or break up space.
➌ Create more dimension in the clothing to change the contour line.
➍ Surround a feature with more space to optically change its size.
➎ Use dominance elsewhere to divert the eye away from the feature.
➏ Surround a feature with a larger item to optically diminish its size.

➊ Use creative exposure to show off the feature.
➋ Repeat and/or extend the line of the feature to emphasize it.
➌ Add more dimension in the clothing to make the feature appear larger.
➍ Surround a feature with more space to optically change its size.
➎ Place an eye-catching element at or around the feature to draw attention to it.

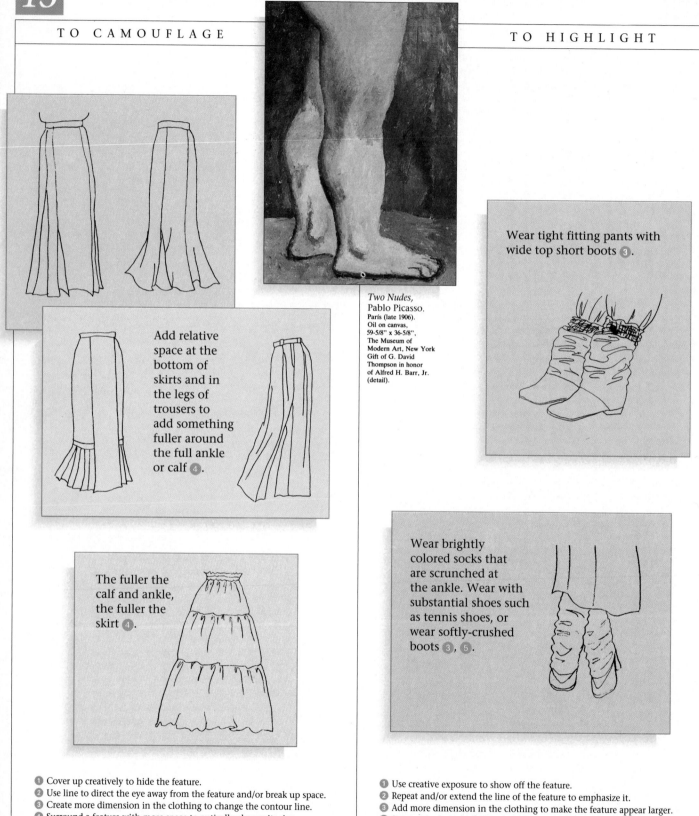

Legs and feet: very thin legs and ankles ✿

TO CAMOUFLAGE

Cover up the leg and ankle with a full pant ❶, ❹.

Wear slightly flared longer skirts ❶. An uneven hem diffuses the eye so the thinness of the ankle is not noticed ❷.

TO HIGHLIGHT

Draw attention to the ankle with eye-catching shoes ❺. Wear a very full skirt that shows the ankles. Remember that the fuller the skirt at the hem, the thinner the ankles look ❹.

Venus in a Landscape,
Lucas Cranach, The Elder,
Musée du Louvre, Paris (detail).

Legs and feet: knock-knees or bow-legs ✿

Wear long skirts or trousers that have some fullness at the bottom ❶, ❸.

Wear skirts with curved diagonals in the construction; uneven hem-lines blend with the curve of the leg ❷.

Repeat the angle and indentation of the knocked-kneed lower body in the construction of the garment ❷.

In the construction of the garment, repeat the curve of the leg, whether curved in or out ❷.

Curved Legs,
D.J. Simison,
Private collection,
C.M. Mathis.

❶ Cover up creatively to hide the feature.
❷ Use line to direct the eye away from the feature and/or break up space.
❸ Create more dimension in the clothing to change the contour line.
❹ Surround a feature with more space to optically change its size.
❺ Use dominance elsewhere to divert the eye away from the feature.
❻ Surround a feature with a larger item to optically diminish its size.

❶ Use creative exposure to show off the feature.
❷ Repeat and/or extend the line of the feature to emphasize it.
❸ Add more dimension in the clothing to make the feature appear larger.
❹ Surround a feature with more space to optically change its size.
❺ Place an eye-catching element at or around the feature to draw attention to it.

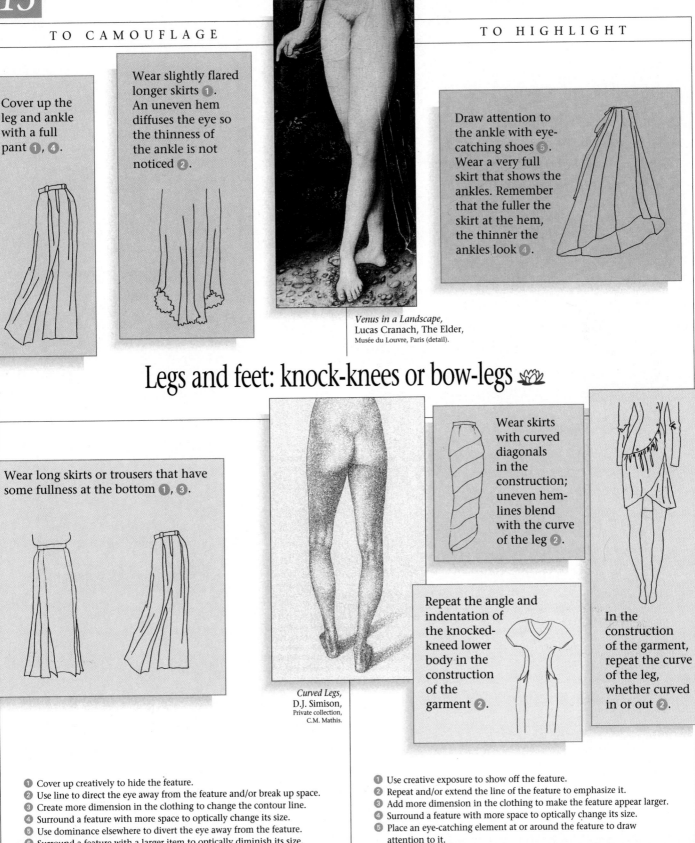

| TO CAMOUFLAGE | TO HIGHLIGHT |

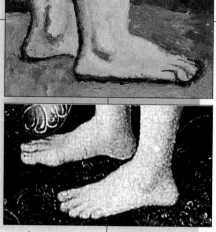

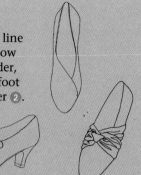

Strange as it may seem, the diagonal line makes a narrow foot look wider, and a wider foot look narrower ❷.

Two Nudes, Pablo Picasso, The Museum of Modern Art, New York (detail).

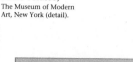

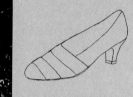

The Judgment of Paris, Lucas Cranach, The Elder, The Metropolitan Museum of Art, 1928 (detail).

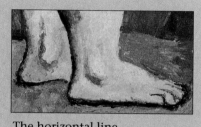

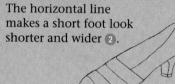

The horizontal line makes a short foot look shorter and wider ❷.

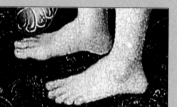

The horizontal line makes a long foot look shorter ❷.

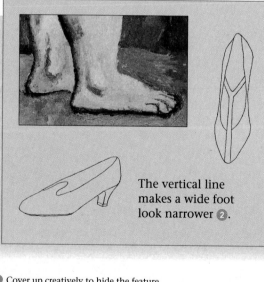

The vertical line makes a wide foot look narrower ❷.

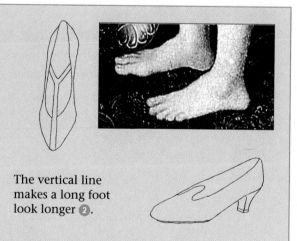

The vertical line makes a long foot look longer ❷.

❶ Cover up creatively to hide the feature.
❷ Use line to direct the eye away from the feature and/or break up space.
❸ Create more dimension in the clothing to change the contour line.
❹ Surround a feature with more space to optically change its size.
❺ Use dominance elsewhere to divert the eye away from the feature.
❻ Surround a feature with a larger item to optically diminish its size.

❶ Use creative exposure to show off the feature.
❷ Repeat and/or extend the line of the feature to emphasize it.
❸ Add more dimension in the clothing to make the feature appear larger.
❹ Surround a feature with more space to optically change its size.
❺ Place an eye-catching element at or around the feature to draw attention to it.

1. Symmetry or asymmetry
   in the face and body
2. Your body's side view
   contour lines

1. Symmetry or asymmetry in the face and body

The styling details in your clothing and especially the cut of a garment should take into consideration your body's overall visual balance. Visual balance can either be symmetrical or asymmetrical. Your face is either relatively symmetrical or asymmetrical, as is your body. It is very simple to determine which visual balance is yours.

Your face

Begin with your face. Imagine a vertical line running down the center of your face dividing the face in half. Now ask: *Do the halves mirror each other for the most part? Or are they different?* If they mirror each other—that is, they are the same or very similar to each other—then your face is symmetrically balanced. If the halves of the face are quite different from each other—for example, perhaps one eyebrow slants while the other is straight, one eye is slightly lower than the other, or any other obvious irregularity—then your face is asymmetrically balanced.

The following art examples clearly illustrate the difference between symmetry and asymmetry.

SYMMETRICAL FACE

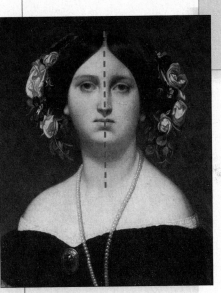

Madame Moitessier,
Jean-Auguste-Dominique Ingres,
National Gallery of Art, Washington;
Samuel H. Cress Collection (detail).

Notice the symmetry in this face: each side is relatively the same. She has chosen to repeat her symmetry in her clothing and ornamentation.

❀ Following our principle of repetition for harmony, if your face is symmetrically balanced, then symmetrical styling details are natural for you.

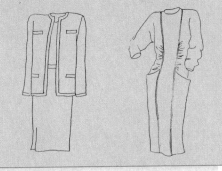

ASYMMETRICAL FACE

In contrast, asymmetry is apparent in this face by Matisse: each side is different from the other in the eyes, nose, cheeks, mouth and chin. Notice she has chosen to repeat her asymmetry in her hairstyle and clothing.

Young Girl with Long Hair, Henri Matisse,
National Gallery of Art, Washington; Rosenwald Collection.

❀ If your face is asymmetrically balanced, then asymmetrical styling details are in harmony with you; and in fact, will make your asymmetrical face more active, emphatic, and exciting.

Your body

Now look at your *body* in a full-length mirror. Again imagine a vertical line running down the center of your body dividing it in half. Look at both the front and back and ask yourself: Do the halves mirror each other for the most part? Or are they different? If they mirror each other, then your body is symmetrically balanced. If the halves of the body are quite different from each other—for example, perhaps one side of the body is less wide than the other, or one hip may be higher than the other, or one leg is shorter than the other, or any other obvious irregularity—then your body is asymmetrically balanced.

If your body is asymmetrical, it will be obvious to you, and you might relate easily to these asymmetrical-looking bodies in Picasso's painting, *Les Demoiselles d' Avignon*.

Les Demoiselles d'Avignon, Pablo Picasso. Paris (begun May, reworked July, 1907). Oil on canvas 8' x 7' 8"; Collection, The Museum of Modern Art, New York. Acquired through the Lillie P. Bliss Bequest (detail).

The question of symmetry versus asymmetry in the body is a consideration for the cut of your garments. Symmetrically cut clothing will not fit or fall properly on the asymmetrical body. Thus, if you have an asymmetrical body, then you will need to make necessary adjustments in your clothing or have your garments custom cut to conform to your body. However, if you are inventive, you can wear some symmetrical pieces in an asymmetrical manner, as in this vest, which is tucked in on one side.

If you want to highlight your asymmetrical body, then use asymmetrical clothing design as shown in the examples on the next page.

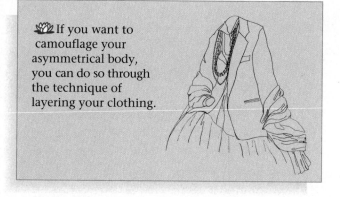

If you want to camouflage your asymmetrical body, you can do so through the technique of layering your clothing.

It is possible to have a symmetrical body with an asymmetrical face.

If you have this body and face combination, you can wear off-the-rack (symmetrically cut) clothing that have asymmetrical styling details.

Or, you can wear symmetrically cut garments in an asymmetrical manner. Though these examples are probably symmetrical pieces of clothing, they are worn in an asymmetrical manner.

It is also possible to have the opposite combination: an asymmetrical body and a symmetrical face. Clothing must be custom cut or adjusted to hang properly on this body, but the garment can have symmetrical details.

All of the examples in this column have symmetry and could be used to relate to a symmetrical face and body.

All of the examples in this column have asymmetry and could be used to relate to an asymmetrical face and/or body. If a person with symmetry would like to wear these designs, she can do so; however, it would be a *dramatic effect* for her because of the *contrast* to her symmetry.

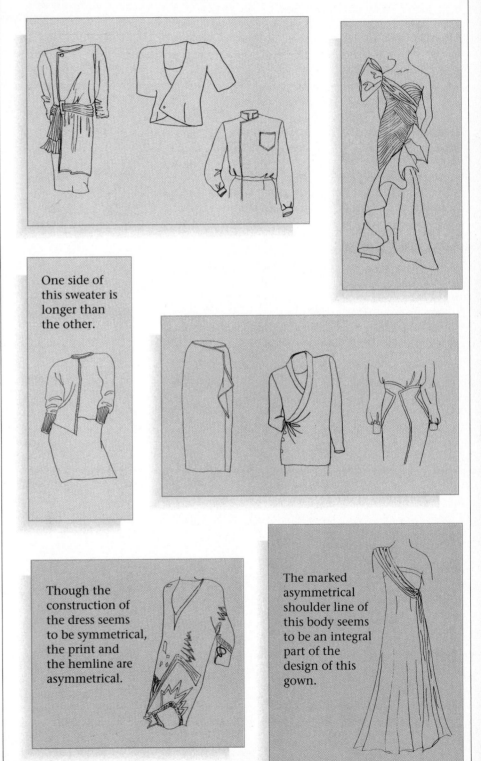

One side of this sweater is longer than the other.

Though the construction of the dress seems to be symmetrical, the print and the hemline are asymmetrical.

The marked asymmetrical shoulder line of this body seems to be an integral part of the design of this gown.

2. Whole body side view contour

We are three-dimensional in shape, so how clothes harmonize with our bodies from the side is just as important as from the front and back. In this next section, we discuss three special body considerations that can be determined only from the side view:

- A waist that slants diagonally (upward or downward) from back to front
- A "wavy" side view contour
- A relatively "flat" side view contour

It is important to determine if you have any one of these body considerations, because they require special clothing construction and design treatments when you wish to highlight rather than camouflage them. It is a question of using the line direction (either vertical, horizontal, and/or diagonal) that best follows the optical flow of your body's contour and waistline as seen from the side.

A waist that slants diagonally (upward or downward) from back to front.

Did you know that even if your waist looks straight and horizontal from side-to-side when viewed from the front or back, it could be slanted diagonally from back to front when viewed from the side? These drawings of the easy-to-dress body show what a straight horizontal waist looks like from both the front and the side.

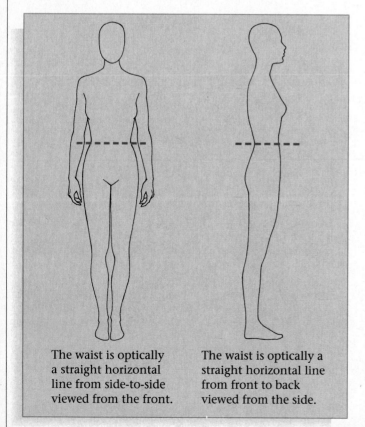

The waist is optically a straight horizontal line from side-to-side viewed from the front.

The waist is optically a straight horizontal line from front to back viewed from the side.

For the straight horizontal waist, jacket bottoms at or near the waist should repeat the straight and horizontal line, thereby creating harmony with the waist.

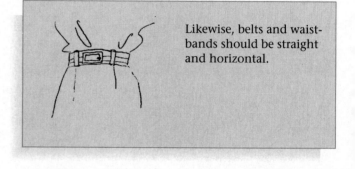

Likewise, belts and waistbands should be straight and horizontal.

Other horizontal lines within the outfit, such as in the pockets of a jacket, can be added to dramatize this waist feature even more.

In contrast, a waist that slants diagonally from back to front when viewed from the side are seen in the artworks on the next page.

The large tummy of Renoir's dancer makes the waist appear to slant upward from back to front. The woman in Lautrec's painting has a swayback, which can make the waist appear slanted downward from back to front.

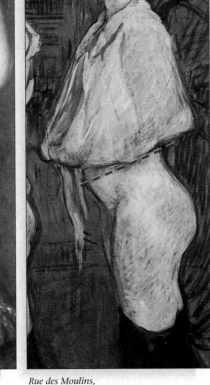

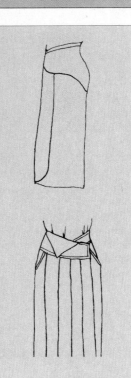

Elasticized
waistbands can
easily conform
to the slanted
waistline.

Dancer with Castanets,
Pierre Auguste Renoir,
National Gallery, London (detail).

Rue des Moulins,
Henri de Toulouse-Lautrec,
1894, National Gallery.of Art, Washington;
Chester Dale Collection (detail).

The diagonally angled waist needs jacket bottoms at or near the waist that repeat its diagonal line. This would make the back of a jacket either higher or lower than the front depending on which way you angle the line. Likewise, belts and waistbands should go in a diagonal direction, and if you wish, repeat the diagonal in other design elements in the outfit as well. Whether you angle the diagonal line upward or downward does not matter, just as long as you repeat the diagonal optical flow of the waist. For instance, in Renoir's dancer, diagonals criss-cross all the way down the skirt via the scarf and the garlands of flowers.

🪷 What all this simply means is that if you are going to highlight or show the waist in your clothing, always follow the line direction of your waist.

A "wavy" side view contour

When we look at the back, bosom, tummy, and derrière from the side, we are able to see how far from the body they protrude. Together they determine the side view contour of the body. Below is a drawing of the side view contour of the easy-to-dress body. First, notice the bosom and derrière curves are moderate in size, and the back and tummy are relatively flat. There is a balance between flat and curved places along the contour. Next, notice that the overall body has an optical effect of being vertically aligned; that is, it appears straight up and down from head-to-toe. This is largely because the straightness of the back and the straightness of the tummy are relatively parallel, and the bosom and derrière are not so large that they pull the eye away from the vertical alignment of the main body.

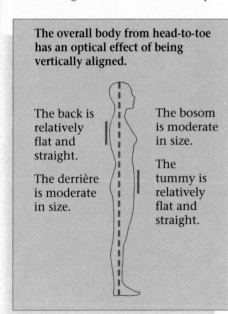

The overall body from head-to-toe has an optical effect of being vertically aligned.

The back is relatively flat and straight.

The derrière is moderate in size.

The bosom is moderate in size.

The tummy is relatively flat and straight.

In Part I of this chapter, you learned the techniques of camouflaging or highlighting certain body particulars, including the dowager's curve, the large bosom, the large tummy, and the large derrière. For each of these features in the examples to highlight, we showed the need to create some balancing element when emphasizing these large body particulars. If you have only one of these features, highlighting can be relatively easy to achieve as long as that balance is created.

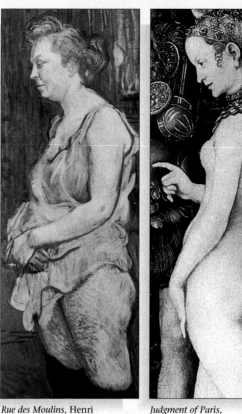

Rue des Moulins, Henri de Toulouse-Lautrec, 1894, National Gallery of Art, Washington; Chester Dale Collection (detail).

Judgment of Paris, Lucas Cranach, The Elder, The Metropolitan Museum of Art, (detail).

Clothes with diagonal construction lines in the bodice or soft diagonals that repeat over and over the curved lines of the body bring out the beauty of this wavy contour.

But what if you have more than one, or even all of these body particulars, as well as a slanted waist? For example, above are two such bodies from the artworks of Toulouse-Lautrec and Cranach, The Elder.

Lautrec's woman has all four features in relatively large proportions. While she is covered around the waist area, we can imagine that her body goes in and out in large curves, pretty much all around the side view contour of her torso. Cranach's more slender woman, also has a prominent dowager's curve, a slightly large derrière, and a protruding tummy. She appears to have a slanted waist, because of her tummy. Her bosom, however, creates a smaller curve from the side.

Both bodies have a "wavy" effect in the side view contour, which appears to optically throw the body off from the vertical alignment that we are accustomed to seeing. Can wavy bodies such as these be highlighted? Indeed they can, and in fact often look best when clothes are allowed to follow the optical flow of the body. Clothes with diagonal construction lines in the bodice or soft diagonals that repeat over and over the curved lines of the body bring out the beauty of this wavy contour.

A relatively flat contour ❧

Finally, perhaps your whole body side view contour is relatively straight and flat, in back and in front as shown in this drawing:

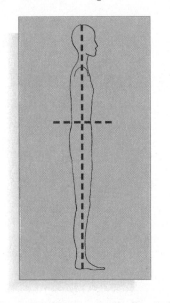

If your body is generally flat and your waist line is horizontal from back to front, then the optical flow of your side view contour lines are basically vertical and horizontal. To highlight the flatness of this body contour, stripes or other details in the bodice that are straight and horizontal and/or vertical are wonderful.

We have found that women who have very flat tummies look their best and feel most comfortable with very flat construction in the front of their skirts and trousers. If you are one of these women, you probably already gravitate toward skirts such as those above.

Girl in a Chemise,
Pablo Picasso,
Tate Gallery, London/Art
Resources, N.Y. (detail).

Picasso's *Girl in a Chemise* is a fine example of the flat contour. While we do not see her entire body, the sudden protrusion of her relatively moderate bosom provides enough contrast to make us immediately aware of her body's flatness, particularly at the tummy.

To highlight the flatness of this body contour, stripes or other details in the bodice that are straight and horizontal and/or vertical are wonderful.

With this chapter you have come halfway in the discovery of your individual design pattern. As you move forward from body particulars to the chapters on scale, color, texture, and finally to your creativity—you will see how more and more of your individuality comes into play.

In this trio of birds you can see differences in their scale: bone structure, facial features, and apparent size.

Scale: your body's bone structure, facial features, and apparent body size

... and how to choose clothing construction, accessories, and jewelry.

Scale is a first cousin to proportion, and it applies especially to the elements of line and shape, and of course inevitably to space.

Like proportion, scale entails the comparison of size of parts, but not in terms of ratios. Rather, scale is concerned only with creating a consistent relationship between your body's scale and the scale of the details found in your clothing, accessories, and jewelry. Again, the goal is to create a balance and harmony, so that we match small scale body features with small scale clothing details, medium scale features with medium scale details, and large scale features with large scale details. Sounds easy enough. But how do you determine your body's scale? And what kinds of details are we talking about? This chapter will give you the answers to these questions in as clear and simple a fashion as possible, so your ability to choose your clothing details becomes highly discriminating.

Your body's three indicators of scale ✿

There are three indicators of scale:

1. The size of your bone structure as seen at your wrists and ankles
2. The size of your facial features
3. Your body's apparent size, or the amount of space your body appears to take.

Each indicator will lead to the most natural scale to use in specific details in your wardrobe pieces. We begin with the first two indicators.

Scale and the element of line

To help you determine the size of your bone structure and of your facial features, we need to look again at the element of line, this time in terms of line width and line length.

1 The size of your bone structure

Line has width. Relative to other lines around it, a line can be thin, medium or thick in width. Matisse gives us an excellent example of this in his painting, *Woman Seated in an Armchair*. Notice the different widths of lines found in the chair arm or those outlining the chest shown in the background.

Woman Seated in an Armchair, Henri Matisse, National Gallery of Art, Washington; given in loving memory of my husband, Taft Schreiber, by Rita Schreiber (detail).

Like line, your wrists and ankles can be seen as being either thin (or narrow), medium, or thick in width, relative to general human dimensions. The narrower the bone structure, the smaller the scale; the thicker the bone structure, the larger the scale. The following artworks illustrate these differences in scale. Look at the wrists and ankles of these figures.

Small scale wrists and ankles

The Judgment of Paris,
Lucas Cranach, The Elder,
The Metropolitan Museum of Art; Rogers Fund, 1928 (detail).

Medium scale wrists and ankles

Diana, Pierre-Auguste Renoir,
National Gallery of Art, Washington; Chester Dale Collection (detail).

Large scale wrists and ankles

Mars and Venus United by Love,
Paolo Veronese, The Metropolitan Museum of Art; John Stewart Kennedy Fund, 1910 (detail).

Walking Woman, Gaston Lachaise, 1922; Hirshhorn Museum and Sculpture Garden, Smithsonian Institution; Gift of Joseph H. Hirshhorn, 1966 (detail).

Notice in the example below that your wrists can be a different scale from that of your ankles. Here, we see a medium-sized looking body with large scale bone structure at the wrists and small scale bone structure at the ankles.

Reclining Nude, Raoul Dufy, National Gallery of Art, Washington; Chester Dale Collection (detail).

It is possible for a small-sized woman to have medium or large scale bone structure. It is also possible for a large-sized woman to have medium or small scale bone structure, as seen in the bronze *Walking Woman* by Gaston Lachaise. This is why we look at the wrists and ankles, because bone structure is most evident there.

What scale is your bone structure?

My bone structure is:

☒ Small   ☐ Medium   ☐ Large   ☐ Combination

My wrists are ___Small___ scale.

My ankles are ___small___ scale.

Details that relate to bone structure

The scale of bone structure determines the appropriate scale of *construction details in garments and accessories* (purses and shoes). When choosing construction details of clothing for the top of the body, look at the scale of your wrists; for the bottom of the body, look at the scale of your ankles. Relate purse details to the bone structure of your wrists. Relate shoe details to the bone structure of your ankles. Construction details include:

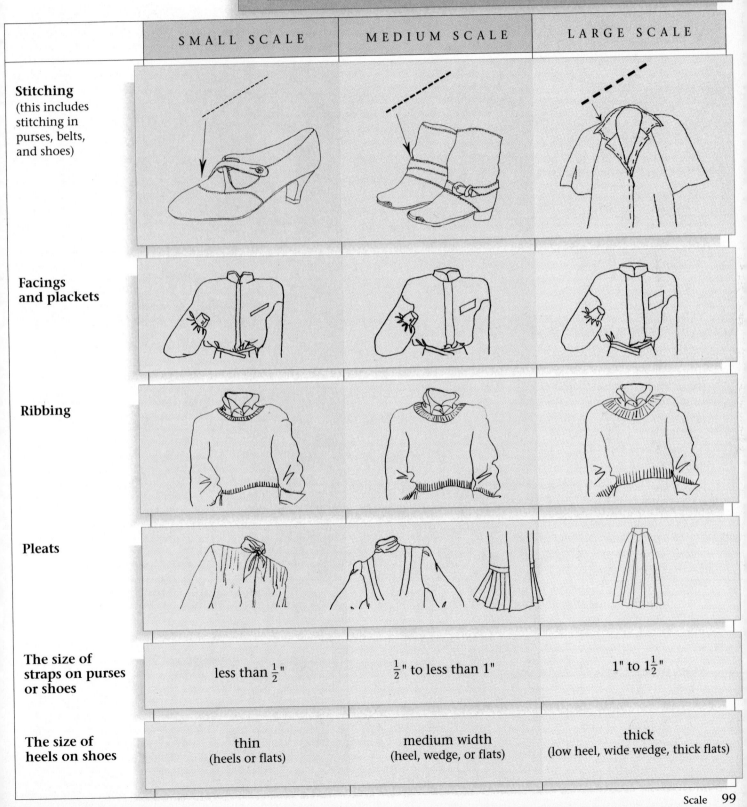

	SMALL SCALE	MEDIUM SCALE	LARGE SCALE
Stitching (this includes stitching in purses, belts, and shoes)			
Facings and plackets			
Ribbing			
Pleats			
The size of straps on purses or shoes	less than $\frac{1}{2}$"	$\frac{1}{2}$" to less than 1"	1" to $1\frac{1}{2}$"
The size of heels on shoes	thin (heels or flats)	medium width (heel, wedge, or flats)	thick (low heel, wide wedge, thick flats)

2 The size of your facial features

*L*ine also has length, being either relatively short, medium, or long. Both length and width of line will help you determine the size of your facial features, which is the second indicator of scale.

The shorter and thinner a line, the smaller its scale. On the contrary, the longer and thicker a line, the larger its scale. Any line that is of moderate width and length is medium scale.

When a line has width and length that cross over, that is, if a line is thin and long or thick and short, it tends towards medium scale.

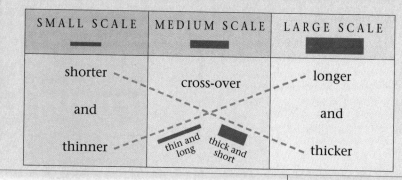

SMALL SCALE	MEDIUM SCALE	LARGE SCALE
shorter and thinner	cross-over — thin and long / thick and short	longer and thicker

The following chart is designed to help you analyze the size of your facial features by determining their length and width of line.

1. Look at yourself in a mirror as you go down the list of features. It might also help if you pretend to draw over each feature with your finger to feel how wide and long it seems to be, especially relative to the size of your face.
2. Then circle the appropriate length or width in the chart.
3. When you have completed the list, count the circled items for each column.

Your features may be all of one scale or be any combination of small, medium, large, or extra-large scale. Each scale value is illustrated with a face from a work of art to help you gauge the relative size of your own facial features. Study these before you begin.

What scale are your facial features?

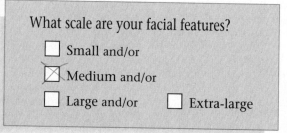

- ☐ Small and/or
- ☒ Medium and/or
- ☐ Large and/or ☐ Extra-large

Looking for line length and width in your facial features

The Nymph of the Spring, Lucas Cranch, The Elder, National Gallery of Art, Washington; Gift of Clarence Y. Palitz (detail).

FEATURE		SMALL SCALE
Eyebrow:	Length	Short
	Width	Thin
Eyes:	Opening	Small
Nose:	Length	Short
	Width: Bridge	(Narrow)
	Tip	Narrow
Mouth:	Length: Upper Lip	Short
	Lower Lip	Short
	Width: Upper Lip	Thin
	Lower Lip	Thin
Total		1

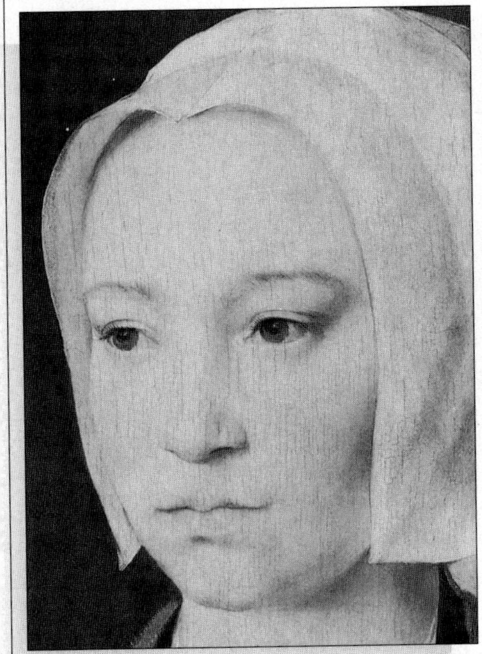

Margaretha Boghe, Wife of Joris Vezeeler, Joos van Cleve,
National Gallery of Art, Washington; Andrew W. Mellon Fund (detail).

Royal Head, Fin de la XVIII Dynastie,
Musée du Louvre, Paris (detail).

Pencil rendering of *Royal Head*, End of ancient Egyptian
XVIIIth dynasty, ornament in colored wood for top of harp, from Tell el
Amarna, by D.J. Simison, artist, San Francisco, CA; as seen in *Great Museums of the
World, Louvre, Paris*, page 26, Newsweek, Inc., and Arnoldo Mondadori Editore,
1967; Pencil rendering in private collection, C.M. Mathis.

MEDIUM SCALE	LARGE SCALE	EXTRA-LARGE SCALE
Medium	Long	Very long
Medium	Thick	Extra thick
Medium	Wide	Very wide
Medium	Long	Very long
Medium	Wide	Very wide
Medium	Wide	Very wide
Medium	Long	Very long
Medium	Long	Very long
Medium	Thick	Very thick
Medium	Thick	Very thick
7	2	0

Faces with a combination of scale in their features

ere are two artworks that illustrate faces with a combination of scale in their features. If you are a combination, you can reflect this combination in your clothing details.

repeats the curvy lines found in her hair, eyebrows and upper lip. Her clothing details are in wonderful harmony with her features.

Tallulah Bockman Bankhead, Augustus John,
The National Portrait Gallery, Smithsonian Institution; Gift of the Hon. and Mrs. John Hay Whitney (detail).

La Mousme, Vincent Van Gogh,
National Gallery of Art, Washington; Chester Dale Collection (detail).

In this portrait of *Tallulah Bockman Bankhead* by Augustus John, we see that her features are mostly medium scale with eyes that are medium-large in scale. Notice that she is wearing medium scale details: medium scale beads in her necklace and medium scale print in her dress. The print also

Van Gogh's *La Mousme* has medium to large scale features—we might even say extra-large eyebrows. Notice the buttons, stripes, and polka dots in her dress print are also medium to large scale. Again, there is harmony between her clothing details and her facial features.

Details that relate to the scale of your facial features

The scale pattern found in your facial features indicates the scale of three important facets of your clothing:
1. Scale of prints and patterns. See the examples on the previous page (*Tallulah Bankhead* and *La Mousme*), or refer back to Chapter 1, page 20 if you wish to review this.
2. Scale of jewelry (rings, earrings, necklaces, bracelets).
3. Scale of style details in the upper part of your garments, which include:

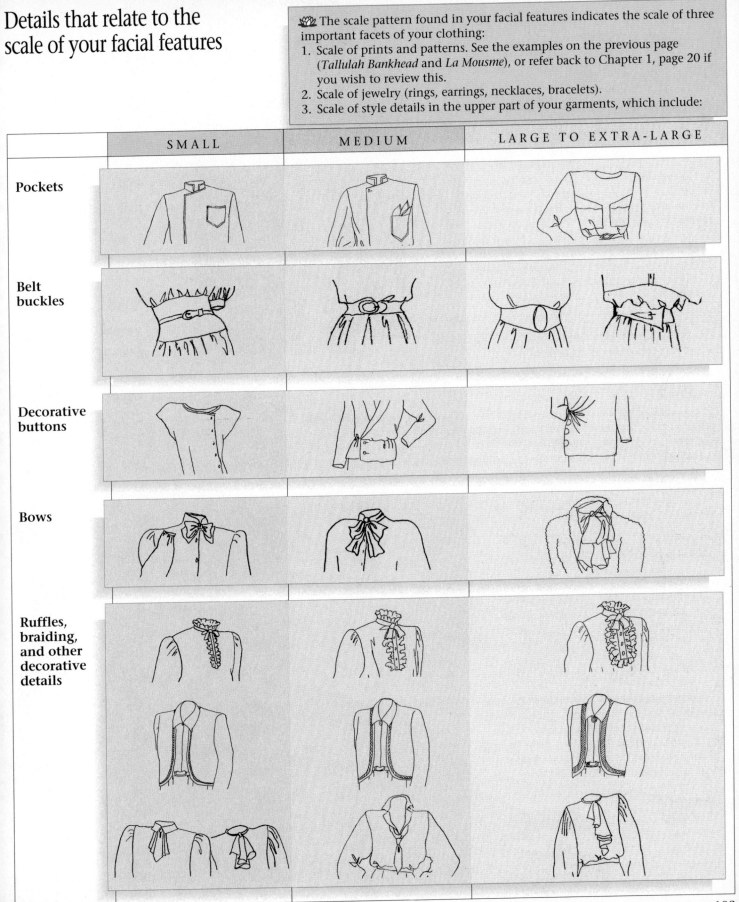

	SMALL	MEDIUM	LARGE TO EXTRA-LARGE
Pockets			
Belt buckles			
Decorative buttons			
Bows			
Ruffles, braiding, and other decorative details			

3 Your body's apparent size

As a general rule, the size of facial features relates to details that are close to the face and in the upper body. Details found in the bottom part of the body relate more to your body's apparent size, which is the third indicator of scale. For example, in the artwork of *Venus* (right), notice that in spite of her body's large apparent size, her small scale jewelry and ornamentation relate to, and are in harmony with, her small scale facial features. The dress shown next to her illustrates how a small scale bow in the bodice, like her jewelry, relates well to her small scale facial features. However, in the lower part of the dress, large pockets are quite appropriate for her large apparent size.

Apparent size indicates the amount of body space you have for your detail and ornamentation.

Mars and Venus United by Love,
Paolo Veronese,
The Metropolitan Museum of Art; John Stewart
Kennedy Fund, 1910 (detail).

You may be as tall as someone else, but your body may be smaller or larger in scale because of the amount of space your body appears to take. Usually, this is because your body width is narrower or wider. For the same reason, you might be short but give an impression, from a distance, of being "bigger" than your actual height suggests. So, regardless of your body's shape or silhouette, you will appear optically small, medium, or large in scale. As a general guide, we think of shape in terms of scale similar to the way we regard line width and length:

The Invisible Object (Hands Holding the Void), Alberto Giacometti, National Gallery of Art, Washington; Alisa Mellon Bruce Fund (detail).

Scale and the element of shape

The narrower and shorter the shape, the smaller its scale.

Conversely, the wider and longer a shape, the larger its scale.

Long and narrow body = medium scale

Short and wide body = medium scale

Any shape that is of moderate width and length is medium scale. Also, when a shape has width and length that crossover, that is, if a silhouette is long and narrow or short and wide, it tends towards medium scale, as illustrated in these artworks that both have the rectangle silhouette.

Reclining Nude, Raoul Dufy,
National Gallery of Art, Washington;
Chester Dale Collection (detail).

When it comes to details and ornamentation, scale is relative to the wearer. What may be large to a small scale body would appear small on a large scale body. These artworks illustrate the point. Both figures have the triangle silhouette, the Cranach nymph being small scale and the Renoir bather, large scale.

Notice the Cranach woman (below) has small scale jewelry around her face to match her small scale facial features, but her bracelet is overall medium scale. This same bracelet on the Renoir beauty (right) would appear small rather than medium because of her large apparent size.

The Nymph of the Spring, Lucas Cranach, The Elder, National Gallery of Art, Washington; Gift of Clarence Y. Palitz (detail).

Bather Arranging Her Hair, Pierre-Auguste Renoir, National Gallery of Art, Washington; Chester Dale Collection (detail)

We liken filling your body's space with detail and ornamentation to the act of furnishing and decorating a room. *The general principle is*: if you have a room that is large and grand, you will fill it with medium to large scale furniture. But if you include small scale decorative items in it, they must appear in large clusters or amounts in order to be in scale with the largeness of the room. Applied to clothing this means if your body's apparent size is large, use medium to large scale detail where appropriate. However, if you have small scale facial features, use small scale detail in large groupings in the upper body. For example, you might wear small scale pearls but in several strands, not just one; or several rows of small ruffles in order to be in scale with your large apparent size.

On the other hand, if your room is small and cozy, fill it with smaller scale items and furniture to be in scale with the room; and if you prefer slightly larger scale, fill the small room with fewer large things—that is, create impact with less. This is to say, if you have a small apparent size, use small scale where appropriate. However, if your facial features are large, use one outstanding detail—for example, a large scale brooch—but nothing else. In this case, less is not only more, it is enough.

Play around with this general principle and see what works for you. In the next section we will be talking about the technique of scaling up or down to give you even greater creativity in this matter. But first, one more detail that relates to apparent size.

Apparent size also determines the overall size of your "everyday" purse. Consider a purse like adding another "room" or space next to your body's apparent size. Together, they must be relatively the same scale: small scale body, small scale purse; medium scale body, medium scale purse; large scale body, large scale purse. Remember, this is just the overall size. The details on the purse, such as stitching, strap width, and/or decorative ornamentation such as a buckle, again, depend on the scale of your bone structure and facial features. For instance, you may have a large purse to match an apparent body size that is large, but the construction and decorative details are medium to small scale to match your medium bone structure at the wrist and your small facial features.

Here now is an array of examples from artworks to demonstrate the interplay of the three indicators of scale and how they manifest themselves in various ways.

*H*ow scale of bone structure, scale of facial features, and apparent size relate to clothing details and ornamentation.

Mrs. William Crowninshield Endicott, John Singer Sargent, National Gallery of Art, Washington; Gift of Louise Thoron Endicott in memory of Mr. and Mrs. William Crowninshield Endicott (detail).

- **Scale of bone structure**: small wrists
  Notice the small scale pleating below her collar.
- **Scale of facial features**: small to medium
  Her brooch and the pattern in the lace shawl is small to medium scale.
- **Apparent body size**: medium

Dancer with Castanets, Pierre-Auguste Renoir, National Gallery, London (detail).

- **Scale of bone structure**: large wrists and ankles
  Notice the hip wrap, as a construction detail, is large scale.
- **Scale of facial features**: small to medium
  Notice her jewelry is small scale.
- **Apparent body size**: large
  Notice the small to medium scale flowers that decorate her dress relate to her facial features, but they are worn in cascading clusters to fill her large apparent size.

- **Scale of bone structure:** large scale wrists
- **Scale of facial features:** large
- **Apparent body size:** large

Mary McLeod Bethune has chosen large scale buttons that are in perfect harmony with her large facial features and apparent body size.

Mary McLeod Bethune, Betsy Graves Reyneau, National Portrait Gallery, Smithsonian Institution; Gift of the Harmon Foundation, (detail).

Madame Rivière, Jean-Auguste-Dominique Ingres, Musée du Louvre; (detail).

Madame Moitessier, Jean-Auguste-Dominique Ingres, National Gallery of Art, Washington; Samuel H. Kress Collection, (detail).

- **Scale of bone structure**: medium scale wrists
  Notice the medium scale facings around the bosom.
- **Scale of facial features**: small to medium
- **Apparent body size**: medium-large

Though her jewelry is small scale, Madame Rivière wears them in clusters to appear medium in scale, which relates to both her facial features and apparent body size. Also her hair, which decorates her otherwise plain outfit, has very prominent medium-size curls.

The border print of her shawl is medium-large scale like her apparent body size; however, notice the detailing of that print is small scale, which relates to her facial features.

- **Scale of bone structure**: large
- **Scale of facial features**: small to medium
- **Apparent body size**: medium to large

As you can see, Madame Moitessier has flowers on either side of her head that are small to medium in scale. They relate to the scale of her facial features as do her bracelets. However, she wears both the flowers and the bracelets in clusters to relate to her large apparent body size. Notice her large brooch does not relate to the scale of her facial features. She has up-scaled this piece, most probably for drama. However, do you see that the brooch has small to medium scale detailing, which *does* relate to her facial features.

This is something to remember:
🪷 If you wear jewelry that is upscaled—that is, overall larger in scale than your facial features—be sure it has detailing that relates to, and helps it harmonize with, the natural scale pattern of your features.

The scaling-up or scaling-down technique

For balancing apparent size 🪷

hen there is a combination of different scale in the three main parts of the body (the head, the top-of-body, and the bottom-of-body), you may scale up or scale down to balance apparent size before you fill in the details and add your ornamentation.

Another example is the triangle silhouette body when the top-of-body is very much smaller in scale than the bottom part of the body as seen here in Dosso Dossi's *Circe*. Again, first create balance between the parts by scaling up the top-of-body, usually done by changing the silhouette and/or by wearing more volume through fabric, as shown in these drawings.

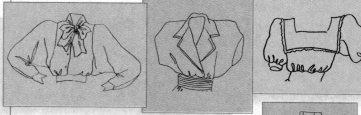

If necessary, you may also scale down the larger bottom-of-body by breaking up the space as shown in this box-pleated skirt. (If you wish, review Chapter 2, page 35.)

Head of a Woman #2, Henri Matisse,
The Santa Barbara Museum of Art, Santa Barbara, CA; Gift of Wright S. Ludington (detail).

When the head is large scale relative to the body, for example, first create balance between the head and body either by scaling the head down with an appropriate hair style, or scaling the body up. If you recall, you can do the latter by changing the natural silhouette so the shoulders appear wider and/or by wearing clothing with more space or volume. (If you wish, review Chapter 2, page 36 on large head/small shoulder relationship.) Of course, if you prefer to highlight the difference as shown in the drawing by Matisse (above), simply use medium scale ornamentation. Notice her brooch is medium in scale and her necklace appears to have both medium and large scale beads, which add drama to the small body, but integrate well with the large head and facial features. The large head, however, is not diminished; it still stands out.

Circe and Her Lovers in a Landscape, Dosso Dossi, The National Gallery, Washington; (detail).

For creating drama ⚜

Perhaps you have noticed that in high-fashion shows the models invariably wear jewelry and ornamentation that are up-scaled, sometimes to the extreme. The purpose of this is to add drama. That drama must be projected from a distance, much like an actor must project his or her voice from the depths of a stage into the hall of the audience.

On certain occasions you might want to project similar drama, and likewise upscale your styling details or ornamentation. The following artwork by Degas gives a simple example. This woman has medium scale facial features. Her ruffles at the neck and sleeves are in scale with her features. But notice the dark trim on her dress. This, too, could have been medium scale, placed perhaps in a two-row pattern to fill in her large apparent size. Instead, this grand oval beauty has upscaled the trim to a large one, used in one row both in the bodice and at the sleeves. This wide dark trim dramatizes her large body. Can you see how one tends to notice her body more immediately than her face?

Gertrude Stein, Pablo Picasso,
The Metropolitan Museum of Art;
Bequest of Gertrude Stein, 1946 (detail).

Girl in Red, Edgar Degas
National Gallery of Art, Washington; Chester Dale Collection (detail).

While some of you may upscale only occasionally, a woman with a strong or dramatic presence will feel very comfortable upscaling most of the time, and will downscale in order to be more approachable. Picasso's portrait of Gertrude Stein is a wonderful example of this. Her presence comes through loud and clear. But notice her ruffle and pin. In terms of scale they do not match or support her drama, even though the pin is in scale with her eyes and the ruffle has the same length as her face. Could you imagine Gertrude Stein wearing even another row or two of ruffles and a much larger brooch and still not be overpowered? They would, in fact, highlight if not magnify her personal presence. Can you also see that she could be perceived as too intimidating if she did upscale in this way?

Indeed, upscaling adds drama. It is also a delicate matter, because if you overdo it, it can fall easily into the comical. Our suggestion is to upscale for drama in one place only, for example, a large belt if you have a waist. And upscale only a notch or two. Make the belt the point of dominance, while keeping other details in the outfit to your scale. Also, the belt could have smaller decorative details that help it harmonize with your natural scheme of scale.

How scale helps you select your jewelry

Because it relates to line, shape and space as we have shown, the concept of scale helps us immensely in refining the way we choose our ornamentation.

It is through our ornamentation that we have a very simple but highly effective way to bring out the beauty of our facial features. First, you identify lines and shapes found in your features. Then, select a feature you wish to highlight and repeat its line or shape in your ornamentation, such as in an earring. Earrings are a good choice because they are so close to the face.

You might repeat the shape of your eye, nose, mouth, or even the shape of your face. It might even be a shape that is suggested with both the eyebrow and eye together, or an interesting line made by the contour of the side of your face. By repeating its shape, you enhance, emphasize and reinforce a feature and make it prominent to the viewer.

The important thing to remember is:

Whenever you repeat a shape of a feature, always keep it in scale with that feature, keeping the length-to-width relationship.

The following examples demonstrate how this technique of repetition works to highlight any facial feature you have. Discover the exciting results of such a simple and inexpensive way to enhance your unique characteristics. Do it and you will add even more of your individuality to your personal style.

The shape of beautiful paisley eyes can be repeated in jewelry or in a paisley print, close to the face.

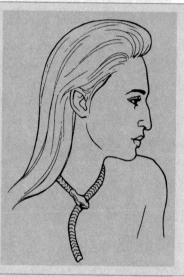

Notice how the curve of the necklace and the shape of her hair style relate to the curve of her forehead; also notice how the shape of the clasp mirrors the shape of her nose.

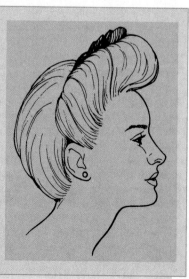

Here hair is treated like an ornamentation that repeats the round line of her forehead. If the curve were flatter, it would not have the same effect.

The large centerpiece of her necklace repeats the shape of her lips, which are full and wide. Though the centerpiece is upscaled for drama, notice the length-to-width relationship is similar to that of her lips.

In these examples, notice that the earring shapes repeat the facial shapes, keeping length and width to scale:

Rippled earrings repeat the ripple in the facial contour and in the same scale; the ripples are neither too narrow nor too wide.

Diamond-shaped earrings repeat the shape and scale of the face, eyes, and eyebrow creating a visual resonance that dramatizes these features. If the diamond shape of the earrings were narrower or wider, the earrings would not be to scale, thus losing that resonance.

The round earrings are in keeping with the scale of her features and repeat the round line found in the nose tip, cheeks and eyes—highlighting all three features.

Notice her earrings are the exact shape of her little bow mouth, and they repeat the angles of her brows and eyes, which are also mirrored in the angle of her neckline.

Madame Amédée (Woman with Cigarette), Amedeo Modigliani, National Gallery of Art, Washington; Chester Dale Collection (detail).

Notice that the shape of her earring repeats the shape of her jawline, facial shape, and the angles of her ear, eyebrows, nose and mouth.

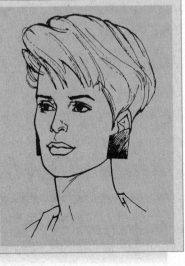

In a manner of speaking, with the element of scale you have completed a picture of your personal style that is quite tangible. You began with simple lines that led to uncomplicated silhouette shapes, moved to more dimension and style options through proportion and body particulars, and finally, discovered the functional and decorative details, prints, and ornamentation to dress-up your silhouette—all of which support your one-of-a-kind physical design. But that picture is still in black and white and relatively flat in its tactile dimensions. And while scale does apply especially to line, shape, and space, we know that advancing colors and textures also suggest bold scale, and receding colors suggest smaller scale, at least in terms of presence. So the time has come to endow your personal style picture with the exciting sensations and beauty that only color and its inseparable partner, texture, can give.

"The sounds of colors are so definite that it would be hard to find anyone who would express bright yellow with bass notes or a dark lake in the treble."
—Wassily Kandinsky

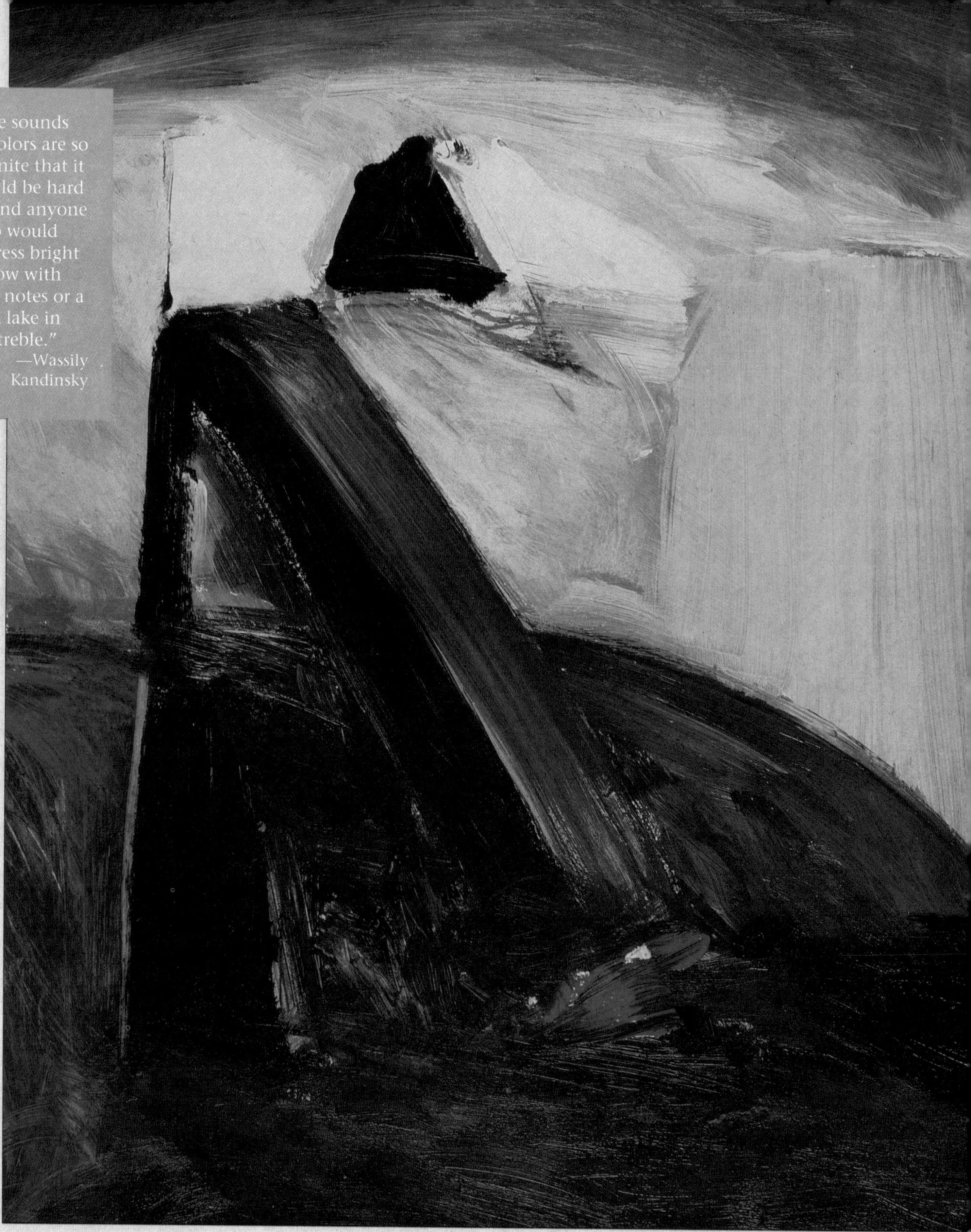

Acrylic on Board, 1988, Albert Smith (detail).

6 Your body's unique color pattern

...and how to choose colors that enhance it.

Color is the most immediate of all the elements of art. It demands attention; stimulates the senses of smell, touch, and even sound; excites emotions; and opens doors to memories.

Color is a natural system organized in harmonious patterns everywhere—in the sky, the landscape, and in our skin, hair, and eyes.

> "I understand how scarlet can differ from crimson because I know that the smell of an orange is not the smell of a grapefruit... In smell and taste there are variations not broad enough to be fundamental; so I call them shades... The force of association drives me to say that white is exalted and pure, green is exuberant, red suggests love, or shame, or strength. Without the color or its equivalent life to me would be dark, barren, a vast blackness."
>
> —Helen Keller (1880–1968), blind and deaf from infancy.

Duck

Iris

Color in the human body is not as brilliant as that found in nature. We have to look more closely to find the color in the human body, and we learn to express it more brilliantly in our clothing. We put color in our art and on ourselves as works of art. We "paint" our faces with make-up and sometimes color our hair, and we create colorful "collages" on our bodies with fabrics, woods, precious stones and other materials through the clothing and jewelry we wear.

Through the countless ways they are displayed, from simple to breathtaking, nature inspires us to be creative with the beauty of all colors. And for centuries humankind has extracted colorants from plants, trees, insects, earth, rocks and minerals to color all manner of human dwellings and articles. As time passed, we developed the technology to replace nature's sources of color with synthetic dyes and pigments, making colors more readily available. It is through the following simple study of modern-day pigments, specifically those found in the artist's paint tubes, that we can show you the best way to develop a sense of your body's natural colors and how to relate them to the myriad of colors available to us today. In this chapter you will learn to choose and work with a palette of colors that are in harmony with your one-of-a-kind body, your unique personality at this point of your life, and even your mood on any given day.

Turkey Mushrooms

❀ A different language of color for creative dressing

When you buy clothing, the colors are already there, pre-chosen and designed into the outfits. Your task is to judge not only the suitability of the silhouette and style, but also to assess the beauty of the colors on you. In this light, we present the language of color in a slightly different way than what you might find in a book written for artists and painters. For example, in this book you will not find the color wheel showing the primary colors, (red, yellow, blue), and how other colors are derived from them by mixing (green, orange, violet). Instead, we will present two different color wheels: The first we call The Pure Pigment Color Wheel; the second, we call The Harmony Color Wheel. Each has a specific purpose in guiding you to create your own individualized palette of colors and to understand its full design potential.

Rhododendron
Bill Terry Photography

The Pure Pigment Color Wheel ❧

As we have said, *pure pigments* are nature's colors captured in synthetic paints. If you walk into any well-stocked art supply store, you would discover artist paint tubes in at least a hundred different colors of pure pigments. We have selected only 25 pure pigments for our Pure Pigment Color Wheel below. Through these 25 pure pigments we will define the *five basic properties* of all color; whether it is other pure pigments, or the colors of your skin, hair, and eyes, or that of fabric or other textures. These five color properties are: *hue, temperature, value, resonance,* and *intensity.*

We will begin by defining the properties of *hue, temperature, value,* and *resonance* first. This is followed by the *Hue Family Color Charts.* These charts show how hues are derived from pure pigments through techniques of lightening or darkening—the results of which are the various *values* and *resonances* of a pigment. Even the most subtle skintone colors can be traced back to one or more specific pure pigments.

Following the charts we will present an exercise to show you how to create a personal palette of colors based on these four properties. You will start by identifying your skin, hair, and eye colors—in terms of hue, color temperature, and value. Then you will be asked to choose a range of colors from the *Hue Family Color Charts* that have the same temperature and value as your natural coloring. In the process, you will discover how the different resonances of color within your color range can help you express your unique personality and its many moods. Finally, you will complete your personal color discovery with the fifth and last property of color, *intensity.* You will learn how color intensity is used to support a strong personal presence, or to create drama in your appearance.

Hue

If you were asked to describe a color, you would probably begin by naming it. Typically, hue has been defined as the name of a color—that is, when you say that something is red or blue-green you are naming its hue. We would like to expand that definition just a little. In our Pure Pigment Color Wheel we show hue families and pure pigment hues.

A *hue family* is the name given a group of like pure pigments. If you recall the rainbow color order you learned as a child, you can name the six basic hue families: 1. the reds, 2. the oranges, 3. the yellows, 4. the greens, 5. the blues, and 6. the violets (children sometimes call these the purples).

Within the hue families, each member has a *pure pigment hue* or name which can give us clues to its origin in nature. For example, under the hue family, the Reds, we have six pure pigments hues which are: Magenta, Carmine, Alizarine Crimson, Cadmium Red, Geranium Lake, and Scarlet Lake. If you were to research these pigment names, you would find their reference in nature—for instance, Alizarine Crimson is defined in the *Oxford Universal Dictionary* as "the red coloring matter of the madder root. The chemical formula is $C14\ H8\ 04$."

Just as members of a human family have different personalities, each pigment in a hue family is different from all the others in some way. Within the reds, for instance: Cadmium is a heavy and thick red, powerful and strong; Carmine, on the other hand, is light and transparent making it charming and pretty; Magenta, like Cadmium, also has strength and presence, but unlike both Cadmium and Carmine, Magenta is a rich and luscious red.

When we alter the pure pigments, we begin to describe colors with what we call their *familiar or fashion hues.* Familiar or fashion

The Pure Pigment Color Wheel ❧

hues are the common names we give to colors that are derived from the pure pigments. For example, the pure pigment Vermillion from the orange hue family can be so lightened that it appears a "peach" color. Most familiar colors will keep some of the personality of the pure pigment or pigments from which it came.

From a parent pure pigment come "offspring" hues or derivatives: A very light value of Vermillion is the *familiar hue*, "peach."

A dark value of Vermillion is the *familiar hue*, "rust."

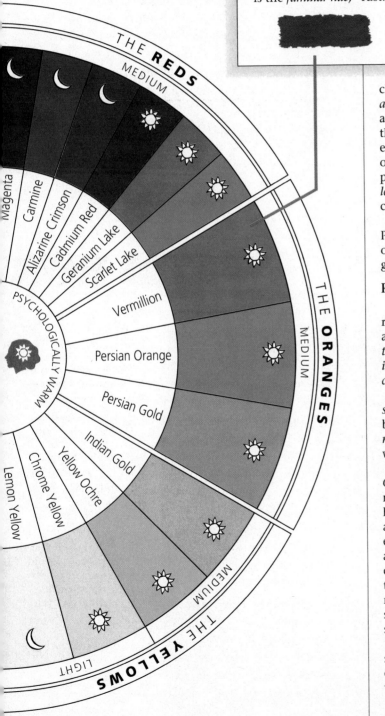

Color Temperature

Artists frequently categorize colors as *warm or cool*. On our Pure Pigment Color Wheel, we show that we have two ways of talking about color temperature which is defined as the warmth or coolness of a hue:
1. there is *psychological temperature* which is more commonly known, and 2. there is *relative temperature*, which is more subtle but is just as important to know for developing an individualized palette of colors for your wardrobe.

Psychological temperature

Our experience with the golden rays of a sunrise or the warmth of sunlight at noon, the red flames of a blazing fire or the yellow glow of its embers, psychologically suggest that *the reds, the oranges, and the yellows are warm hues*. These colors are also commonly regarded as aggressive, unabashedly forward or at least highly visible. On the other hand, our experience of shade in a deep green forest, the soothing blue of a cloudless sky, the cold splash of an ocean wave, the violet shadows of distant mountain tops all psychologically suggest that *the greens, the blues, and the violets are cool hues*. These colors are also often thought of as calming, distant and quiet.

As you can see psychological temperature divides the Pure Pigment Color Wheel in half with the so-called warm reds, oranges, and yellows to the right side, and the so-called cool greens, blues, and violets to the left.

Relative temperature

When we compare the warmth and coolness of a hue relative to other hues within the same family, we are talking about relative temperature. *Notice that we have shown the relative temperature of each pigment either with a sun symbol indicating it is warmer than the other family members, or a moon indicating that it is cooler.*

Remember, relative temperature concerns only members of the same hue family, so the sun and moon symbols appear on both sides of the color wheel. *Yet to see relative temperature, you must be aware of psychological temperature.* To understand what we mean, first look at the Greens and the Violets.

Although placed on the cool side of the color wheel, the *Greens* can seem warmer or cooler because green is commonly seen as a mixture of yellow (a psychologically warm hue), and blue (a psychologically cool hue). So a green that appears more yellow when compared to other greens, for example Sap Green, is relatively warmer; and one that appears bluer, for example Transparent Viridian, is relatively cooler. Likewise, when we think of the *Violets*, we often think of them as composed of a psychologically warm hue, red, and a cool hue, blue. So a violet that leans toward red, such as Thio Violet, is relatively warm; and toward blue, such as Parma, is relatively cool.

Now look at the rest of the hue families: In the *Reds* we see that of the six pure pigments. Three of them lean toward orange and so are relatively warmer than the other three, which lean toward cool violet.

Notice that all the *Oranges* are warm, because we often think of orange as composed of red and yellow, both psychologically warm hues. Oranges are in the depths of warmth.

Like the Oranges, the *Blues* are in the depths of their color territory, which might lead you to believe that all blues are cool. On the contrary, there are blues that can be seen as relatively warm; one of these is Manganese Blue. Manganese is the warmest of the blues, because it leans towards green. Green is quite versatile in its influence on the relative temperature of a hue. On our color wheel, did you notice that of the five greens, three of them are considered relatively warm? Because of the yellow influence brought in through green, Manganese is considered a relatively warm blue. On the other hand, when the already warm *Yellows* lean toward green—for example the Lemon Yellow—they appear cool because of the blue influence brought in through green!

Value

When you describe an orange as dark or a blue as light, then you are talking about the *value* of a color. Value is the lightness or darkness of a hue relative to other hues. When colors are photographed with black-and-white film, each color shows up as a shade of gray—some lighter, some darker; a few look almost black and others look almost white. As shown below with Renoir's painting of *Madame Hagen*, the black-and-white photograph eliminates the hues and allows you to see only the relative darkness or lightness of each color. This relative darkness or lightness is called value.

Like temperature, we should look at relative value in two ways:

First, compare value levels amongst pure pigments only. On our Pure Pigment Color Wheel, notice we have designated a value—either light, medium, or dark—to each pigment. That is, each pigment is light or dark relative to the other pure pigments on the color wheel. Some hue families have pigments in all values, others have no light value and/or dark value pigments.

Second, compare value levels between a pure pigment and its derivatives. Through certain lightening and darkening techniques, from a "parent" pure pigment come "offspring" hues. These techniques require the use of the neutral pigments. These value-changing neutral pigments are shown below grouped by color temperature:

PURE PIGMENT NEUTRALS		
Color Temperature	☾ Cool	☀ Warm
White lightens a pigment.		
Black darkens a pigment.	▬	
Brown can either darken or lighten, depending on the pigment with which it is mixed.	▬	▬

More will be said about these neutrals in the next section on the resonance of color. For now, go back to the Pure Pigment Color Wheel and look again at the examples of value pulled from Vermillion (a medium value pigment). When we add a lot of white to it, Vermillion becomes a very light value color called "peach". If we add black to it instead, Vermillion changes to another familiar hue, "rust", which is a dark value color.

Madame Hagen, Pierre-Auguste Renoir, National Gallery of Art, Washington; Gift of Angelika Wertheim Frink (detail).

Resonance of color

In the following Hue Family Color Charts (pages 120–125), we expand the 25 pure pigments to show how other hues are derived from them. The overall organization of these charts is simple:

1. First, notice that the pigments are grouped in their respective *hue families* (the Reds, the Oranges, etc.), with *psychological temperature* noted at the top right hand corner of each hue family chart.
2. Then, notice within each family, the pigments are grouped again according to *relative temperature* when a family has both warm and cool. These are indicated with the moon or sun symbols in the far left column of each chart.
3. Next, notice that each *pure pigment* within a family is placed in the chart according to relative value (either light, medium, or dark) along a gray scale. This gray scale appears along the top of each hue family chart. The gray scale, of course, allows you to see the relative lightness or darkness of the pigment without the color.
4. Finally, notice that around each pure pigment are *eight derivative hues arranged according to value along the gray scale.* Five of these are the basic resonances of color: *Washed, Tinted, Shaded, Toasted, Muted.*

The other three derivative hues are those that were first shaded, toasted, or muted and then lightened—that is, washed or tinted. The result are more complex derivative hues.

PURE PIGMENT	BASIC RESONANCES	COMPLEX RESONANCES
	💧 water = washed	
	⬜ white = tinted	
⚫ +	⬛ black = shaded	+ 💧 ⬜
	🟫 brown = toasted	water or white
	▦ complement = muted	

Washed, Tinted, Shaded, Toasted, Muted. As these five words suggest, resonance is the visual impression of a hue as it moves away from the pure pigment. No matter what value a hue has, its resonance is a result of what was used to lighten or darken the original pigment. The diagram below summarizes how the eight different resonances are derived and how they are arranged around the pure pigment in the Hue Family Charts. We use the pure pigment Thio Violet for our example.

Though it was not practical to do so on the Hue Family Color Charts, our diagram shows that each of these hues can be run across the gray scale to give you a full range of values for each resonance.

Psychological Temperature: **Cool**

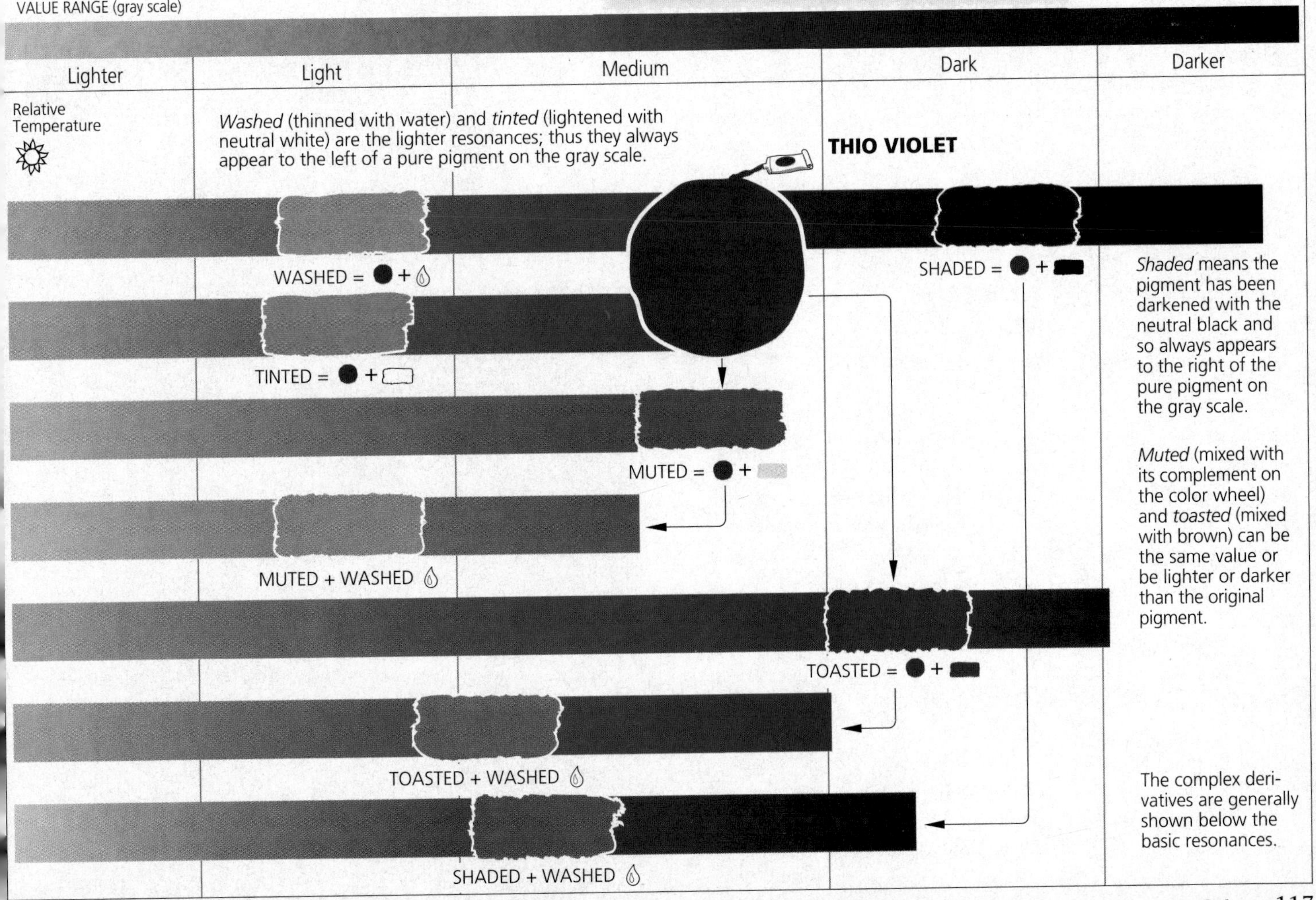

VALUE RANGE (gray scale)

Lighter	Light	Medium	Dark	Darker

Relative Temperature ☀

Washed (thinned with water) and *tinted* (lightened with neutral white) are the lighter resonances; thus they always appear to the left of a pure pigment on the gray scale.

THIO VIOLET

SHADED = ⚫ + ⬛

WASHED = ⚫ + 💧

TINTED = ⚫ + ⬜

MUTED = ⚫ + ▦

MUTED + WASHED 💧

TOASTED = ⚫ + ▬

TOASTED + WASHED 💧

SHADED + WASHED 💧

Shaded means the pigment has been darkened with the neutral black and so always appears to the right of the pure pigment on the gray scale.

Muted (mixed with its complement on the color wheel) and *toasted* (mixed with brown) can be the same value or be lighter or darker than the original pigment.

The complex derivatives are generally shown below the basic resonances.

How the five resonances appear to the eye—in words and in artworks

*J*ust as each pure pigment has its own special "personality" or quality, each resonance has a distinctive quality that you can learn to see and use when creating certain effects in your clothing. Washed, Tinted, Shaded, Muted, Toasted—here now are the five basic color resonances with descriptions on how they are derived from the pure pigment and how they appear to the eye—both in words and in artworks. Study them to understand how the resonance of a color can reflect your personality and/or enhance your various moods. (For a closer look at pure pigments and how they can be used to enhance innate color intensity and/or innate personal intensity, turn to page 150.)

Mrs. Joseph Chamberlain,
John Singer Sargent,
National Gallery of Art, Washington;
Gift of the sitter, Mary Endicott
Chamberlain Carnegie (detail).

TWO WAYS TO LIGHTEN A PIGMENT:

Resonance—how we get it	How it appears to the eye

Washed

Pure pigment + Thin w/ water.

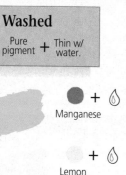

Manganese

Lemon Yellow

It appears transparent and lightweight. The original pure pigment is still readily apparent. Thus, while water dilutes a pigment it does not change its original color temperature.

Personality/Mood
Washed colors are clear, crisp and/or pretty.

Tinted

Pure pigment + White (warm or cool)

Geranium Lake

Yellow Ochre

Chrome Green

Verde Green

It appears opaque and milky. The color temperature of tints depends on which white is used in the mix—a warm or a cool white. A warm pigment remains warm when mixed with a warm white, but can be made cooler if mixed with a cool white.

Personality/Mood
Tinted colors are lighthearted, innocent and/or sweet.

The Lovers,
Pablo Picasso,
National Gallery of Art,
Washington; Chester
Dale Collection (detail).

TO DARKEN A PIGMENT:

Resonance—how we get it **How it appears to the eye**

Shaded

Pure pigment **+** Black

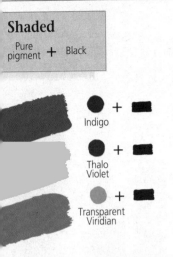

Indigo **+** ▬

Thalo Violet **+** ▬

Transparent Viridian **+** ▬

It appears shadowed, deepened, weighty. Black is a cool neutral and will make all warm pigments appear cooler, and cool pigments cooler still. In Glackens' *Family Group*, shaded colors appear side-by-side with intense pure pigment colors.

Personality/Mood

Shaded colors are serious, profound, and/or mysterious.

Family Group, William Glackens, National Gallery of Art, Washington; Gift of Mr. and Mrs. Ira Glackens (detail).

TWO WAYS TO LIGHTEN OR DARKEN A PIGMENT:

Toasted

Pure pigment **+** Warm or cool brown

Chrome Green **+** ▬

Verde Green **+** ▬

Indian Gold **+** ▬

The relative color temperature of toasted colors depends on whether a cool or warm brown is used. But, toasting will always warm up any color. Toasting a cool color, even with a cool brown, will warm it.

Personality/Mood

Toasted colors are warm, mellow, and/or luscious.

The Magdalene, Bernardino Luini, National Gallery of Art, Washington; Samuel H. Kress Collection (detail).

Muted

Pure pigment **+** Complement*

Thio Violet **+** Lemon Yellow

Thalo Violet **+** Yellow Ochre

Ultramarine **+** Persian Orange

It appears misty, veiled, mysterious or complex. When complements are side by side, they intensify each other. When they are mixed with each other, they mute or de-intensify each other.

Personality/Mood

Muted colors are soft, gentle, and/or subtle.

Duchess de Fitz-James, Henri Fantin-Latour, National Gallery of Art, Washington; Chester Dale Collection (detail).

*Mix with its complement—any pure pigment from the hue family opposite it on the Pure Pigment Color Wheel (see page 114). For example, the reds and the greens are complementary colors.

The Reds

Psychological
Temperature: **Warm**

VALUE RANGE (gray scale)

Lighter _____ Darker

Lighter | Light | Medium | Dark | Darker

Relative
Temperature

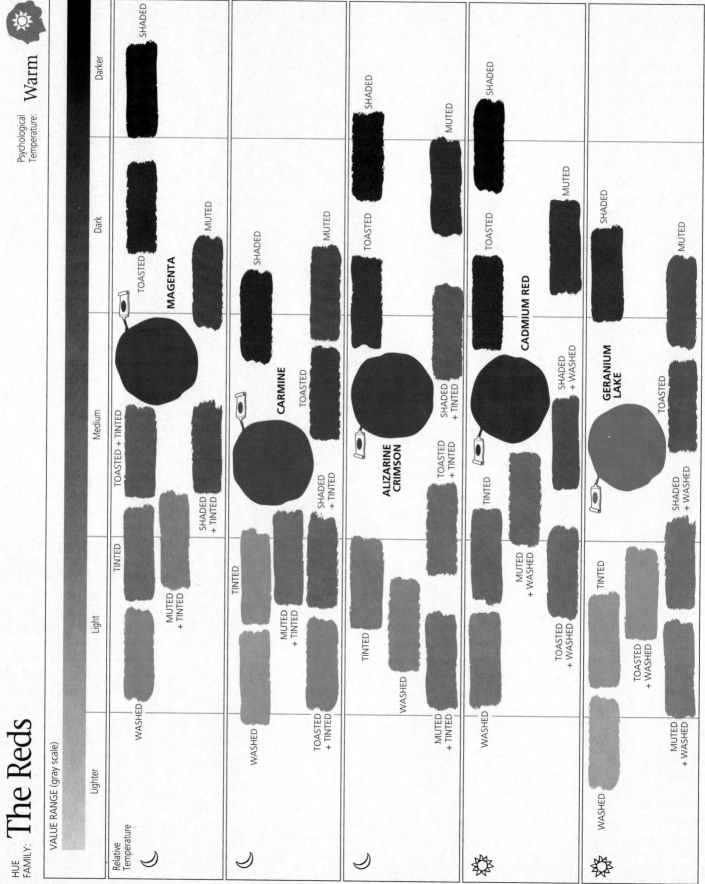

MAGENTA

SHADED

TOASTED

MUTED

TOASTED + TINTED

TINTED

SHADED
+ TINTED

MUTED
+ TINTED

WASHED

CARMINE

SHADED

MUTED

TOASTED

TINTED

SHADED
+ TINTED

MUTED
+ TINTED

TOASTED
+ TINTED

WASHED

**ALIZARINE
CRIMSON**

SHADED

TOASTED

MUTED

SHADED
+ TINTED

TOASTED
+ TINTED

TINTED

MUTED
+ TINTED

WASHED

CADMIUM RED

SHADED

TOASTED

MUTED

SHADED
+ WASHED

TINTED

MUTED
+ WASHED

TOASTED
+ WASHED

WASHED

**GERANIUM
LAKE**

SHADED

MUTED

TOASTED

SHADED
+ WASHED

TINTED

TOASTED
+ WASHED

MUTED
+ WASHED

WASHED

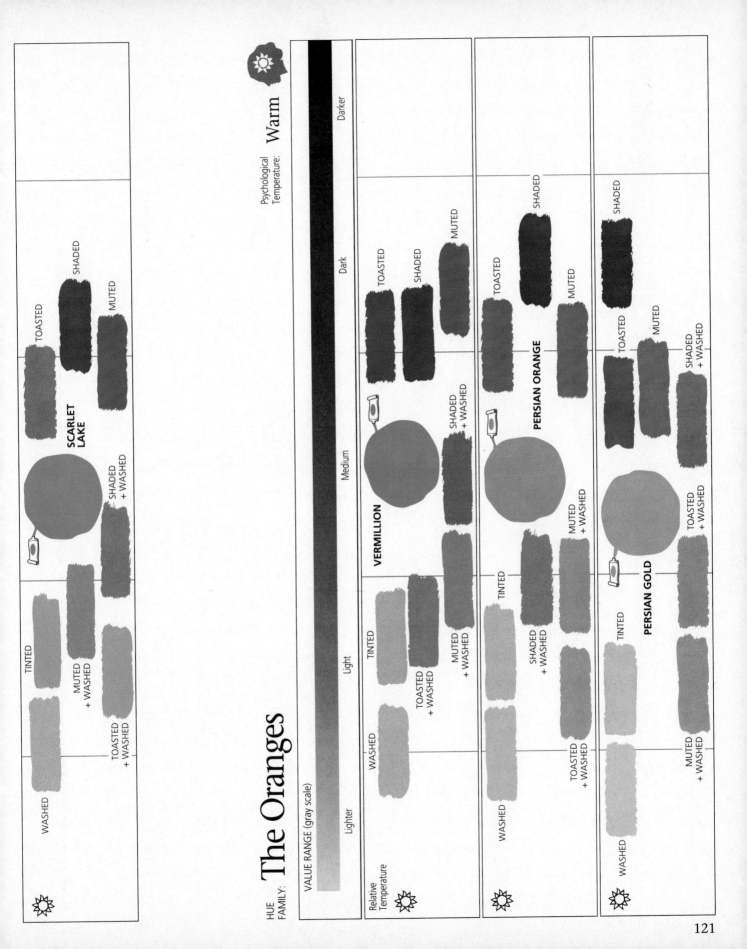

The Oranges

HUE FAMILY:

Psychological Temperature: **Warm**

VALUE RANGE (gray scale)

Lighter — Light — Medium — Dark — Darker

Relative Temperature

SCARLET LAKE

WASHED · TINTED · MUTED + WASHED · TOASTED + WASHED · SHADED + WASHED · TOASTED · SHADED · MUTED

VERMILLION

WASHED · TINTED · TOASTED + WASHED · MUTED + WASHED · SHADED + WASHED · TOASTED · SHADED · MUTED

PERSIAN ORANGE

WASHED · TINTED · SHADED + WASHED · MUTED + WASHED · TOASTED · SHADED · MUTED

PERSIAN GOLD

WASHED · TINTED · MUTED + WASHED · TOASTED + WASHED · SHADED + WASHED · TOASTED · MUTED · SHADED

121

Psychological
Temperature: **Warm**

VALUE RANGE (gray scale)

Lighter — Light — Medium — Dark — Darker

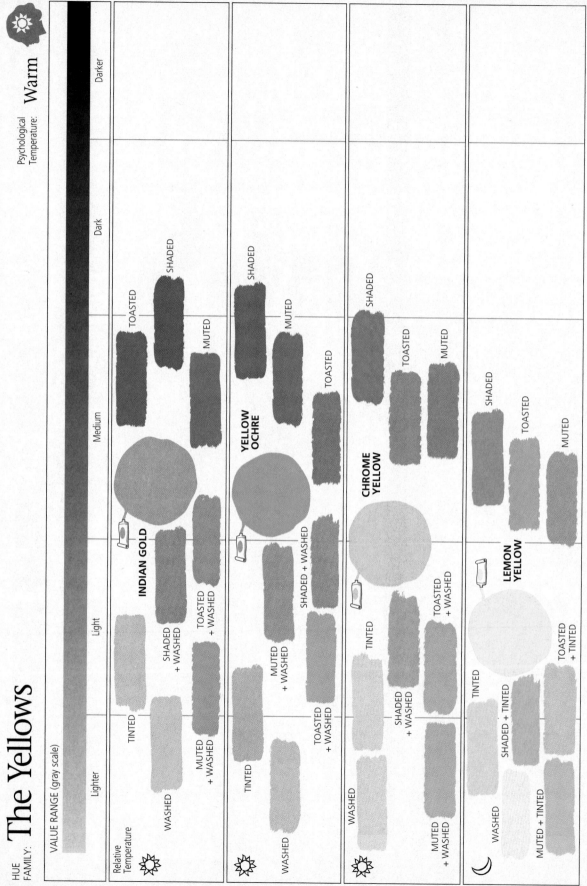

Relative
Temperature

INDIAN GOLD
TOASTED
SHADED
MUTED
TINTED
SHADED + WASHED
WASHED
MUTED + WASHED
TOASTED + WASHED

YELLOW OCHRE
SHADED
MUTED
TOASTED
MUTED + WASHED
TINTED
TOASTED + WASHED
WASHED
SHADED + WASHED

CHROME YELLOW
SHADED
TOASTED
MUTED
TINTED
SHADED + WASHED
TOASTED + WASHED
WASHED
MUTED + WASHED

LEMON YELLOW
SHADED
TOASTED
MUTED
TINTED
SHADED + TINTED
TOASTED + TINTED
WASHED
MUTED + TINTED

The Violets

Psychological
Temperature: Cool

HUE
FAMILY:

VALUE RANGE (gray scale)

Lighter	Light	Medium	Dark	Darker

Relative
Temperature

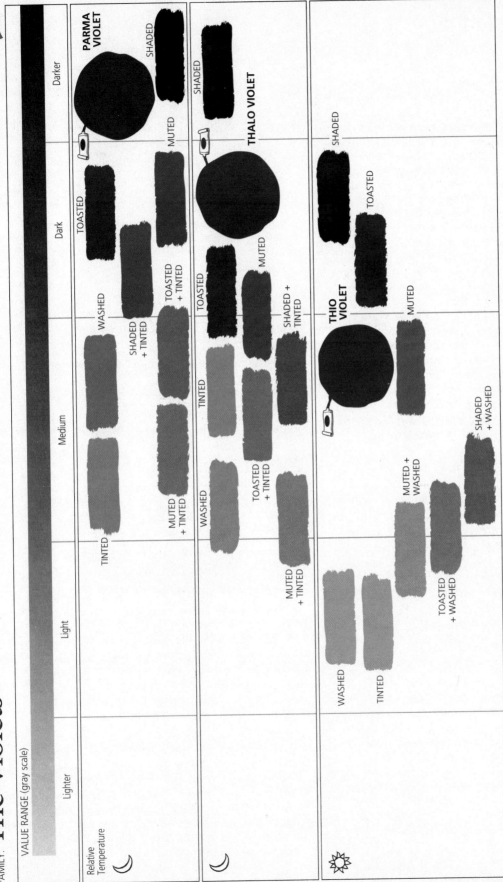

PARMA VIOLET

SHADED

MUTED

TOASTED

WASHED

SHADED + TINTED

TOASTED + TINTED

MUTED + TINTED

TINTED

THALO VIOLET

SHADED

MUTED

TOASTED

TINTED

SHADED + TINTED

TOASTED + TINTED

WASHED

MUTED + TINTED

THIO VIOLET

SHADED

TOASTED

MUTED

MUTED + WASHED

SHADED + WASHED

TOASTED + WASHED

WASHED

TINTED

125

Creating your personal palette of colors

In this section, we will walk you through an "exercise" that will show you how to create your own personal palette of colors, based on hue, color temperature, and value range. We emphasize the word "exercise" because we don't expect you to create your definitive palette here. Though we've tried our best, limitations inherent in the printing process prevent us from always printing true color. So, while we believe you will not find in any other publication a better method for building an individualized palette, ours is not a substitute for a professional personal color analysis. It is only the next best thing. In this light, let's approach the following exercise as a way to put the information you have just learned about color to practical use by selecting colors that enhance your beauty. Then, should you ever "get your colors done," your eyes will already be attuned to your body's special language of color.

There are some hues that are naturally easier for you to wear than others and you probably already "know" instinctively what some of these are. If you have green eyes, for example, you probably gravitate toward certain greens, or if you have black hair, you naturally wear that neutral very well. To build a personal palette, we will show you how you can select colors from all the hue families if you wish. But like anything that is built well, you need to establish a strong foundation first.

The foundation of any personal palette is composed of the natural colors found in the skin, hair, and eyes. Why do we look to these colors first? Like all hues, the colors in your body have the properties of hue, color temperature, and value. Once you determine these properties in your inherent coloration, then by the principal of repetition you can go back to the Hue Family Color Charts and choose colors that match your color temperature and color value schemes. These colors will include the different resonances to enhance your various moods. It's as simple as that.

On the following pages are Skin/Hair/Eye Color Charts. In these charts, we've made it easy to determine the temperature and value of your natural pigmentation. Notice above each sample are three or more of the following special symbols which indicate its temperature, value and whether the sample is a skin, hair, and/or eye color. The "feature" symbols will help you determine which samples to look at as you go through the following analysis of your colors. The hand indicates that a sample is a skin color. The hair curl designates a hair color. If it also has the eye symbol, it is also an eye color.

Color Temperature	☀ warm	☽ cool	☾ warm & cool
Value	L light	M medium	D dark
Feature	🖐 skin	〰 hair	👁 eye

The samples are placed along the outside edge of the pages so that as you look in a mirror you can slowly turn the book around and easily see each color relative to your own skin, hair, or eye colors.

In this process of discovering your colors, you will find the answers to the following questions:

- What are your natural hues?
- What are your natural color temperature and color value schemes?
- What colors complete your palette?
- What is your level of contrast?

What are your natural hues?

Let's begin your personal color discovery.

If you are inside as you go through the following color self-analysis, be near a window so you will be in natural light. However, do not stand in direct sunlight.

1 🖐 Scope out your skin

(If you tan, you may want to do this part of the exercise twice—once without your tan, and again with it.)

Skintones can be very subtle to the untrained eye, but if you remember that there are only two types of skintones to look for, and that they are easiest to see in certain areas of the body, then the process of skintone analysis is not so difficult. (Also, you might want a friend, whose eye for color is more acute than your own, to help you.)

Hemoglobin

The first type of skintone to look for is called your hemoglobin color. Your hemoglobin is a value of red (pink or rose), a value of orange (peach), and/or a value of violet (light violet or mauve). Your hemoglobin color(s) can usually be found in the palm of your hand and/or in your ear. If your palm and ear are a value of brown or black, then look at your gums which will be a value of red (pink, rose, or burgundy), of orange (peach or coral), or of violet (mauve or plum).

Hair
Eyes: iris
Eyes: whites

Skin: Melanin
Skin: Hemoglobin

Adrienne (Woman with Bangs), Amedeo Modigliani, National Gallery of Art, Washington; Chester Dale Collection (detail).

Melanin color

The second type of skintone to look for is called your melanin color. Your melanin color(s) is a form of the neutrals black (ebony, blue black), or brown (from a dark black-brown to warm yellow-brown, or light beige, or a cool violet rose-brown), gray (taupe), and/or white (from ivory and milky white to brownish, grayish or cooler whites). It can also be a derivative of green (olive), or yellow (pale yellow, or golden tones). Your melanin color can usually be found at the bottom of your palm and inside your wrist, your neck, and/or your forehead.

Turn now to the Skin/Hair/Eye Color Charts. Find all the places where skin colors appear. Mark the samples that blend best with your hemoglobin and melanin colors. You will cut

and paste the samples you've marked later. But first let's continue your analysis.

2 ❧ Next, hone in on your hair

You might have one general color, or you might have several colors if you are graying or if your hair is sun-streaked. Look at your hairline at the back of your neck or at the roots of your hair to find the natural color that has not been lightened by the sun, by chlorine, or permanent wave solution. If you have two obvious natural hair colors, identify both of these colors on the charts. As before, mark your samples, and we will explain how you will cut and paste these later.

If you dye your hair—first ask if your hair color relates to your skin color. For example, if you have yellow tones in your skin and you dye your hair blonde, be sure the "yellow" in the blonde relates to the pigment of "yellow" in your skin. If you have golden-yellow skin, your hair needs to be golden-blonde; if you have golden-peach skin, then your blonde could be a strawberry blonde that has some orange in it.

If your helped-along hair color and your skin color are not in harmony, you may choose to overlook this part of your color decisions and wait for some roots to grow out in order to discover your natural color.

Whether you choose to dye your hair, or choose to leave it your natural color is not an issue. Keeping the dyed hair in harmony with your skin and eye colors is of the utmost importance.

3 👁 Finally, look into your eyes

Looking into a mirror, look directly into your eye. Be sure to face the light. You will look for the basic color or colors of your iris.

First, choose an overall color of the iris—blue, gray, green, brown, black, orange (rust), or yellow (golden). Next turn to the Skin/Hair/Eye Color Charts. Find all the places your "overall" color appears. Mark the sample that blends the most with the main color of your eye.

Next, look for subsidiary colors, for your eyes may have more than one color. For example, your iris might have a different colored ring around it. If your hair is naturally gray, you might find that you have a gray ring around your iris. Or you might have light flecks of color within the main field. For example, many brown eyes have gold, yellow, or green flecks in them. Only choose brown or black as your eye color if you do not have any lighter highlights that show. You may notice some rust colored spots in your eyes. That color is often indicative of impurities in your system. Only choose a rusty color for your eye color if you also have a similar rusty tone in your skin and/or your hair. Mark off each color you find to cut and paste later as directed.

What about the whites of the eyes surrounding the iris? If the whites of your eyes really show, then you can wear that color of white quite nicely. Find and mark your white.

What are your natural color temperature and color value schemes?

Once you have identified your skintones, hair color(s), and eye color(s), you may cut the samples out. Then cut each sample again along the dotted line so it is divided into two pieces. Paste the larger piece of each sample in the appropriate boxes below, and paste the smaller piece according to its hue family on the Harmony Color Wheel (see page 146), or on The Four Neutral Families Chart next to it.

The hue family in which a sample belongs is written just under the symbols on each sample. We will talk about harmony shortly. For now, note that each color you have chosen has a temperature symbol (either a sun, or a moon, or a combination sun/moon symbol), and it has a capital letter (L, or M, or D) indicating its value level. Finally, check-off the appropriate spaces below according to these symbols and you will have completed your Skin/Hair/Eye color analysis.

Skintones

Color Temperature: ☐ ☀ Warm ☐ ☾ Cool ☐ ☾☀ Both Warm & Cool

Color Value: ☐ L Light, and/or ☐ M Medium and/or ☐ D Dark

Hemoglobin hues

Melanin hues

Hair hues

Color Temperature: ☐ ☀ Warm ☐ ☾ Cool ☐ ☾☀ Both Warm & Cool

Color Value: ☐ L Light, and/or ☐ M Medium and/or ☐ D Dark

Eye hues

Color Temperature: ☐ ☀ Warm ☐ ☾ Cool ☐ ☾☀ Both Warm & Cool

Color Value: ☐ L Light, and/or ☐ M Medium and/or ☐ D Dark

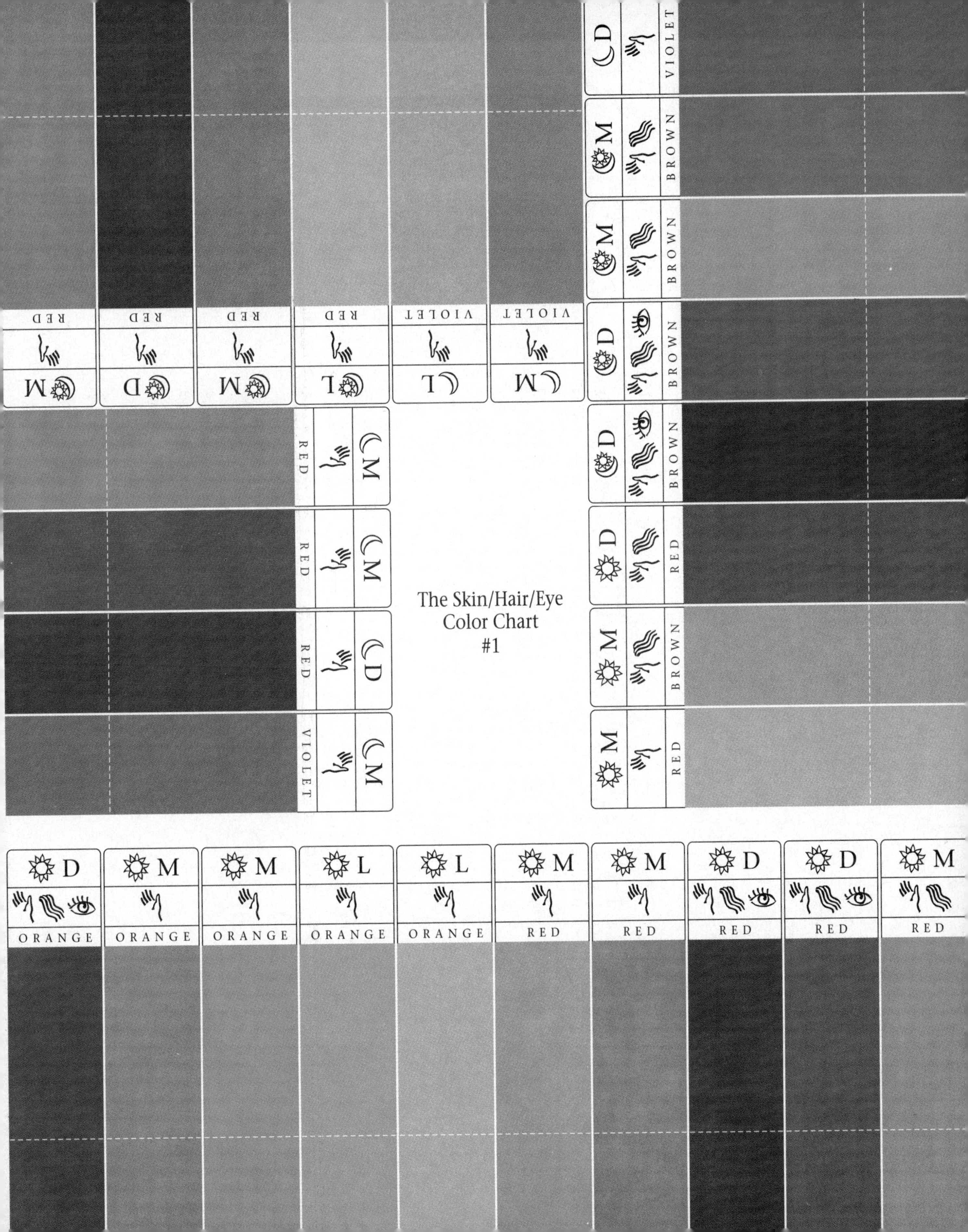

The Skin/Hair/Eye
Color Chart
#1

VIOLET

BROWN

BROWN

BROWN

BROWN

RED

BROWN

RED

RED

RED

RED

RED

VIOLET

RED

RED

RED

RED

VIOLET

VIOLET

D	M	M	L	L	M	M	D	D	M
ORANGE	ORANGE	ORANGE	ORANGE	ORANGE	RED	RED	RED	RED	RED

The Skin/Hair/Eye Color Chart #2

ORANGE M

ORANGE M

ORANGE L

ORANGE L

ORANGE M

ORANGE M

BROWN D

BROWN D

BROWN M

BROWN L

BROWN M

BROWN D

BROWN D

BROWN D

D	D	M	M	M	D	D	D	M	M
GREEN	GREEN	GREEN	GREEN	GREEN	GREEN	BROWN	GREEN	GREEN	GRAY

The Skin/Hair/Eye Color Chart
#3

GREEN · YELLOW · YELLOW · YELLOW · YELLOW · BROWN · YELLOW · YELLOW · YELLOW · YELLOW

BROWN · BROWN · BROWN · ORANGE · ORANGE · BROWN

BROWN
BROWN
BROWN
BROWN
BROWN
BROWN
BROWN
ORANGE

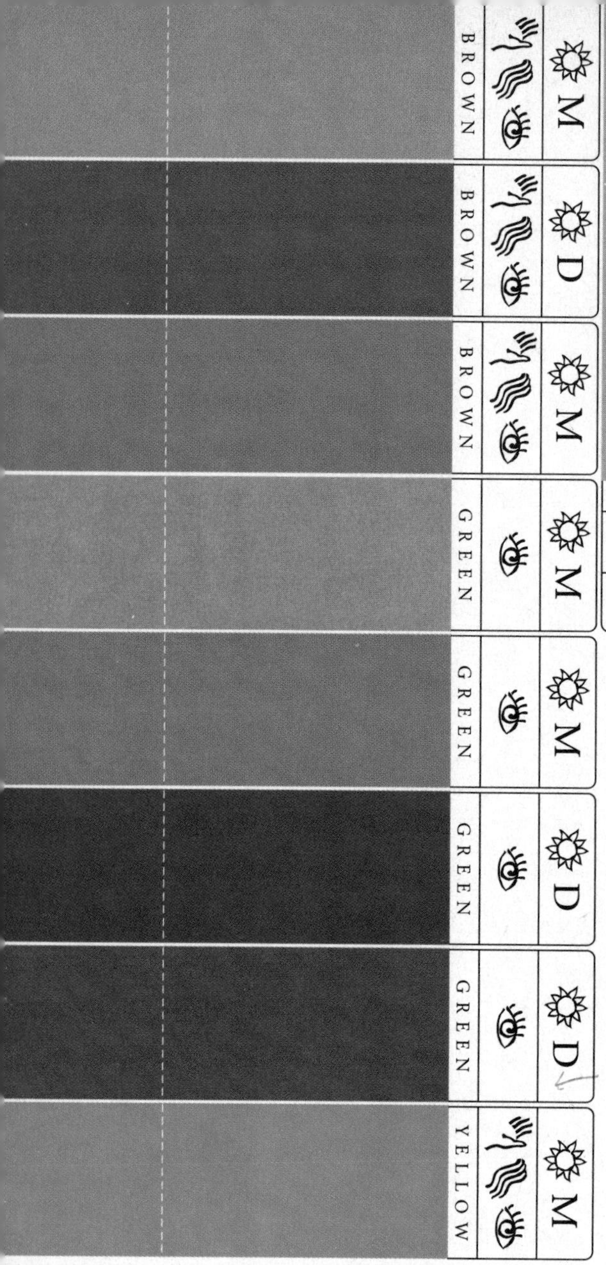

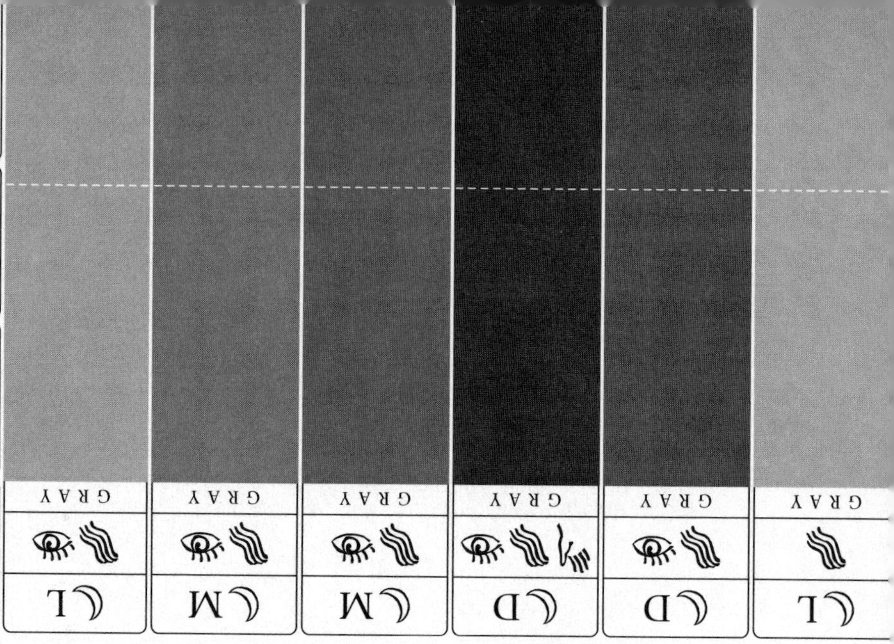

The Skin/Hair/Eye Color Chart
#4

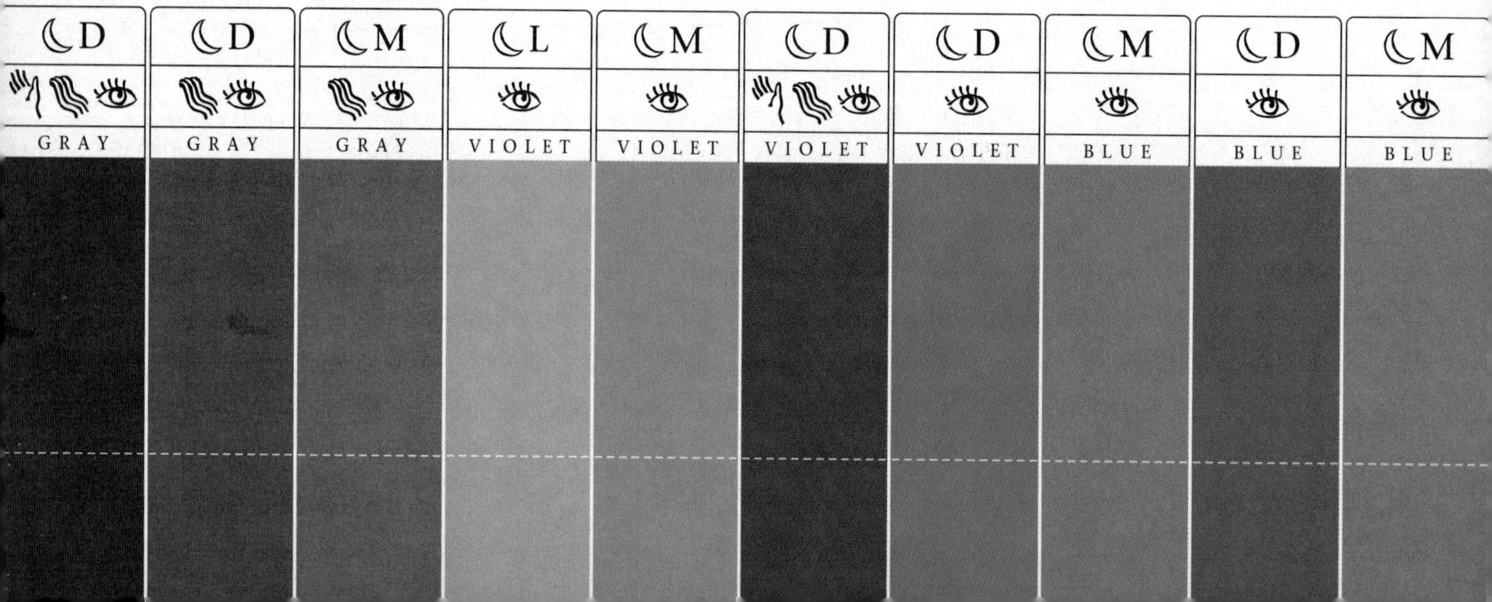

The Skin/Hair/Eye Color Chart
#5

M GREEN
L GREEN
L GRAY
M GREEN
M GREEN
D BROWN

L GREEN
D GREEN
M GREEN
M GREEN
M GREEN
L BLUE
L GRAY
M GRAY

M BLUE
L BLUE
M BLUE
M BLUE
M GREEN
D GREEN
M GREEN
M GREEN
M BLUE
D GRAY

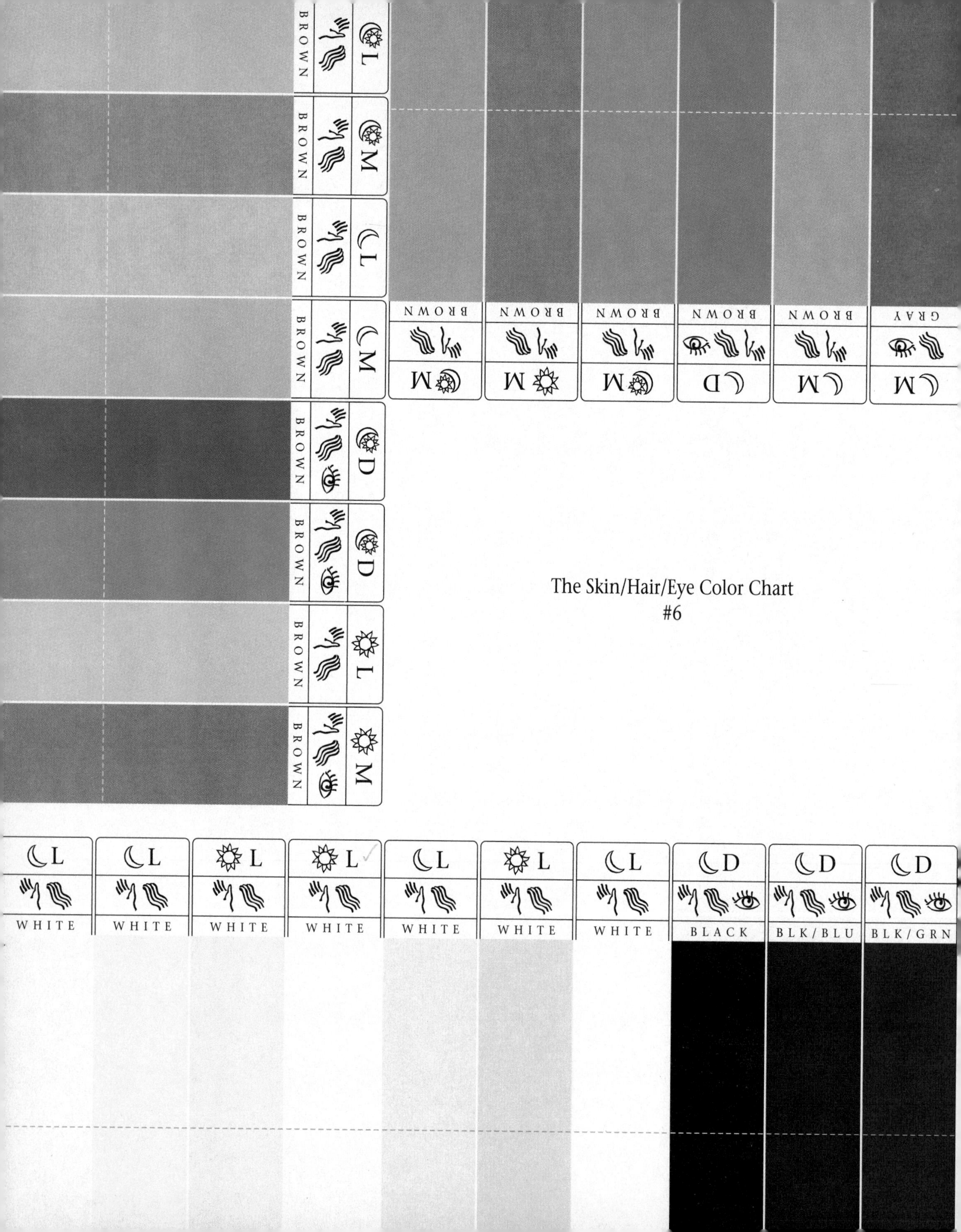

The Skin/Hair/Eye Color Chart
#6

BROWN
BROWN
BROWN
BROWN
BROWN
BROWN
BROWN
BROWN

BROWN
BROWN
BROWN
BROWN
BROWN
GRAY

WHITE | WHITE | WHITE | WHITE | WHITE | WHITE | WHITE | BLACK | BLK/BLU | BLK/GRN

The Skin/Hair/Eye Color Chart
#7

BROWN · VIOLET · VIOLET · VIOLET · RED · BROWN · BROWN · BROWN

VIOLET · VIOLET · VIOLET · VIOLET · VIOLET · VIOLET

BLACK · BLACK · BLACK · BLACK · BROWN · BROWN · BROWN · BROWN · BROWN · BROWN

What colors complete your palette?

Let's begin with color temperature.

Now it's time to go back to the Hue Family Color Charts and select colors from all the hue families that complement your natural coloring. By choosing colors that have the same color temperature and color value as your skin, hair, and eyes, which you determined on page 128, you will be able to create a color palette that will always be in harmony with you.

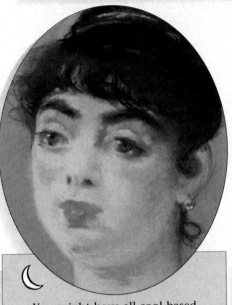

If your coloring is all warm, you can safely choose colors from all the psychologically warm hue families (red, orange, and yellow) regardless of their relative temperature within the hue family.

In Fragonard's Painting, *A Young Girl Reading*, we see one such warm-based coloring: yellow-brown or ivory skin, golden brown hair, and we've taken the liberty to imagine she also has golden brown eyes! If you wish to wear a psychologically cool color (from the violet, blue or green hue families), choose the members of these hue families that have the warm relative temperature; and wear them in combination with your reds, oranges, and/or yellows.

A Young Girl Reading, Jean-Honoré Fragonard, National Gallery of Art, Washington; Gift of Mrs. Mellon Bruce in memory of her father, Andrew W. Mellon (detail).

You might have all cool-based coloring, such as *Madame Michel-Levy* by Manet—violet-rose-brown skin, gray-blue eyes, cool grayish-brown hair.

If your coloring is cool, you can safely choose colors from all the psychologically cool hue families regardless of their relative temperature within the hue family. If you wish to wear a psychologically warm color, choose the members of these hue families that have the cool relative temperature, and wear them in combination with your greens, blues, and violets.

Madame Michel-Levy, Edouard Manet, National Gallery of Art, Washington; Chester Dale Collection (detail).

You might have a combination of temperature—warm skin, cool eyes, warm/cool hair. Or you might have chosen a shade or two that have the combination sun/moon symbol—that means it can be considered both warm and cool. In either case, your color temperature is both warm and cool as in the woman in *The Plum* by Manet. She has warm red hair and cool pink-violet skin.

If you naturally have both warm and cool coloring, you can choose both warm and cool colors from all the hue families. Another way to wear warm and cool in combination is to wear gold jewelry (warm) when you wear cool colors, and silver jewelry (cool) when you wear warm colors.

The Plum, Edouard Manet, National Gallery of Art, Washington; Collection of Mr. and Mrs. Paul Mellon (detail).

Next choose your value range.

After your color temperature, your color value level(s) will help you define your color range even further. In each of the six hue families, next choose your value column or columns.

For example, you may have all light value coloring. By applying the principle of repetition, you would select within your temperature range only the colors that are under the light value columns. Or you might have light and dark coloring, in which case you would select colors from both the light and dark value columns.

What is your level of color contrast?

The value levels found in your natural coloration, generally should be repeated in the value scheme in your clothing. By doing so, you will also discover another aspect of combining colors that relates to your value level(s)—the level of color contrast you can wear.

There are three levels of color contrast—low, medium, or high—which are illustrated by the seven artworks in this chart. Study these examples and their accompanying notes to help you determine which one is your level of color contrast. Notice that only (7) has two levels of contrast, while the others have one. Check the picture that is your level of color contrast.

If your skin, hair, and eyes are all light value, or all medium value, or all dark value colors, you will most easily wear low color contrast in your clothing.

🪷 This means you will wear a dark value color with another dark value color if you are all dark value like (1); a medium value color with another medium value color if you are all medium value like example (2); or a light value color with another light value color if your natural color combination is all light value like (3).

☐ **2**

All medium value colors in skin, hair, and eyes.

Tallulah Brockman Bankhead, Augustus John, The Portrait Gallery, Smithsonian Institution; Gift of the Honorable and Mrs. John Hay Whitney (detail).

☐ **1**

All dark value colors in skin, hair, and eyes.

Note: If you are all dark value, but the whites of your eyes are white and really show and sparkle, then you may consider yourself to have high contrast coloring like (6), *Madame Leblanc,* rather than low contrast.

Mary McLeod Bethune, Educator, Betsy Graves Reyneau, National Portrait Gallery, Smithsonian Institution, Washington; Gift of the Harmon Foundation (detail).

☐ **3**

All light value colors in skin, hair, and eyes.

Young Girl with Long Hair, Henri Matisse, National Gallery of Art, Washington (detail).

MEDIUM COLOR CONTRAST	HIGH COLOR CONTRAST	BOTH MEDIUM & HIGH COLOR CONTRAST

MEDIUM COLOR CONTRAST

If you have light and medium values in your coloring (4), or medium and dark values (5), you will most naturally wear *medium level contrast* in your clothing.

❧ This means you will wear a light color with a medium color if you are like (4), or a medium color with a dark color if you are like (5).

☐ **4**

Light and medium values in any combination of skin, hair, and eyes. Here we have light skin, medium value hair and eye colors.

Ginevra Bentivoglio, Ercole de Roberti, National Gallery of Art, Washington; Samuel H. Kress Collection (detail).

☐ **5**

Medium and dark values in any combination of skin, hair, and eyes. Here we have medium skin, medium-dark hair, and dark value eye color.

Tilla Durieux, Pierre Auguste Renoir, The Metropolitan Museum of Art; Bequest of Stephen C. Clark. (detail).

HIGH COLOR CONTRAST

If you have light and dark values in your coloring (6), you can easily wear *high color contrast.*

❧ This means you can wear a dark color with a light color. Black and white is the most obvious use of high contrast.

☐ **6**

Light and dark values in any combination of skin, hair and eyes. Here we have light value skin and dark value hair and eye colors. Also, see the note for example (1) under Low Color Contrast (all dark value).

Madame Jacques Louis Leblanc, Jean-Auguste-Dominique Ingres, The Metropolitan Museum of Art; Wolfe Fund, 1918, Catharine Lorillard Wolfe Collection (detail).

BOTH MEDIUM & HIGH COLOR CONTRAST

Finally, if you have all three values, then you can wear *a light color, a medium value color, and a dark color at the same time.*

❧ If the whites of your eyes are dramatically noticeable, then they are considered in your value pattern. This is one way to bring light value into your scheme, if your other colors are of medium or dark value. *The three different values together would give you the play of both medium and high contrast in your clothing.*

☐ **7**

A combination of values: light, medium, and dark. Here we have medium value skin, light and dark values in the hair and eyes. Notice how the whites of her eyes really show.

Woman in a Chemise, Andre Derain, National Gallery of Art, Washington; Chester Dale Collection (detail).

The Harmony Color Wheel and The Four Neutral Families Chart

Now that you have discovered how to create a personal palette of colors, it's time to present The Harmony Color Wheel and its adjunct, The Four Neutral Families Chart (both cool and warm). You have by now filled these in with your skin/hair/eye colors. By placing them on the Harmony Color Wheel and Neutrals Chart you automatically have the clues to color harmonies or combinations that are inherently beautiful for you to wear.

The Harmony Color Wheel

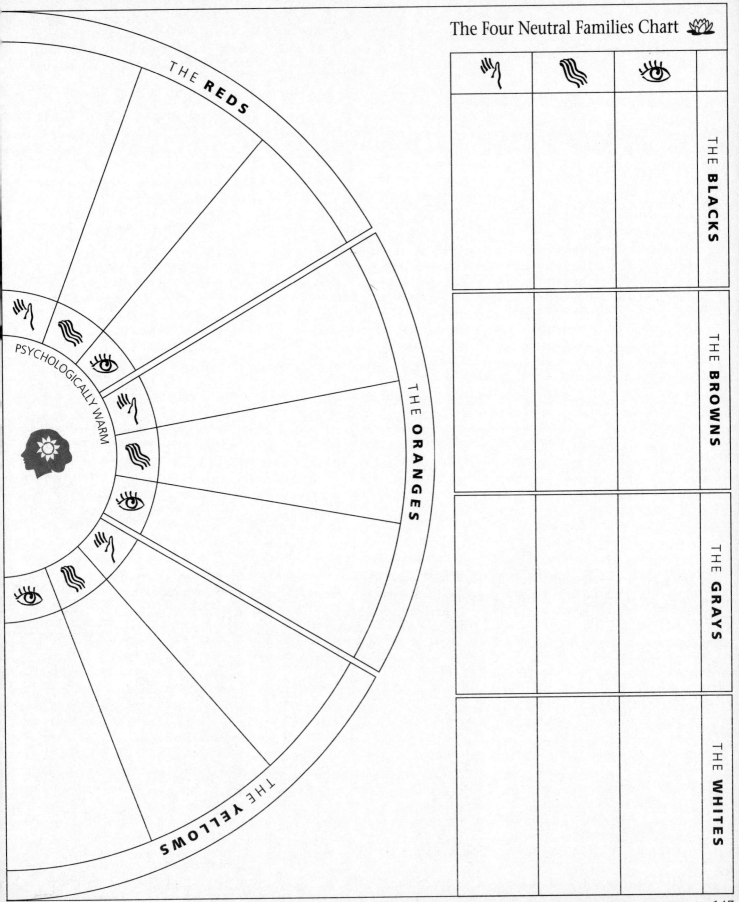

The Four Neutral Families Chart

PSYCHOLOGICALLY WARM

THE **REDS**

THE **ORANGES**

THE **YELLOWS**

THE **BLACKS**

THE **BROWNS**

THE **GRAYS**

THE **WHITES**

The five basic harmonies of color

The purpose of The Harmony Color Wheel is to help you remember how to relate colors in the four most commonly known color harmonies: monochromatic, complementary, analogous, and triadic. A fifth harmony is the neutral harmony, which is a combination of any of the neutrals shown in the neutrals chart. Your skin, hair, and eye colors relate to one another in one or more of these harmonies. Check which one(s) are yours. Notice that each harmony has certain inherent effects.

MONOCHROMATIC

☐ A harmony where the same hue is presented in gradations of value from light to dark. The hue can come from the Color Wheel or gradations of brown from the Neutrals Chart. An example of brown monochromatic coloring can be seen in the painting, *Portrait of a Lady* by van der Weyden below: medium-light brown skin, medium brown hair, dark brown eyes.

Monochromatic combinations are:

🖐 Skin	〰 Hair	👁 Eyes
Brown	Brown	Brown
Orange (peach)	Orange (rust)	Brown
Red (pink)	Red (mahogony)	Red (mahog.)
Yellow (ivory)	Yellow (blonde)	Yellow (gold)
Green (olive)	Green (khaki)	Green

Effect: restful, expected, and/or elegant.

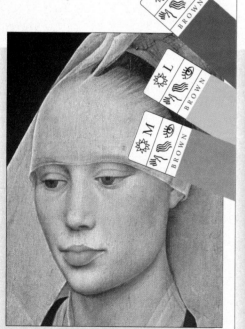

Portrait of a Lady, Rogier van der Weyden, National Gallery of Art, Washington, Andrew W. Mellon Collection (detail).

COMPLEMENTARY

☐ A harmony of two hues that are opposite each other on the color wheel. Combinations are: Red/Green, Orange/Blue, and Yellow/Violet.

See Modigliani's painting, *Girl in a Green Blouse*, below. She has orange hair, orange (peach) skin, and blue eyes.

Note: Where there are two columns that have the same hue, you could replace one with a neutral color and still maintain the harmony.

Complementary combinations are:

🖐 Skin	〰 Hair	👁 Eyes
Orange (peach)	Orange (rust)	Blue
Red (pink)	Red (mahogony)	Green
Yellow	Yellow (blonde)	Violet
Violet (mauve)	Yellow (blonde)	Brown

Effect: dramatic and/or intense, if you use colors of equal value and intensity.

Girl in a Green Blouse, Amedeo Modigliani, National Gallery of Art, Washington; Chester Dale Collection (detail).

ANALOGOUS

☐ A harmony of two to three hues that are side-by-side on the color wheel. For example: Reds/Violets/Blues; or Oranges/Reds/Violets. Look below at the woman in the painting, *The Plum* by Manet, who has this harmony: pink and violet skintone (red and violet), and red-orange hair, and neutral eyes.

Note: Where there are two columns that have the same hue, you could replace one with a neutral color and still maintain the harmony.

Analogous combinations are:

🖐 Skin	〰 Hair	👁 Eyes
Red (pink)/Viol.	Orange (red-or.)	Red-or. or Neu.
Orange (peach)	Yellow	Yel. or Neutral
Yellow (ivory)	Yellow (blonde)	Green
Red (pink)	Red-orange	Viol. or Neutral
Red (pink)	Red-orange	Red-orange
Yellow (golden)	Orang. or Yel.	Orang. or Yel.

Effect: calm, friendly, and/or restful.

The Plum, Edouard Manet, National Gallery of Art, Washington; Collection of Mr. and Mrs. Paul Mellon (detail).

Your natural harmony or harmonies tells you the most enhancing way to combine colors in your clothing. Again, the principle of repetition is the key.

For example, if you are complementary in your coloring, you can do all complementary combinations of color in your clothes very effectively. You might even choose to wear two or more pairs of complementary colors, which would give you a multi-colored effect—especially if you are in a festive mood. Another example, if you are neutral in your overall color impression, then you wear neutral schemes quite naturally and beautifully.

TRIADIC

☐ A harmony of three hues that are equidistant from each other on the wheel: Reds/Yellows/Blues or Greens/Oranges/Violets. The following painting of *Nude With Red Hair* by George Bellows demonstrates this harmony: yellow skintone, red hair, blue eyes. Triadic combinations are:

🖐 Skin	〰 Hair	👁 Eyes
Yellow (golden)	Red	Blue
Red (pink)	Yellow (blonde)	Blue
Violet (mauve)	Orange (rust)	Green
Orange (peach)	Green (khaki)	Violet
Green (khaki)	Orange	Violet

Effect: active, energetic, and/or playful.

Nude with Red Hair, George Wesley Bellows, National Gallery of Art, Washington; Chester Dale Collection (detail).

✿ NEUTRAL

The chart of The Four Neutral Families shows the fifth color harmony.

☐ Two or more of the neutrals combine to create this harmony. Gauguin's *Tahitian Women* gives us a fine example of this harmony: brown skintone, black hair and eyes, and the whites of her eyes add a third neutral. Neutral combinations are:

🖐 Skin	〰 Hair	👁 Eyes
Brown	Black	Brown
Black	Brown	Brown
Brown	Gray	Brown
Black	Gray	Brown
White	Gray	Gray
White	Black	Brown

Effect: stable, sophisticated, and/or elegant.

Two Tahitian Women, Paul Gauguin, The Metropolitan Museum of Art, New York (detail).

✿ You may have more than one natural harmony and the Harmony Color Wheel and Neutrals chart will reveal this. What you should look for initially is the harmony that is your first visual impression. We call this your *primary harmony*. Other less obvious harmonies we call your *secondary harmonies*.

For example, your primary harmony may be neutral like Gauguin's Tahitian woman, but in your palm you also show yellow and violet skintones, which are complementary colors. So you could also wear complementary color combinations as a *secondary natural harmony*. In addition, you might also have a blue ring around your overall brown eyes. Now blue and violet are analogous colors, giving you yet another secondary harmony. Not to get too complex, but we could also point out that while yellow and violet are complementary, if we added the blue to them, we would create yet another harmony—called a split-complement! In other words, a split-complement combines a complementary pair with a hue that is to one side or the other of one of the complements.

Of course, you can adapt any of the five harmonies to your wardrobe depending on the effects you want. If your primary harmony is the Neutral one, you have the most versatile backdrop upon which to adapt the other harmonies. For example, you might wear a colorful scarf—which could be in either a complementary, or analogous, or triadic color combination—to accessorize a neutral ensemble.

While your primary harmony will be the one in which you will feel most at home, allow yourself to experiment from time to time with the different effects of other harmonies. Challenge your creativity!

Refining your color palette
through the concept of intensity 🪷

Perhaps you've noticed we have yet to talk about the fifth and last property of color: *intensity.* We have left it to the last, because:

> In the art of dressing, intensity is not just a property of color, it is also an aspect of personality or at least a personal mood that can be expressed through color if you so choose.

Color intensity and resonance 🪷

Intensity is defined as the relative brightness of a color. So we can say a hue has a low, a medium, or a high intensity level relative to other hues.

Like color temperature and value, color intensity can also be regarded in two ways:

First, in our Hue Family Color Charts, *we can compare the intensity of each pure pigment relative to its different resonances.*

All of the light value pure pigments (see Sap Green, Lemon Yellow and Chrome Yellow), and all but one of the medium value ones appear as bright and intense as they can

possibly be. These pure pigments have a high intensity level. Notice as these pigments move into the lighter or darker resonances. the intensity level decreases. That is, these resonances are not as bright as the original pure pigment.

Of the medium value pigments, only *Yellow Ochre* is like the dark value pigments—*Hooker's Green, Verde Green, Indigo, Parma Violet,* and *Thalo Violet*—in that they *need to be lightened* in order to appear brighter and more intense. The intensity level of these pure pigments is low. However, notice if they are washed with water or tinted with white, their intensity level increases; they appear brighter.

Second, we can also talk about changing a hue's intensity level relative to itself—that is, raise or reduce its brightness without changing its value. An easy way to understand this is to imagine that all the colors on the Hue Family Color Charts have a light bulb behind them. When you pump up the electricity into these bulbs, the colors will appear brighter and more intense; when you turn it down, the colors become less bright. You aren't changing the color, just the intensity.

🪷 A light bulb is a nice analogy you say, but how do you achieve this in clothing? The answer is simple: You can change the intensity of a color by the fabric surfaces you use. Fabrics that have shine, shimmer, luster, a reflective surface,

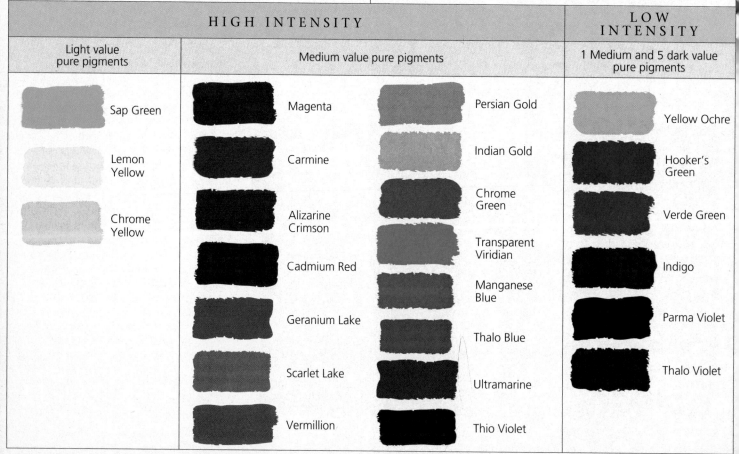

HIGH INTENSITY			LOW INTENSITY
Light value pure pigments	Medium value pure pigments		1 Medium and 5 dark value pure pigments
Sap Green	Magenta	Persian Gold	Yellow Ochre
Lemon Yellow	Carmine	Indian Gold	Hooker's Green
Chrome Yellow	Alizarine Crimson	Chrome Green	Verde Green
	Cadmium Red	Transparent Viridian	Indigo
	Geranium Lake	Manganese Blue	Parma Violet
	Scarlet Lake	Thalo Blue	Thalo Violet
	Vermillion	Ultramarine	
		Thio Violet	

or a flickering quality such as a shiny jacquard—all have built-in electricity, so to speak, which can make a color appear brighter than if it were on a dull fabric surface. For example, even the neutral black will appear brighter if it appears on a shiny velvet than if it were on a dull cotton fabric. By the same token, we can make even the most intense pure pigment such as chrome yellow less bright by using it, say, on a lackluster wool fabric. Compare this with chrome yellow on silk or polished cotton—can you imagine how much brighter it would be? All colors, whether pure or in its various resonances, can be intensified or de-intensified in this way.

Do you have innate *color* intensity? ❀

Madame X (Mme. Gautreau), John Singer Sargent, The Metropolitan Museum of Art, New York; Arthur H. Hearn Fund, 1916 (detail).

When complementary colors are mixed together, they reduce each other's brightness creating a muted resonance. But when placed next to each other, complementary colors intensify each other. High contrast color combinations such as black and white are also high in intensity because of the tension between opposites—each making the other appear stronger by contrast. If your innate harmony is complementary (for example red hair, pink skin and green eyes), or if your natural value scheme is high contrast (for example dark skin and light hair, or vice versa, as seen in Sargent's *Madame X*), then you have natural color intensity relative to other human coloring.

> To support your natural color intensity, use the colors in your range that are the most intense.

Depending on your value range, for the most part these colors would be the high intensity light or medium value pure pigments, or some *lightened* resonances of the low intensity medium or dark value pure pigments. If you have high contrast coloring, the intense black and white scheme is also a natural combination for you.

There may be times when you want to subdue your natural intensity—perhaps the occasion warrants it or your mood requires it. At these times, stay away from high contrast com-

binations. Instead, use your lightened colors or the colors in the shaded or muted resonances. You might even go to the toasted hues if you are feeling "earthy" or "yummy".

> However, when you wear these more subdued colors always have something in the outfit that has luster or shine, be it in the fabric or in your accessories. Your natural color intensity should always have some support in whatever you wear.

Do you have innate *personal* intensity? ❀

There is another natural intensity that is not in the coloring but in the personality.

> Like the electricity of our light bulb analogy, personal intensity is a kind of energy level that shines through regardless of the person's coloring.

A high level of personal intensity is often expressed in two ways:

First, there is the kind of personal intensity that is projected through the person's eyes and her bearing which is seen as having *a powerful strength*. This kind of energy is concentrated and seemingly contained within the body which gives it tensile strength. This personality is often described as "intense" and "magnetic". Picasso's portrait of *Gertrude Stein* illustrates this type of intensity.

Gertrude Stein, Pablo Picasso,
The Metropolitan Museum of Art, New York; Bequest of Gertrude Stein, 1946 (detail).

You can even be all light value in your coloring and have this intensity. In fact, this would be the type of blonde woman who wears black very well. However, it must be a bright black, never dull and not to be worn all over the body. That is, much of her skin must show in order to create a balanced high contrast look between her light value coloring and the black clothing. High contrast color combinations, as we already know, support high intensity.

Then, there is the other type of personal intensity that is rarely contained, but is, on the contrary, very effusive. We often describe this type of intensity or brightness in a personality as "sparkling", "electric", and "energetic".

It is possible for a personality to have both contained and outwardly-directed intensity. It is also possible to find someone with both high intensity coloring and high personal intensity. In both cases we would have individuals with *extremely* high personal intensity.

Low personal intensity

The Mother and Sister of the Artist,
Berthe Morisot,
National Gallery of Art, Washington;
Chester Dale Collection (detail).

Sparkling personal intensity

Mlle. Marcelle Lender en buste,
Henri Toulouse-Lautrec-Monfa,
The Metropolitan Museum of Art,
The Alfred Stieglitz Collection, 1949 (detail).

It is also possible to be "magnetic" or "sparkling" in lesser degrees. That is, your personal intensity is still evident, but not at such a high pitch. Whatever the level, you will want to support it with colors that are naturally brighter or with colors that are intensified through fabrics with shine, luster, and/or sparkle. On the other hand, if your personal intensity is relatively low, you may want to eliminate from your palette all pure colors that are intense and all other colors that are bright. You will probably not wear these colors and prefer the more complex and deeper resonances. Yet, in fact almost everyone, at one time or another will feel intense. It doesn't have to be an aspect of your personality, it could simply be a mood that comes over you at certain times of your life. When this happens, simply wear your preferred colors through fabrics and materials with "built-in electricity" as we have described.

At this point, we have related all five properties of color to human pigmentation. In the next chapter we will look at the properties of texture, color's inevitable partner, and relate them to the textural qualities found in the human body.

Sometime at your leisure, go back to each Hue Family Chart and look carefully at the colors within your range.

Imagine them in different textures.

Allow your feelings then to decide which colors are among your very favorites. Have the confidence that with your present knowledge of color, your intuition will work wonders as you use them! Call it intuition backed by attention.

Let your innate creativity reach out and play with color in ways you have never tried before. Very soon you may even extend the meaning of the word "color" to other aspects of your life: that there is color in the fragrances you wear, the music you love, and in the way you speak; color in preparing food and decorating your surroundings.

Let color lead you to extend your individual style beyond just the things you wear. Let color, as the most immediate element of design, lead you to begin seeing the other elements—line and space, shape, proportion, and texture—in your home environment, in the world around you, and in the design pattern of other people. When you do, you will be well on your way to seeing your world with the artist's eye.

Would you rather have someone help you with this process?

Tips on how to find a color consultant

Look for individualization.
Look for a consultant who:

- individualizes your range of colors. (Beware of those who give pre-packaged color palettes without breaking them apart to create individualized color harmonies.)
- individualizes your range of textures.
- understands how to identify your skintone, eye color, and hair color. (Beware of those who generalize all Asians and all Blacks in one color category. Remember that there is a wide range of coloring in all racial groups.)
- gets excited by the possibilities of dressing your unique body shape.

Look for background.
Research the consultant's training or experience.

- Is there a strong background in color, texture, and design principles? Or, is there sufficient evidence based upon client results, that this consultant understands personal design as related to lifestyle, dressing purpose, and budget?

Look for service.
Ask yourself, does the consultant:

- listen to your needs and answer your questions? Or, does she tell you what she thinks you need to hear.
- show a strong interest in what makes you a unique and creative being?
- stay focused on you and your color or styling needs? Or, does she spend time telling you about other clients or herself?
- also provide individualized design and style information?
- provide or suggest someone who can finish the "picture" with makeup and hair styling, closet editing, or personal shopping expertise?

Look for presentation.
Trust your first impression.

- When you phone for information, how does the consultant impress you over the phone? Does the consultant seem to understand your needs and answer your questions sincerely and professionally?
- During your visit, does the consultant's own personal presentation give a beautiful first impression? Does the consultant's studio or home office have a professional appearance?

Our response to texture in painting depends a great deal on the close tie between our visual and tactile senses. In Fantin-Latour's *Still Life*, we comprehend the coarseness of wicker, the roughness of the book cover, the softness of ripe fruit, the smoothness of glass, the waxy quality of a thick camellia petal, not only by looking, but by many experiences of touching their surfaces. In fact, it is the brain's capacity for what is called tactile memory which can make depicted textures in painting seem almost as true as real ones. From the many experiences you've had of touching your skin and hair, and touching different fabrics over the years, you have developed tactile memory for them which will, and probably already has helped you develop a keen sensitivity for your most harmonious textures to wear.

7

Your body's textural qualities

...and how they interact with your clothing textures.

exture is the other side of color. We learn about texture by everything we touch from the time we are babies. At birth, our newborn vision is estimated to be between 20/250 to 20/500—this is legally blind! We could say that we come into this world greeting it with our sense of touch more than with our sight—knowing first the texture and warmth rather than the color of our mothers' skins. As we grow and eyesight becomes more acute, our senses of sight and touch come closer together. And at some point we no longer need to touch a familiar surface or substance to know how it feels, because we have developed what is called tactile memory. That is, the mere *sight* of a surface or substance stimulates a memory of how it *feels*. Do you remember a favorite warm blanket or a cuddly teddy bear you couldn't be without?

Our eyes tell us whether a surface looks **shiny** or **matte**. Tactile memory also gives us more information, for example, about whether something *feels* **rough** or **smooth**, **soft** or **hard**, and **heavy** or **light-weight.**

Rough and matte

Smooth and shiny

Soft

Light-weight

Heavy-weight

Hard

Lizard on Bark, Shiny Green Frog, Milkweed Pod, Pink Flower, Variegated Flower, Tortoise, Bill Terry Photography

These textural qualities actually determine the "feel" of a color on a surface. The quality of a color—its brightness, for instance—varies depending on the textures. Our opening painting can help us to imagine that smooth and shiny textures like the glass vase or polished wood table reflect light, whereas matte surfaces like the book cover or wicker basket absorb it. Some textures both reflect and absorb light, and some let light through, as in the transparent skin of each orange wedge. Compare for yourself the white of the camellia flower with the white of the porcelain cup or the white of the inside of the orange peel—can you see how the white color is affected by the different textures? Can you see how tactile memory forces us to see a shiny brittle white from the cup and a softer almost cushiony quality in the yellowish white of the peel, while the white in the flower petal seems thick and opaque? In fact, it is this intricate relationship between color and texture that makes it possible for us to make almost literal translations of nature's colors into fabrics. For instance, it is easy to imagine the shiny red of an apple interpreted in red taffeta, or sand in beige raw silk, or peach skin in peach velveteen, or the effects of water ripples in lustrous blue moiré. Can you think of others?

Still Life, Henri Fantin-Latour, National Gallery of Art, Washington; Chester Dale Collection (detail).

Choosing textures is just as important as choosing colors

Colors grab us; textures affect us in more subtle ways. But affect us they do, and in no more potent way than in the fabrics and other materials we choose to wear. In chapter 1 you learned the four categories of fabric in terms of how they support your body type or hold a line in the construction of an outfit. You saw fabrics in terms of their relative drape or tautness. In Chapters 1 and 5 you learned to relate prints to the scale of your facial features. In Chapter 6 you learned more about fabric with respect to increasing the intensity of any color through the shine or luster of a fabric surface. Indeed, more than any of the other elements of art, texture has been woven in and out, so to speak, throughout this book. In this chapter it seems natural then, that from time to time we will look back to previous chapters whenever we need to site examples. Looking back also serves to remind us how truly interrelated are the elements of art.

In this chapter you will use tactile memory to discover the last component of Your Body's Design Pattern—*the textural qualities found in your skin and hair*—and learn how these personal textures interact visually with clothing textures to create the effects you want. We begin this discovery by first defining the three basic types of textures that can be found in your wardrobe pieces.

In the three artworks shown on this page and the next, the women have combined different types of clothing textures to create visual and tactile interest and beauty.

Portrait of a Young Woman,
Piero del Pollaiulol,
The Metropolitan Museum of Art; Bequest of
Edward S. Harkness, 1940 (detail).

Madame Picasso, Pablo Picasso,
National Gallery of Art, Washington; Chester Dale Collection (detail).

The three basic types of clothing textures

1. **Woven fabrics:** The different weaves include plain, twill, satin, jacquard, loop pile, cut pile, and double. Because they have the most stable fabric structure, woven fabrics generally are most used for all pieces of clothing, except for pieces like sweaters that are knitted.

2. **Nonwoven fabrics:** generally comprise two categories:
   - Knits—Knits are less stable than woven fabrics, but are flexible and wrinkle resistant, and can also be used for most pieces of clothing including sweaters, socks, and accessories.
   - Fragile fabrics—These have little tensile strength and include fabrics like lace, net, braid and crochet. Nonwoven fabrics are most often used as decorative trim. When used for entire pieces of clothing, they need to be supported by stronger fabrics.

3. **Non-fabric textures:** These are other materials that add both visual and tactile variety and character. Generally, they are divided into two categories according to their use:
   - Leather, suede, fur—(can be used for entire pieces of clothing and accessories, or as trim)
   - Metals, wood, glass, bone, shells, pearls, semi-precious stones, ceramics, plastic, paper, flowers, etc. (used in jewelry, accessories, buttons, beading and other trim or ornamentation).

Personal textures and clothing textures

All textures, whether they are in the three types of clothing textures mentioned on the previous page or in personal textures of skin and hair, can be described for our purposes by answering the following two questions:

1. What is the surface quality—smooth, or textured, or both?
2. What is the relative textural weight—light-weight, medium-weight, or heavy-weight?

1 What is the surface quality— smooth, or textured, or both?

In surface quality we find either absolute smoothness or its opposite—texturedness; or we have a combination of both smoothness and texturedness.

Smoothness: plain and patterned

Smooth fabrics are made from the finest yarns and the most compact and simple weaves or knits. When you run your hand across these textures, you see and definitely feel the flat, smooth quality; this is true for smooth non-fabric textures as well. We describe smoothness in two ways: there is *plain smoothness* and *patterned smoothness*. If one were to depict them in a painting, fabrics that are plain and smooth would appear as though they were painted with fluid paint and with very fine brushes, so brush strokes are barely perceptible. However, any smooth fabric can be made to look textured because of variations of coloring or if it is in a print of any kind—this is patterned smoothness. These fabrics are the silk jacquards that flicker from matte to shine in their finish, or any smooth fabrics with prints such as the silk kimono in this Japanese print, *An Oiran.*

An Oiran, Japanese, 18th century print, K. Utamaro, The Metropolitan Museum of Art; H.O. Havemeyer Collection, Bequest of Mrs. H.O. Havemeyer, 1929 (detail).

Texturedness

Texturedness includes all other fabrics and materials that do not look and feel smooth. Texturedness is created when there is a variation of loft (or depth) in the surface of the fabric or non-fabric. That is, systematically in the weave or plane, threads or variations are allowed to come above absolute flatness or planeness.

When you run your hand across these textures, you *feel and see* the variations in the surface. This large group runs the gamut of finely textured to moderately textured to highly textured.

Combination smooth and textured

Typically, we achieve this combination by simply putting plain smooth and textured fabrics or materials together. Smooth fabrics can be made "textured" in certain places by manipulating the fabric through smocking, shirring, gathers, pleats, or designed stitchery as shown in *Portrait of a Young Woman* on the preceding page. You will also find many examples of this throughout this book—for example *Maud Dale* on page 12.

In this Japanese print notice that, for the most part, the surface quality of both the personal and clothing textures are either plain or patterned smoothness.

Identify the surface quality of your skin and hair 🪷

Identify what surface quality you find in your skin and hair, using the descriptions and examples to guide you. See how personal textures correspond to fabric textures as we have just described.

	PLAIN SMOOTHNESS	PATTERNED SMOOTHNESS (OR VISUALLY TEXTURED)	ALL-OVER TEXTURED	COMBINATION SMOOTH AND TEXTURED
		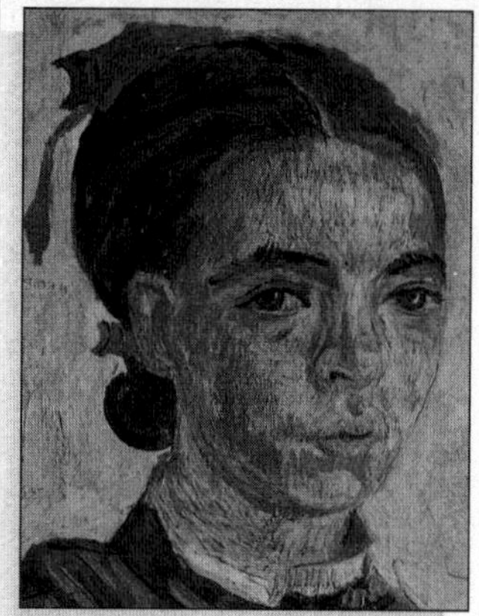		
Skin	☐ Skin is overall smooth and flawless	☐ Skin feels smooth, but looks textured because of freckles all over, or because of obvious variations in pigmentation as in *La Mousme* above. We can also describe this skin as being smooth but "visually textured."	☐ Opposite of smooth and flawless, skin has some surface depth because of general wrinkling or is overall porous, grainy and/or pocked (as in Modigliani's *Head of a Woman*, right). 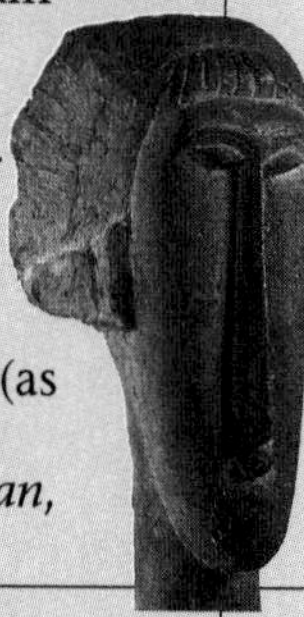	☐ Skin is plain and smooth in certain areas and textured in others (for example, smooth and wrinkled, or smooth and pocked in some areas).
Hair	☐ Hair is overall straight, smooth and one-colored	☐ Hair is all straight and smooth, but has overall color variations as in highly streaked hair or in salt and pepper hair (seen here in Derain's *Woman in a Chemise*). 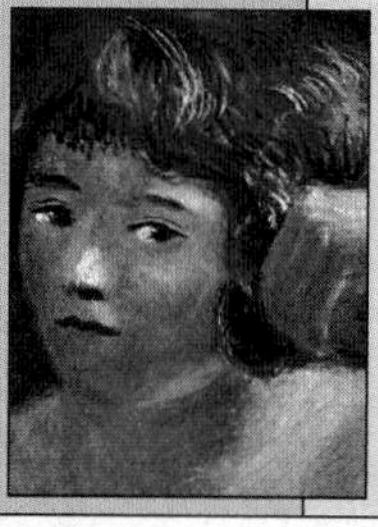	☐ Opposite of straight and smooth regardless of color, this hair has loft because it is wavy, curly, or kinky all over. (For examples of these, see chart on textural weight on page 160–161.)	☐ Hair like that of Mrs. Endicott (above) is smooth and wavy combined. Da Vinci's *Ginevra* (below) also has combination hair—straight and smooth in back, and curly and textured in front. 

Nude with Red Hair, George Wesley Bellows, National Gallery of Art, Washington; Chester Dale Collection (detail).

La Mousme, Vincent van Gogh, and
Woman in a Chemise, Andre Derain, National Gallery of Art, Washington; Chester Dale Collection (detail).

Old Market Woman, Greek sculpture, 2nd century B.C., The Metropolitan Museum of Art, New York; Rogers Fund, 1909 (detail).
Head of a Woman, Amedeo Modigliani, National Gallery of Art, Washington; Chester Dale Collection (detail).

Mrs. William Crowninshield Endicott, John Singer Sargent, National Gallery of Art, Washington; Gift of Louise Thoron Endicott in memory of Mr. and Mrs. William Crowninshield Endicott (detail).
Ginevra de'Benci, Leonardo da Vinci, National Gallery of Art, Washington; Ailsa Mellon Bruce Fund (detail).

The surface quality of my hair and skin is (check one):

☐ Plain smoothness,   ☐ All-over textured, or
☐ Patterned smoothness   ☐ Combination smooth and textured.

Note: If you've check-marked your hair in one column and your skin in another, then you are a combination.

2 What is the textural weight—light, medium, heavy, or a combination weight?

Whether the surface quality is smooth, textured or a combination, each fabric will also have weight. There are two kinds of weight in fabric—tactile weight and visual weight. *Tactile weight* refers to how heavy a fabric *feels* relative to others. Your tactile memory helps you to decide this. Often a fabric looks heavier or lighter than it feels because of its color or print—this is called *visual weight*. Both kinds of weight can be described as relatively light-weight, medium-weight, or heavy-weight.

Most of us wear *medium-weight* fabrics easily. If you have a moulded body type and have chosen to use fluid and medium-drape fabrics, these fabrics are either light-weight or medium-weight. Medium-taut to taut fabrics are generally

Compared to medium or heavy-weight fabrics, light-weight fabrics such as those worn by Renoir's Tilla *are not as practical for everyday use.*

Tilla Durieux, Pierre-Auguste Renoir, Metropolitan Museum of Art, New York; Bequest of Stephen C. Clark, (detail).

medium-weight and heavy-weight. For some reason, we have not met any woman who effectively wears only heavy-weight fabrics, so we venture to say there are few woman who can. Most heavy-weight fabrics are used in outer wear such as in coats, or in some outdoor or casual wear such as heavy denim. If you can wear heavy-weight fabrics, you will wear them in combination with other lighter-weight fabrics.

Light-weight fabrics can be either sheer or opaque, and are not as practical as medium or heavy-weight fabrics, especially if they are also sheer. *Medium-weight* fabrics are chosen most often because they are more practical than light-weight fabrics, and unlike heavy-weight fabrics, they adapt most easily to different clothing purposes. They avoid extremes and can be dressed "up" or "down." (See page 14 to see examples of these different weights in fabrics).

Few women can wear all heavy-weight fabrics. Here, Picasso's Gertrude Stein *wears a combination of heavy and medium-weight fabrics.*

Gertrude Stein, Pablo Picasso, Metropolitan Museum of Art, New York; Bequest of Gertrude Stein, 1946 (detail).

This chart is designed to help you determine the relative textural weight of your hair and skin. There are five qualities in hair, and one quality in skin that help to determine your body's textural weight. Use the examples and descriptions to guide you as you check mark your qualities. Like fabric, the overall textural weight of your skin and hair is either predominantly light-weight, medium-weight, or heavy-weight, or it is a combination of light and medium-weight or medium and heavy-weight. Note that any check-marks you make in the extreme columns will cancel each other out and you will choose fabrics that are medium-weight. For instance, if your hair length is below the shoulder (listed under heavy-weight column), but your hair is not full and lies close to the head (listed under the light-weight column)—then consider that these two qualities even out into a check-mark for medium-weight instead. (For an illustration of this, turn to Luini's *The Magdalene* on page 119.)

Being aware of your textural weight will help you know how to use the different weight fabrics in your clothing, which we will discuss in the next section. For now, here is something to remember: Most women will try to find ways to use medium-weight fabrics because of their practicality. In order to wear medium-weight fabrics effectively, some may even adjust the weight of their hair to create medium-weight in their appearance. For example, women with

---

The textural weight of my skin and hair is (check one):

- [ ] All light-weight
- [ ] All medium-weight
- [ ] All heavy-weight
- [ ] Combination light and medium-weight
- [x] Combination medium and heavy-weight

If your skin is translucent, you can easily wear soft, sheer fabrics.

Madame Henriot, Pierre-Auguste Renoir, National Gallery of Art; Washington; Gift of the Adele R. Levy Fund, Inc. (detail).

Identify the textural weight of your skin and hair

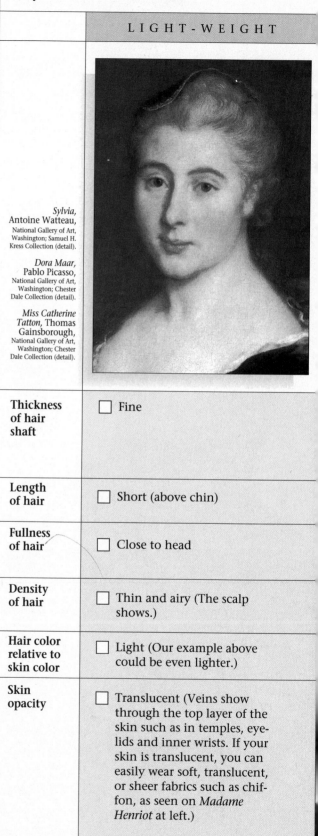

	LIGHT-WEIGHT
Sylvia, Antoine Watteau, National Gallery of Art, Washington; Samuel H. Kress Collection (detail). *Dora Maar,* Pablo Picasso, National Gallery of Art, Washington; Chester Dale Collection (detail). *Miss Catherine Tatton,* Thomas Gainsborough, National Gallery of Art, Washington; Chester Dale Collection (detail).	
Thickness of hair shaft	☐ Fine
Length of hair	☐ Short (above chin)
Fullness of hair	☐ Close to head
Density of hair	☐ Thin and airy (The scalp shows.)
Hair color relative to skin color	☐ Light (Our example above could be even lighter.)
Skin opacity	☐ Translucent (Veins show through the top layer of the skin such as in temples, eye-lids and inner wrists. If your skin is translucent, you can easily wear soft, translucent, or sheer fabrics such as chiffon, as seen on *Madame Henriot* at left.)

MEDIUM-WEIGHT	HEAVY-WEIGHT
☐ Medium	☑ Thick, coarse, and/or wiry (Many Asians have hair shaft that is thick and coarse; see the Japanese print, *An Oiran*, on page 157.)
☐ Medium (chin to shoulder length)	☑ Long (below shoulder)
☐ Moderate volume	☑ Voluminous (The hair has bulk and fullness.)
☐ Medium thickness (There is some air space between the strands.)	☑ Thick and compact (The scalp does not show.)
☑ Medium	☐ Dark
☑ Opaque (Most women have skin that is opaque, which is considered medium-weight.)	☐ Overly exposed to the sun, leathery appearance (This type of skin appears heavy-weight as illustrated here in van Gogh's *Girl in White* at right.)

(above) *Portrait of a Young Lady*,
Leonardo da Vinci,
National Gallery of Art, Washington;
Chester Dale Collection (detail).

light-weight hair will add volume to their hair, usually by curling or perming, to help it move more toward medium-weight (especially if their skin is also light-weight). Women with heavy-weight hair often trim the thickness out of it or pull it back, or perhaps even lighten it to make it appear less weighty (especially if the skin is also heavy-weight).

Girl in White, Vincent van Gogh,
National Gallery of Art, Washington; Chester Dale Collection (detail).

Repeat or contrast your body's textural qualities ❧

*N*ow that you are aware of the textural qualities of your skin and hair, let us see how they interact with clothing textures. Perhaps you are beginning to see that clothing textures with qualities similar to or very different from your personal textures will emphasize your personal textures. That is, you always have a choice between repeating or contrasting your personal textures—between selecting fabrics and other materials that have the same textural qualities as your hair and skin, or fabrics that are opposite them.

Repeating and/or contrasting surface quality ❧

First, how does this work with surface quality? Look at the chart below. This chart summarizes how the surface quality of clothing textures (listed down the left side) interacts with the surface quality of your skin and hair (listed across the top) in terms of repetition and/or contrast. Go to the column that describes your personal textures as found in your skin and hair. Notice the numbers in each of the boxes which indicate the following: ❶ the most natural fabric surface for you to wear; ❷ still easy to wear, but adds some contrast to your personal texture; ❸ provides even more contrast to your personal textures; and ❹ provides the most contrast to your personal textures.

Combination smooth and textured ❧

If your skin and hair are a combination of smooth and textured, then you have natural textural contrast. Your combination can be like that of Mrs. Endicott shown above, where the hair and/or skin are smooth in some areas and are textured in other areas. Or, you can have plain smooth hair and all-over textured skin or vice versa—all-over textured hair and smooth skin as seen in our two examples on the next page. Look at ❶, de'Landi's *Portrait of a Lady*. Notice how the smooth and textured combination found in her personal textures was repeated in her clothing textures. If your personal textures are both smooth and textured, you may also choose to just repeat one or the other quality, as in example ❷, Reyneau's *Mary McLeod Bethune*. Bethune has chosen to repeat only her skin's smoothness in her dress and buttons, which contrasts with her textured hair. Notice, however, that while her dress is smooth like her skin, its matte fabric finish relates to the matte quality of her hair; only the buttons repeat both the shine and smoothness of her skin.

CLOTHING TEXTURES (Surface quality of fabrics and other materials)	PERSONAL TEXTURES (Skin and Hair)			
	Plain Smoothness	Patterned Smoothness	All-over Textured	Combination Smooth and Textured
All Plain Smoothness	❶ Repeats your personal textures and is most natural for you to wear.	❹ Provides the most contrast to your personal textures and is difficult to do.	❹ Provides the most contrast to your personal textures and is difficult to do.	❸ Repeats your smoothness and adds some contrast to your texturedness.
All Patterned Smoothness	❸ Repeats your personal smoothness while the visual texture contrasts it.	❶ Repeats your personal textures and is most natural for you to wear.	❷ Overall visual texture repeats your texturedness, but the smooth surface provides some contrast.	❷ All patterned smoothness repeats your combination, but visually the pattern adds some contrast to your smoothness.
All Textured	❹ Provides the most contrast to your personal textures.	❸ Repeats your visual texturedness and contrasts the smooth surface quality of your skin and hair.	❶ Repeats your personal textures and is most natural for you to wear.	❸ Repeats your texturedness but adds some contrast to your smoothness.
Combination of Smooth and Textured	❷ Adds some contrast to your personal textures.	❷ Repeats the personal textures in a contrasting way.	❸ Though the texturedness supports your texturedness, the visually and tactilely smooth surface provides even more contrast.	❶ Repeats your personal textures and is most natural for you to wear.

Credits are on page 158.

Two examples of natural textural contrast in personal textures

 Hair: all-over textured
Skin: plain smoothness

Portrait of a Lady, Neroccio de'Landi,
National Gallery of Art, Washington; Widener Collection (detail).

2 Hair: all-over textured
Skin: plain smoothness

Mary McLeod Bethune, Betsy Graves Reyneau
The National Portrait Gallery, Smithsonian Institution, Washington (detail).

All-over textured

If your skin and hair are all-over textured, then all textured fabrics as well as smooth printed fabrics would repeat your textured quality. For contrast, you would wear textured surfaces with some smooth ones. If smoothness in the garment is around the face, limit the amount of smoothness to a small area such as in a collar, keeping it surrounded by lots of texture as shown in van Gogh's *Girl in White* (page 161). All plain smoothness would provide the greatest contrast, but it is difficult to do well, if you are all-over textured. Instead, try wearing plain smooth pieces of clothing in layered fashion as shown in this drawing.

The different depths created by layered clothing would give an impression of some texturedness in the total outfit in spite of the smoothness of each piece of clothing. Also, use smooth fabrics with a matte rather than a shiny finish. Shiny fabrics would flatter a fine smooth skin, but would make porous or wrinkled skin look even more so. At the end of this chapter, we will have more to say about the use of shiny and matte finishes in creating the effects you want.

Patterned smoothness

If van Gogh's *La Mousme* shown above had highly streaked or salt and pepper hair, she would be an example of someone with all patterned smoothness. Her skin and hair would both be smooth but be visually textured. Smooth patterned or printed fabric would repeat her textural quality. Like someone who is all-over textured, she would need plain smooth fabrics for contrast. Like van Gogh's *Girl in White*, on page 161, all plain smoothness would give La Mousme the greatest contrast, but again, would be difficult to do well. However, she, too, could wear plain smooth clothing worn in layered fashion, for the same reason noted above. Or, she could wear plain smooth fabrics that are manipulated to look textured in some areas, such as in these blouses.

Finally, we come to all plain smoothness in personal textures. Look at the artworks in the chart below. All four of these women have both smooth hair and smooth skin. Notice Picasso's *Lady with a Fan* has *repeated her plain smoothness* in her clothing—only the tie of the sash gives a hint of texture.

In the second painting, van der Weyden's *Portrait of a Lady* is dressed predominantly in smooth clothing that *repeats her smoothness, with touches of contrast* in the print of her belt and its textured buckle. The braiding in her thin light-weight hair also adds to the contrast, which is like manipulating a smooth fabric to create texture. Next, we see that Ingres' *Mme. Moitessier* has *almost entirely contrasted* her smoothness in the various textures of her ensemble, including the gathers and tiers of the dress which create an impression of texturedness from smooth fabric. Her necklace is a smooth surface, but the long string of pearls creates a certain texture of its own from a distance. In the last painting by de'Predis, *Bianca Maria Sforza's* outfit is *completely textured, which contrasts* dramatically with the smoothness of her skin and hair.

Examples of plain smoothness with clothing from simple to complex design

🌸 *Whether you like simple or more complex design, plain surfaces or more textured ones, always keep in mind to balance your body's textural weight in the overall look. This concept is illustrated here in these four artworks of women who all have both smooth hair and smooth skin.*

1

Lady with a Fan, Pablo Picasso
National Gallery of Art, Washington; Andrew W. Mellon Collection (detail).

2

Portrait of a Lady, Roger van der Weyden
National Gallery of Art, Washington; Andrew W. Mellon Collection (detail).

Little textural variety; simple and uncomplicated design.	A little more textural variety; relatively simple and large spaces where the eye can rest.

Surface quality:
   Hair and skin—plain smoothness
   Clothes—repeat her plain smoothness
Textural weight:
   Hair and skin—medium-weight
   Clothes—repeat her medium-weight

Surface quality:
   Hair and skin—plain smoothness
   Clothes—repeat her plain smoothness with a touch of texture in her belt for contrast
Textural weight:
   Hair—light-weight
   Skin—medium-weight
   Clothes—repeat her combination light and medium-weight

Repeating and/or contrasting textural weight 🪷

Repetition and contrast have their own interesting dynamics with respect to your body's textural weight. It involves the concept of *simplicity versus complexity of design*. In our two examples on page 164 notice how plain smooth fabrics and surfaces allow our eyes to slip easily from surface to surface while texturedness of any kind, as shown on this page, slows down our scrutiny from surface to surface. This phenomenon allows us to use textures to create different looks that range from simple, to moderate, to complex in their design.

🪷 Generally speaking, simple design means plain smooth (or even finely textured) fabrics in clean uncluttered lines. The more textural variety you add through fabrics or accessories, the more complex the design becomes, because you are giving the eye more at which to look.

Regardless of how much design you wear, you must always keep in mind the overall textural weight. Study how our four beauties have repeated their textural weight in the textures they are wearing. **1** has medium textural weight

Madame Moitessier, Jean-Auguste-Dominique Ingres,
National Gallery of Art, Washington; Samuel H. Kress Collection (detail).

Bianca Maria Sforza, de'Predis,
National Gallery of Art, Washington; Samuel H. Kress Collection (detail).

A lot of textural variety; quite complex design.	Completely textured; highly complex design.

Surface quality:
  Hair and skin—plain smoothness
  Clothes—contrast with her plain smoothness
Textural weight:
  Hair—heavy-weight
  Skin—medium-weight
  Clothes—the fabric weight of her dress is light, but she has balanced her personal textural weight by using the lightweight fabric in volume and in a dark, heavy color.

Surface quality:
  Hair and skin—plain smoothness
  Clothes—contrast dramatically
Textural weight:
  Hair—heavy-weight
  Skin—medium-weight
  Clothes—repeat her combination medium and heavy-weight

of hair and skin, which is repeated in her medium-weight clothing textures.

2 has a combination of light and medium weight personal textures, which are repeated in her light-weight head piece and collar, and in the medium-weight fabric of her dress. The metal of her belt buckle is also medium-weight.

3 and 4 both have a combination heavy and medium-weight personal textures. 4 has repeated her textural weight in her dress, jewelry, and accessories. 3 has also repeated her textural weight, but notice she has light-weight fabrics in her dress. However, she has used the following principle to bring the light-weight fabric into balance with her personal textural weight:

> 🪷 The color or the volume of the fabric can increase or decrease the visual weight of a fabric.

For example, if you are heavy or medium-weight as she is, but wish to use a lighter weight fabric, use it in greater volume or in layered fashion so it gives the impression of being weightier. Or, use lighter weight fabrics that are in "heavier" or darkened colors. For example, Mme. Moitessier's dress is black which appears heavy. Bright vivid colors and prints that have depth can also increase visual weight. Another example of visually altering fabric weights is Renoir's *Odalisque* (below) who is wearing light-weight fabrics even though she appears to have medium and heavy textural weight. However, she has created balance by increasing the outfit's visual weight through much layering,

Renoir's Odalisque *is wearing light-weight fabrics even though her personal textures appear to be medium and heavy-weight. However, she has created balance by increasing the outfit's visual weight through layering, a mix of prints in deep and bright colors, and a shiny gold fabric trim at the pant legs.*

Odalisque, Pierre-Auguste Renoir, National Gallery, Washington; Chester Dale Collection (detail).

Creating the effect you want with textures

a great mix of prints in deep and bright colors, and a shiny gold (metallic-looking) fabric trim at the pant legs.

If you have medium and/or heavy textural weight in your hair and skin, a simple way to test this technique for yourself is to see how it works when you wear a scarf in light-weight fabric. Notice how volume in the fabric of the scarf and/or weightier colors bring the scarf into balance with your textural weight.

❀ If you are all light-weight in your hair and skin, and you do not want to change your hair so it has more weight, then in general, you must keep your design simple. Sheer fabrics in dressy clothes are wonderful on you. Here is where you can wear a little more volume and complexity without it becoming too heavy on you.

If you wish to wear medium-weight fabrics, use them in the finest weaves and combine them with light-weight pieces. Wear knitted sweaters with the softest and finest yarns, and if they have any loft, then keep the knit loose and open so it appears light-weight. And, you can create textural variety with your accessories, which should all be visually light-weight.

Your mood greatly influences how much simplicity or complexity you choose in your clothing. Here are some points to remember when creating various effects in your outfits:

- In general, plain smooth surfaces look hard-edged and textured surfaces look softer.
- ❀ All plain smoothness can sometimes look too static, too quiet, or too hard. Color can enliven this look, or you can add a touch of texture in your accessories or jewelry.
- ❀ On the other hand, all texturedness can appear too soft or too busy, and be tiring to the eye. Often it is easier, and more pleasing to the eye, to create a mix of contrasting textural surfaces—you still have textural variety, but you give the eye places to rest.

❀ Take special note of this principle: Whether you begin with smoothness or texturedness in your personal textures, in general—when you go toward textural contrast to whatever degree of design complexity you wish, you will always have places in the design where the eyes can rest, even if those places are just your hair and skin.

For example, *Bianca Maria Sforza's* outfit, 4 on page 165, is so textured, her contrasting smooth face, neck, and hair provide "breathing spaces" for our eyes. The highly textured ensemble may draw our attention at first, but it will ultimately force us to focus and rest our eyes on her face.

- All textures, whether smooth or textured, can also be loosely divided as either shiny or matte. A moderately shiny finish is often described as lustrous—compare the difference between a diamond, which has a brilliant shine, and a pearl, which has luster.
- As we have said, we often think of smooth as looking hard-edged, textured as soft-edged. A shiny finish creates an even harder look, and a matte finish softens a surface.
- Shine visually comes forward; matte recedes.
- We can say that the smoother and shinier the surface, the harder, even colder the effect, (similar to the look of glass compared to a dull-finished brick).
- You can tone down any shiny, smooth, hard look by contrasting it with a textured matte finish, say on buttons, decorative detail, or jewelry and accessories. Or, vice versa, to create greater visual interest and punch, sharpen the smooth, matte look with shine in buttons, other decorative details, or in your jewelry and accessories.

Deciding on which textures to wear—smooth or textured or both; light-weight, medium-weight, or heavy-weight or a combination; plain or printed; matte or shiny, hard or soft, in simple, moderate, or complex designs—is important, because texture is the medium for the different messages and effects you create through your colors, and through the shapes or lines in your clothing.

And so, we have come full circle in the discovery of Your Body's Design Pattern through the elements of art, and we have shown how clothes can enhance your innate beauty through the concepts of balance and harmony. Now, it is time to challenge your creativity.

"There is an ancient myth about the image asleep in the block of marble until it is carefully disengaged by the sculptor. The sculptor must himself feel that he is not so much inventing or shaping the curve of breast or shoulder as delivering the image from its prison."
—Antoine de Saint-Exupery

Every woman has a beauty that is special to her; it is her birthright, as it is for every child that is born. Whatever your prison that keeps you from recognizing your beauty—be it the memory of an unkind word said about your appearance by a stranger or insensitive friend, be it the media images or social trends that keep you separated from a healthy view of your body, or be it even traumatic abuse you've endured, either physically or emotionally, that robbed you of your self-worth—we believe, you can regain a sense of wonder about your body by learning to exercise your innate creativity, through your personal style.

Louise Brongniart,
Jean-Antoine Houdon,
National Gallery of Art, Washington;
Widener Collection (detail).

The Surprise, Clodion,
National Gallery of Art, Washington;
Gift of Irma I. Straus in memory of her
husband, Jesse Isidor Straus (detail).

Aphrodite, Greek sculpture,
Copy, probably Hellinistic,
of IV c. B.C., The Metropolitan
Museum of Art; Fletcher
Fund, 1952 (detail).

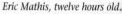

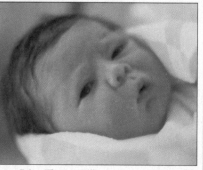
Eric Mathis, twelve hours old.

Alexandra von Klan, seven hours old.

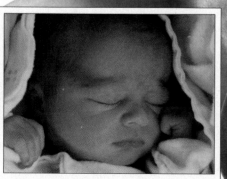
Gwendolyn von Klan, six hours old.

Brian Thomas Villa Connor, two hours old.

CHAPTER 8

Your innate creativity

...and how to use it to develop your personal style.

> "My feeling is that the concept of creativeness and the concept of the healthy, self-actualizing, fully human person seem to be coming closer and closer together, and may perhaps turn out to be the same thing."
>
> —Abraham Maslow,
> *The Farther Reaches of Human Nature*

Creativity is the heart of personal style; self-acceptance is its soul. The more contented the soul—that is, the more you esteem yourself and honor your body as beautiful, the stronger that creative pulse will beat—and the more life you will give to your personal style.

Personal style is an act of self-definition that is driven by the human need to exercise and proclaim our sense of beauty and creativity about our bodies. It happens best when we can say, "No!", to the general culture's messages on what is, or is not, beautiful—because almost all of us are left out of the definition. Lowered self-esteem is often the result of our allowing outside sources to define our body image for us. From the start of this book, we have shown you how to demystify beauty and fashion. By looking at yourself through the eyes of the artist, you've learned how to express aesthetically your own standard of beauty.

Personal style demands a commitment to your inner well-being, and the first step toward that commitment is to reclaim the power of beauty from those who would put us "in boxes" which can stifle the joy and block the triumph of individual style. By knowing Your Body's Design Pattern and seeing how it relates to clothing, you've begun this takeover by enhancing your instincts to make good choices in clothing a good percentage of the time. This alone will save you needless experimentation and expense. On a practical level, knowing your unique body in this way is economical. This is the tangible side of being the master of your own beauty. There is an intangible value as well—for on the surface, we may be talking merely about clothes, but underneath the overall message is about being fully human.

In the end, personal style is not about how much money you can spend on clothes; but about how creative you are with the money that you do spend. It is not about being obsessive about fashion or style; but about possessing a clear sense of your style. It is not about comparing yourself to others and feeling unequal; but about discovering the point of view that sees the specialness of each individual—a perspective that can lead you to feel connected rather than compared to all humanity. Clothes are merely a vehicle for showing this specialness, if and whenever you choose.

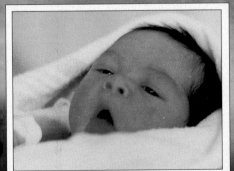

Caroline Amanda Villa Connor, four hours old.

Creativity is a process first and a product last

T he full play of your personal style involves getting in touch with your innate creativity. At this moment, many of you may be saying to yourselves, "But I don't feel I'm a very 'creative' person." Take heart and take note: Creativity is not something that belongs to only the gifted few, nor is it something you can add to someone's person, in the words of Maslow, "like a coat of paint"; it is a mental capacity that resides in all of us. Your creativity—your capacity to solve problems in new ways, to see the familiar with fresh eyes, to express new ideas and to do things in novel ways—this ability may be buried deep down within you, unnoticed, but it is there.

There is a state of being where creativeness is so integrated in an individual that it shines through again and again as a quality of the whole person. Here creativeness flows forth easily from within the person into many aspects of her life, including her personal style. You may not be at this state of creativeness yet, but this is an excellent goal toward which to strive. We believe a good way to begin is to look at creativity not only as a means to an end product, but also as a process that you can enter into over and over, until you've become comfortable with the idea of being "creative". In fact, in terms of personal style, the process may be more important than the final results; because styles change, your body changes over the years, and consequently your clothing choices will also change. However, the creative process of putting the pieces and elements together so there is a sense of "just rightness", harmony, and balance—its dynamics remain relatively the same, regardless of circumstances.

Personal style and the 4 stages of the creative process

It is widely accepted by researchers in the field of creativity that the creative process is basically a problem-solving process that consists of four stages. The central problem *we* have been dealing with in this book is stated in these questions:

- How does one go about developing a genuine personal style?
- How does one achieve the "triumph of individual style?"

Let's look at the four stages of the creative process to see how it works in our quest for solid answers.

Stage 1 Preparation

T his is the stage where we prepare ourselves to think creatively. Here we consciously feed our minds with information and data, images and ideas, and gather any other materials that seem pertinent to the problem.

In terms of personal style development, we can say that the information you have gleaned from this entire book is part of this stage. You have learned about:

- Your Body's Design Pattern
  - How the elements of art (line, space, shape, proportion, scale, texture and color) can help you discover it
  - What components are in Your Bo Design Pattern:
    body type, basic body shape (si houette), length proportions, b particulars, scale pattern, natur coloration, textural qualities
  - What clothing images relate to Yo Body's Design Pattern
- Your Proportions
  - The techniques for balancing you proportions
  - How to find your upper body balance points
- Your Body Particulars and the tech niques to camouflage and highlig them
- Your personal coloring and how to create a palette of colors to expres different effects and moods
- The principle of repetition for creat harmony
- The technique of contrast for creati visual design interest.

In *Lady with a Dog* by Toulouse-Lautrec, we see the technique of **contrast** expressed through color (light against dark), texture (lightweight against medium-weight), and print motifs (dots against stripes). In fact, as you can see by now, these various contrasting elements also repeat certain aspects of her features. Thus, she is using the principle of **repetition** as well.

Lady with a Dog, Henri de Toulouse-Lautrec, National Gallery of Art, Washington; Gift of the W. Averell Harriman Foundation in memory of Marie N. Harriman (detail).

Three more techniques for creating visual interest

There will be many times when you will want to add to your store of information, especially as the information you already have becomes second nature to you, and as you become better at tapping into your creativity. For instance, you might be ready at this point to include three more techniques for creating design interest in your personal presentation.

Rhythm

Rhythm is a dominant visual path that carries the eye easily through the design. This is usually achieved through repetition (of shape or hue in interior parts), gradation (i.e. gradual changes in size, weight, texture, and/or color of similar parts), and/or the use of line movement and direction (where a dynamic use of line in the design moves the eye in a definite direction).

Whistler's *L'Andalouse Mother-of-Pearl and Silver* is a wonderful example of the use of repetition and the use of line movement and direction in rhythm. First, notice the strong line movement downward that begins with the chignon at the top of her head, and goes down her back to the bow, and then extends all the way down to the floor with the long pleat at the back of the skirt. Next, notice how the repetition of shape in the ruffled sleeves creates interest in the bodice, which helps to direct our eyes downward along this dominant visual path in the design.

The pose of this white bird creates a similar visual image with the painting. The repetition of the bird's feathers creates a pattern that directs our eyes in a somewhat downward spiral fashion, moving us gracefully through the design of the bird.

Bird drying feathers,
Bill Terry Photography

Finally, in Alfred Stevens' *Young Woman in White Holding a Bouquet*, we see a fine example of rhythm through gradation. Notice the gradual change in size of the ruffles—from small ruffle at the neck, to medium-sized ruffle in the bodice, to large ruffles at the sleeves.

L'Andalouse, Mother-of-Pearl and Silver, James McNeil Whistler,
National Gallery of Art, Washington; Harris Whitmore Collection (detail).

Young Woman in White Holding a Bouquet, Alfred Stevens,
National Gallery of Art, Washington; Chester Dale Collection (detail).

Visual grouping 🪷

The technique of visual grouping is like rhythm in that it also helps to carry the eye around a design. However, visual grouping does not necessarily create a dominant visual path. Instead in visual grouping, strong similarities between different and widely separated parts in a design allow our eyes to jump to-and-fro between them in such a way that they are seen as a kind of "network".

Similarities can be seen in terms of size, shape, texture, and/or color. Look at the photo of the flowering plant. What do your eyes group together? Do you see how the opened flower is seen together with the slightly opened bud because of their violet color; which, in fact, delineates them from the green parts of the plant? What about shape? The leaves group by similar shape even though they are of different sizes, as do the unopened buds. The buds can also be visually grouped by texture. Can you see how these visual groupings have helped you move around the photograph, even though you would probably not have been aware of them had you just been looking casually at the picture? Visual grouping in clothing works in the same way.

Ingres' *Madame Moitessier* is a familiar figure to you by now, because she has been an excellent example for several concepts throughout the book. She is also wonderful for showing visual grouping. Notice how your eyes group together the brooch, bracelets, rings, and fan because of their common metal material. A larger grouping can be seen with the brooch, bracelets, rings, and the pearl necklace, and the flowered ornaments in her hair. This time, the round shapes common to all of them is what makes our eyes see these different items as a group.

Flower and buds,
Bill Terry
Photography.

Madame Moitessier, Jean-Auguste-Dominique Ingres, National Gallery of Art, Washington; Samuel H. Kress Collection (detail).

Portrait of an Elderly Lady, Mary Cassatt, National Gallery of Art, Washington; Chester Dale Collection (detail).

Dominance

Dominance has to do with creating an eye-catching element in an outfit that dominates the entire look. The flower in the hat of Mary Cassatt's painting of *Portrait of an Elderly Lady* is a good example of dominance. These drawings also demonstrate how dominance can be executed in many different ways, through all the elements of design. For example:

line, as in the large diagonal ruffle of this dress

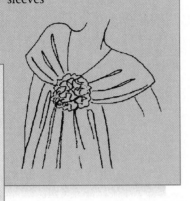

shape and scale, as in the large flower and triangular sleeves

texture, as in the long scarf around the neck

Of course, color can be used in all of the above to create even greater dominance.

Finally, when your outfit is very simple and clean in its design, your face can become the dominant element as in Jean-Jacques Henner's *Madame Uhring*. Her face stands out, not only because of the outward direction of her profile, but because of her skin's contrast with the surrounding solid black of her ensemble.

Because analysis is a major part of stage 1, before you move on to stage 2 of the creative process, you will also want to survey your current wardrobe pieces (including jewelry) to determine which ones relate to Your Body's Design Pattern.

Madame Uhring,
Jean-Jacques Henner,
National Gallery of Art, Washington;
Chester Dale Collection (detail).

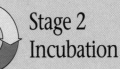

Stage 2
Incubation

In this stage of the creative process, we let go of our conscious hold of the problem and let the subconscious mind take over. Most research on creativity agree that this stage is the critical one. The theory is that during this stage all the information, images, ideas, and other materials you gathered in stage 1 shift and realign themselves into orderly and meaningful patterns. In terms of personal style, we would think of the unconscious mind as selecting, arranging, and correlating your ideas and images into aesthetically pleasing patterns of body and clothing. The unconscious mind sees, according to the framework of Your Body's Design Pattern, certain combinations as beautiful and rejects others as incompatible or unattractive. All this will happen while your conscious mind has turned its attention to other things and activities. Even while you are relaxing, behind the calm, things are simmering in the subconscious: at this point, you are developing a sensitivity to pattern, and moving toward growth and wholeness in your perception of self and style. Is it any wonder that this stage is often compared to the growth of a child in the womb—where at every moment, a life is striving to grow towards wholeness, and uniqueness?

Like the gestation period in the womb, this stage requires your patience and time to allow your ideas to grow and spring to life.

One reason art masterpieces were chosen to illustrate this book is that art has a way of cutting quickly through to the human subconscious, surprising us with the truth of our beauty and bestowing us a gift: a greater sense of our uniqueness. The words of Robert Henri (1865–1929), the famous American artist and teacher, give us yet another reason:

> "Art also tends towards balance, order, judgment of relative values, the laws of growth, the economy of living—very good things for anyone to be interested in."
>
> —Robert Henri, *The Art Spirit*

Stage 3
Illumination

This is the stage when the answer spontaneously appears. It is the time when new paradigms—new ideas and fresh ways of looking at things —come into being. It is the "Aha!", symbolized by the switched-on light bulb, although it often strikes us like a thunderbolt. This is the moment of discovery and inspiration that overflows with feelings of joy and certainty. It is the moment when the artist sees the images of a new painting, the writer the outline of his new plot, the composer hears the themes of her new symphony.

Similarly, in style development not only do you begin to see how you would put together your outfits, but you will also have new insights. Light is often the symbol of wisdom, and wise you are when you begin to experience the artistic potential of your unique human form. You feel a sense of wholeness and pleasure about your body similar to the way Robert Henri described how one might think when painting the human body:

> "In your painting think of the neck, head and body as having a liking for each other. There is a love of the hand for the head. No cold lack of sympathy between the parts of a human being, but a beautiful fellowship exists. The parts are joyous in their play together, and an absolute confidence exists between them."
>
> —Robert Henri,
> *The Art Spirit*

You also become acutely aware of that delicate monitor inside that recognizes balance, harmony, and aesthetic pleasure. You understand clearly now the reasons why certain clothing choices you have made over the years have remained among your favorite purchases. You realize that you must practice listening to your inner voice—your instinct—that directs you to pull together from random choices only those things that truly relate to your special design. When you join correct knowledge with your instinct, it becomes a powerful force for tearing down any barriers you may have to your creative freedom, which you will fully express in Stage 4 of the creative process.

Dancing Figure,
Auguste Rodin,
National Gallery of Art,
Washington; Gift of Mrs.
John W. Simpson.

Stage 4
Verification

If you feel you are already highly attuned to your creative instinct, and have always had a flair for dress and style, then stage 4 comes naturally to you.

This verification stage—sometimes we call it the validation or implementation stage—is the time for conscious effort to apply our talents, learned skills and techniques, so that we can bring our ideas to life.

Giving form and detail to your ideas may not come easily to you at first, but remember, you are not alone. As you progress, be confident that you will experience many times when you will express yourself through your clothes in a way that is well-integrated with Your Body's Design Pattern and with the healthy, confident person within.

Ultimately the playing out of your personal style should be effortless. But just as a musical performer (or any artist) must spend hours of study and practice at her instrument in order to make her performance appear natural and easy and unstudied, so does personal style take practice for it to develop—especially if it is to honestly reflect your intrinsic nature and personality. If you are creatively putting together your outfits, you will discover it is almost impossible not to express your personality in some way. *Your personality is your overlay of originality onto Your Body's Design Pattern.* Here are some questions that might lead you to a better understanding of it:

1. How would you describe your personality at your very best? (These are the times when you feel the most alive, loved, and cared for.)

2. How do the people who are your greatest fans describe you?

3. How would these descriptions express themselves in the way you dress? for business? for leisure? for other occasions? For example, if your friends describe you as "creative and intelligent", you might express these qualities in a business outfit this way: a suit in a conservative cut and color, accented with an unusual scarf or accessory. What else might you do? Remember these qualities and any other

quality can be interpreted in many different ways depending upon the personality through whom the qualities are filtered.

4. Finally, what are some of your favorite things? Do you like large earrings, brooches, a certain period in history, birds, flowers, abstract art, for example? How might you integrate or reflect these things and/or themes you love into the way you dress?

Some practical application

Finally, when building a wardrobe to showcase your personal style, you might consider the following hints.

Basically, there are only two approaches to dressing that will determine how you build your wardrobe:

1. The One-look-outfits approach

2. The Adaptable Basics approach

In the One-look-outfits wardrobe, each outfit is always worn with the same accessories and jewelry to make it work; rarely can an outfit be separated into its pieces. Generally, this is a very expensive way of dressing. Any woman who builds a wardrobe in this way usually has no budget consideration. What she does need to consider is how well each outfit suits her personality and her Body's Design Pattern.

The Adaptable Basics wardrobe consists mainly of basic pieces in solids or very subtle fine blends that can go anywhere, any time of day or night. They can be dressed up or down because they generally have no eye-catching buttons or trims; although some tops can have subtle patterns (for example, a blouse in a subtle silk jacquard fabric). As long as the basics you choose combine into your natural silhouette(s) and can mix and match in terms of line, color, and texture, all they need are accessories (shoes, belts, handbags, scarves), jewelry and other ornamentation to make them work in multiple ways for different occasions. This concept is the most economical way to approach dressing, but requires the most imagination and creativity.

Accessories and jewelry are the key to making the "Adaptable Basics" wardrobe work to get the most outfits out of relatively few pieces. In general, update accessories and jewelry every year, or add as needed, or as your budget allows.

The Adaptable Basics wardrobe

Items you need:

(How many of each item you have depends on your lifestyle, seasonal needs, and budget.)

- Tops
  - suit jackets in solid colors
  - sweaters with different necklines
  - blouses in various colors
  - under tops in various colors
- Bottoms
  - suit skirts in solid colors
  - other skirts in solid colors and/or subtle patterns
  - trousers in solid colors and/or subtle patterns
- Dresses—work to evening
- Outer wear
  - coats
  - jackets

Accessories and jewelry you need:

- Shoes (basic and non-basic)
  - flats, pumps, loafer, boots and evening sandals or shoes
- Purses and bags (basic and non-basic)
  - clutch, day and evening
  - casual shoulder for everyday
  - briefcase and/or carryalls
- Scarves and shawls—day and evening
- Belts (if you can wear them)—day and evening
- Jewelry—you may want only a few versatile pieces. Or you may want a variety to express different needs, character, moods and effects, etc.: for example, dressy, casual, costume, for evening, for drama, or for elegance—whatever purpose and look you desire.

In the Adaptable Basics wardrobe, shoes, scarves, belts, and jewelry are an easy way to create any effect you want. Here are just four examples of how to create different effects:

Dramatic—use extreme line and shape (say in an earring), or, vivid colors in an ensemble, a scarf or belt.

Elegant—use classic accessories like pearls, fine jewelry, scarves in fine fabrics and choose middle to low value colors.

Exotic—wear ethnic jewelry or use belts or scarves with unexpected color combinations and/or worn in an asymmetrical fashion.

Romantic—use scarves in lace or caressable fabrics, romantic jewelry such as pearls or gold filigree or any piece of ornamentation that has antique quality and design.

Once you have the basics, then you can add to your wardrobe in this way:
- other suits, dresses, and ensembles that are One-look-outfits.
- casual clothes that are either Adaptable Basics and/or One-look-outfits
- active wear—these are sports clothes for exercise, tennis, golf, skiing, etc. (Whatever your lifestyle, you may also need active wear.)

Creating a wardrobe is an open-ended process, and how it develops is a product of your unique imagination.

Fearfully and wonderfully made

very woman wants a style that is recognizably hers, just as we can recognize a Picasso from a Lautrec, or a Rembrandt from a Renoir. Even when two artists have similar styles, there will always be something that will distinguish one artist from the other. It is a difference that comes from the spontaneous expression of the personality. Even in the realm of music, we know that any piece can be interpreted in many different ways, according to the style of the artist who performs it. Likewise, in the art of dressing, "Style" with a capital "S", means that a woman's unique personality is very clearly reflected in the way she dresses. We liken it to music that is expressed with the heart, so that we may hear the sounds of the soul—ringing true, clear, and free. This is *The Triumph of Individual Style.*

We have come to the end of your journey in this book. You have discovered that within Your Body's Design Pattern are the secrets to the harmonious and artistic expression of your uniqueness through your clothes. Much beauty can be created with just a few elements, each in its special and proper place. Personal expressiveness is a fundamental human desire, and you have learned that aspiring for beauty and creativity in yourself is a move towards psychological health, in as much as it moves toward self-acceptance, self-esteem, and a mutual enrichment of your body and inner being. This is *The Triumph of Individual Style.*

In these last pages you have also learned that the creative process depends least of all upon accident: First we must learn through logic and sequence and open our eyes to "see", not just look; then we submerge what we've scoped and amassed into the subconscious, to learn even more through "silence"; finally, we are pushed outward again by our inner impulses to create in the spirit of art with complete self-trust. We like to think that the four stages of the creative process flow one into the other in a circular fashion, constant and continuous, as shown here (below). Seen in this way, the four stages represent the idea of creativeness when it has become such an integral part of one's being that it is expressed in some way on a daily basis. This, too, is *The Triumph of Individual Style.*

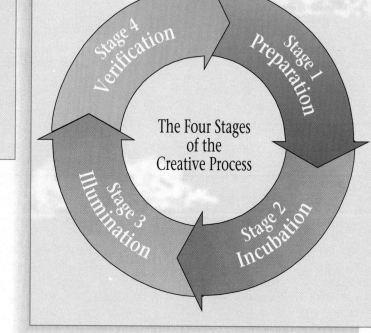

The Four Stages of the Creative Process

Stage 1 Preparation
Stage 2 Incubation
Stage 3 Illumination
Stage 4 Verification

Recommended classic readings

Henri, Robert, *The Art Spirit*, compiled by Margery A. Ryerson. Philadelphia and New York: J. B. Lippincott Company, 1960.

Maslow, Abraham, *The Farther Reaches of Human Nature.* New York:The Viking Press, 1971.

Ghiselin, Brewster, *The Creative Process.* New York: Mentor Books, 1964.

The sense of freedom. The sense of wonder. Both must always be at the core of your creativity to keep your individual style alive and dynamic, changing with you as you go through life.

The sense of freedom means an ability to feel detached from the restraints of conventional wisdom or known ideas. It is a kind of openness that is found in all healthy children, because they are the least bound by inhibition or tradition,which allows them to be at their most creative. The image of that little girl playing dress-up shows us how little children give themselves permission to be themselves, to follow their instincts, to play, to be spontaneous. Look back to that little girl within yourself from time to time, lest you forget.

A sense of wonder is the ability to recapture the poetic, the timeless, the feeling of being out of time and place. Seeing a newborn baby can give us that sense of wonder, which is the miracle of life itself.

When you honor your body's unique design pattern and yield to the authority of its being, you are reaffirming that little miracle that you were at birth and that you are every day of your life. If you hold on to that feeling of awe, you can move into loving and joyfully approving that your body be itself—unconditionally, in its own nature and in its own style. Then if you want to make changes in yourself, you will do so without rejecting, but rather with great respect for both your potentials and your limitations. If there were just one message we hope to have given you, it is that your beauty was always there, from the beginning. Lest you forget this, we invite you to write the words of this timeless psalm within your heart:

Girl in Front of Mirror; Norman Rockwell,
The Norman Rockwell Museum at Stockbridge.

Liesl Mathis von Klan, ten hours ol

...and twenty-seven years

For thou didst form my inward parts;
Thou didst weave me in my mother's womb.

I will give thanks to Thee, for I am
fearfully and wonderfully made.
Wonderful are Thy works,
and my soul knows it
very well.

—Psalm 139:13-14

Index

Acknowledgments

We thank you, Lord, for giving us these working orders for the past eleven years and for blessing us each with our different gifts and talents that have combined to truly create a project whose whole is greater than the sum of its parts.

We thank our respective families and friends who encouraged, listened, critiqued, and often filled in for us in other areas of our lives:

Carla's family...

Husband, Robert, a true knight in shining armor whose wisdom, encouragement and unconditional love have been my mainstay... and who is my very best friend.

My children, Eric (29 years old) and Liesl (27 years old), whose courage, exuberance for life and natural creativity are an inspiration to me. Their instincts regarding their environment of clothing and interiors started my questioning those many years ago...

My mother Gwendolyn, late father Carl, and step father, Lou—who have been my greatest fans, who have faithfully helped and supported every endeavor... and taught me by example that every man and woman has dignity and is a unique gift from God.

...and friends...

Thank you to my mentor, personal color and design pioneer, Suzanne Caygill, whose intuitive personal design brilliance and genius I was able to observe for 19 years; to Martena Sasnett, Suzanne's dear friend, for her encouragement and enthusiasm for this project; and to Julie Rogers who gave me the gift of having my colors done by Suzanne Caygill in 1961.

Thank you to my Bible study prayer group, who every Tuesday morning band together for prayer: Gini Bunnell, Pat Cawood, Margaret Erickson, Jeannie Gee, Joan Jack, Nancy Lammerding, Carolyn Schwartz.

Thank you to my best friend, Joan Jack, and her husband, Bob, who continue to be loyal and loving friends, giving love, lodging, when needed, warmth, laughter, listening, critiquing only when asked, and extra measures of patience when most needed. And thank you to all my friends, headed by Lois Marlow, who have continued to listen, care, and support over these many years.

Thank you to the ColorStyle staff and teachers in the ColorStyle Institute who formed a support team so the personal color and style design consulting and the ColorStyle Institute could continue operation: Patricia Demetrios, Diana Wood, Sharon Chrisman, Metta Gerber, Barbara Menker, Aïda Morano, Cathy Brewer, Karen Snow, Judie Sobrero, Mary DiMenna, Liesl Mathis von Klan, Susan Schwartz, Eadie Agid, and Posey Ferguson.

Ana Duran and Bill French for doing their parts with excellence which allowed me to do mine.

Helen's family...

My parents, Lydia and Romulo Villa, whom I love and honor deeply... who inspire me always with their creativity, zest for life, and immense capacity to garner friendships through their love and respectful acceptance of others... thank you, Mom and Dad, for this legacy.

My husband, Thomas, my dearest and most loving friend and soul mate, whose wonderful sense of humor often came to my rescue during this project... thank you for your faithful strength.

My children, Caroline (8 years old) and Brian (4 years old), whose childlike sense of wonder and creative freedom inspired the words in Chapter 8 and kept me from forgetting these qualities in myself as I researched, learned, and wrote.

My highly creative sisters, Noemi V. James and Daisy V. Mischke, who have given me the pleasure of experiencing all my life that "individuality" is not only possible, even among the closest of siblings, but also fun! Thank you for your love and unfailing support.

Thank you to extended family members—my husband's parents, Ruth and Thomas H. Connor, for 20 years of love and friendship; and caregivers Marina Luces, Nicole Meixner, and Posey Ferguson for their motherly care of my children when I wasn't there.

...and friends...

Thanks to my friends, old and new, for being who you are; whether you know it or not, you constantly renew my faith in our common humanity: my sister-in-law Teresa Connor, Lynda Banks, Robert Robin, Sylvia Chu, Anita Millard, Judith Maurier, Pat Faust, Liesl Mathis von Klan, Mary Ann Smith, Karen Skurnac, and Marie Monohan. Also, Patricia Harrison Rosato, who introduced me to Suzanne Caygill 13 years ago and was instrumental in bringing Carla and me together. And all the moms in my parenting group, especially our leader and mentor, Mary DeLoach, who has guided our abilities to develop the highest levels of self-esteem in our precious children.

Finally, I thank the many artists across the ages whose artworks became familiar friends—masterpieces that illustrate this book and inspired my writing and guided the information design as well as my vision for this book.

We both thank:

The design and production team...
- Premier designer, Lynda Banks of Lynda Banks Design, and her talented graphic design team for their commitment to design excellence:
  - Computer typesetting and layout: Myrna Vladic, Stephanie Eichleay, Lori Robinson, Rick Gordon
  - Administration: Sari Marks
- Robert Flynn, Vice President, Graphics Group, printing manufacturing representatives, who believed in this project and referred us to Theresa Savage at Applied Graphics, pre-press and desktop specialists, and her fine team headed by electronic publishing specialist, Marie Pence
- Sanjay Sakhuja of Digital Pre-press International, and his expert crew: Don Haaga, Judd Vetrone, Jeff Sacilotto, Peter Collins, Michael Lee, Eric C. Hudson.

The artists...
- Bill Terry who volunteered his professional nature transparencies as well as countless hours of sitting with Carla to search his thousands of slides
- Al Smith for his artwork which opens Chapter 6
- D. J. Simison for her drawings that appear on pages 4, 56, 87, 92, 94, 95, 101, 110-111
- Janet Hekking for the initial line drawings which enabled Carla to complete and create hundreds more.

The editorial team...
- Our readers: Susan Schwartz, Julie Rogers, Sharon Chrisman and Karen Skurnac for their insights and comments
- Our editors: Linda Lee Evans, Karen Selikson, and Metta Gerber for their fine expertise
- Color expert, Sharon Chrisman, for reviewing and helping us refine the color charts in Chapter 6.

Permissions...
- The Department of Visual Services of the National Gallery of Art in Washington, D.C., headed by Mr. Ira Bartfield, with Margaret Cooley, Sara Sanders-Buell, and Barbara Bernard, who were stalwart in their efforts to help this project
- Butterick Patterns for allowing us to use their pattern drawings as the basic idea behind many line drawings.

Behind the scenes...
- The thousands of ColorStyle design clients and institute students who believed in the ColorStyle process over the past 12 years, on whom our theories were tested and verified
- Michele Accinelli for his patience and home-made bread during design; Lynda and Michele's daughter, Alessandra, for her three-year old exuberance which gave delightful relief time and time again during the nine months of design
- Caroline and Joe Youmans, and Sherry Thorson who provided many nights of lodging for us
- Ken Brooks for his computer expertise and his computer, and Sandy and Don Keating for their computer
- Financial supporters for their faith and trust: Pat Cawood, Dick and Nancy Lammerding, Helen Mathis, Bill and Lois Scott; and Bob Gee as our financial advisor
- Robert Mischke and Daisy Villa of Vanguard Media whose guiding hands are on the marketing and promotion of this project.

Answers to charts on pages 18-19

Art credit on page 18

page 18

Line Movement	Straight	Curved
Eyebrows	✔	
Eyes		✔
Sides of nose	✔	
Tip of nose	✔	
Mouth when:		
smiling (not shown)		
not smiling	✔	
Hairline		✔
Sides of face		✔
Jaw and/or chin		✔
Total	4	4

The line movement of Madame Moitessier's features is
- ᵂ Predominantly straight
- ᵂ Predominantly curved
- ✔ Evenly distributed

Line Direction	Horizontal	Vertical	Diagonal
Eyebrows	✔		
Eyes	✔		
Nose *(can appear horizontal if very wide and short)*		✔	
Tip of nose *(from nostril to tip to other nostril)*	✔		
Mouth when:			
smiling (not shown)			
not smiling	✔		
Hairline			✔
Sides of face		✔	✔
Jaw and/or chin			✔
Total	4	2	3

- ᵂ Her features go predominantly in a horizontal direction.
- ᵂ Her features go predominantly in a vertical direction.
- ᵂ Her features go predominantly in a diagonal direction.
- ✔ Her features go equally in *horizontal* and *diagonal* directions.

Art credit on page 18

page 19

Line Movement	Straight	Curved
Eyebrows	✔	
Eyes	✔	✔
Sides of nose	✔	✔
Tip of nose	✔	✔
Mouth when:		
smiling (not shown)		
not smiling		✔
Hairline		✔
Sides of face		✔
Jaw and/or chin		✔
Total	4	7

The line movement of the young girl's features is
- ☐ Predominantly straight
- ✔ Predominantly curved
- ☐ Evenly distributed

Line Direction	Horizontal	Vertical	Diagonal
Eyebrows	✔		
Eyes			✔
Nose *(can appear horizontal if very wide and short)*		✔	✔
Tip of nose *(from nostril to tip to other nostril)*			✔
Mouth when:			
smiling (not shown)			
not smiling	✔		✔
Hairline			✔
Sides of face			✔
Jaw and/or chin			✔
Total	2	1	7

- ☐ Her features go predominantly in a horizontal direction.
- ☐ Her features go predominantly in a vertical direction.
- ✔ Her features go predominantly in a diagonal direction.
- ☐ Her features go equally in _____ and _____ directions.

Order Form: analysis of Your Body's Design Pattern by the authors

*I*f you have read this book and would like the authors to verify your own analysis of Your Body's Design Pattern, then this special offer is for YOU!

What you get

For only $50.00, you will receive a complete written analysis of Your Body's Design Pattern (excluding color palette). The analysis will include the following:

- your body type
- the best fabrics for your body
- clothing construction tips for your body and what fabrics to choose for them
- your silhouette(s)
- your length proportions and how to work with them
- your upper body balance points
- your body particulars and how to camouflage and highlight them
- your scale pattern and how to choose accessories, prints and construction details
- your level of color contrast
- your body's textural pattern

This personalized analysis will also include page references to the book for your information.

Allow 4–6 weeks for delivery.

What we need from you

In order for us to be able to do this analysis, please send us the following 5 photos of you:

Close-up of your face

1. front view—(Show your regular hairdo)
2. profile view—(Pull your hair back to show your hairline and the back of your neck; a pony tail would work if you have medium to long hair.)

Full-body photos (Dress in flat shoes or barefeet, and in a plain-colored leotard or swim suit; be sure to show your body from the top of your head to the bottom of your feet.)

3. front view—
   (Pull your hair back to show your hairline and neck.)
4. side view—
   (Pull your hair back to show your hairline and neck.)
5. back view—
   (Pull your hair back to show your hairline and neck.)

Please send pictures on which we can mark. We will return the ones that demonstrate what you can do to create a wardrobe that is in balance with your very special unique body.

☐ If you would like us to include another copy of *The Triumph of Individual Style* that we've marked for you, check here, send the price of another book and we'll personally sign and mark your copy, then send it to you postage-free when we send your analysis.

Simply send the photos and payment to

Timeless Editions
1150 Chestnut Lane, Menlo Park, CA 94025

☐ I enclose a check or money order, payable to Timeless Editions

☐ Charge my: ☐ MasterCard or ☐ Visa
(Please Print)

Name _____
(as it appears on your card)

Account # _____ Exp. date _____

Signature _____

Mailing Address _____

City _____ Zip _____ State _____

What can I do with my hair?

Can ColorStyle personal design consultants help you find a hair style that relates to your design pattern? YES!

If you have ever wondered how to find the perfect hair style for you, ColorStyle has a personal hair design system to help you discover it.

☐ Check here if you wish ColorStyle, Inc. to send you more information on how to get your personal hair design based upon your silhouette, body proportions, face shape, hair type, length preference, lifestyle, and hair management skill level.

The ColorStyle Institute

☐ Check here if you wish to receive a catalog and course schedule, or call (415) 321-5997 to find out if the ColorStyle Institute, a leader in the field of personal color and style designing, suits your educational goals.